PETER QUINN

THE OUTSIDER

Published by Irish Sports Publishing (ISP)
Unit 11, Tandy's Lane
Lucan, Co Dublin
Ireland
www.irishsportspublishing.com

First published, 2013

A CIP record for this book is available from the British Library

ISBN 978-0-9573954-6-6

Printed in Ireland with Print Procedure Ltd
Cover Design and Typesetting: Anú Design www.anu-design.ie
Cover Photographs: © Inpho Sports Agency
Inside Photographs: Inpho Sports Agency and Peter Quinn's Private Collection

Contents

	Reamhrá	vii
1.	Death's Door	1
2.	In the Beginning	5
3.	Living with the Border	17
4.	Born and Reared to be a Farmer	22
5.	Farming Interrupted	29
6.	Play – Whatever the Price	48
7.	Student Life and Disenchantment	56
8.	A New Impetus	68
9.	Escape from Accountancy	74
10.	A Short Career	95
11.	Winning a Championship	102
12.	Entering GAA Administration	113
13.	Events Produce Change	116
14.	Manchester	119
15.	Back in Ireland	128
16.	In Business	137
17.	Ulster Calling	141
18.	Second Time Round	162
19.	Becoming a Target	171
20.	Back to Building	194
21.	There's Nothing so Past as a Past President	221
22.	Where Are We Now?	238
23.	In the End	253

To all those who played our games and enjoyed them,
even though they never won a medal.

Reamhrá

To quote Julius Caesar in the first sentence of De Bello Gallico, his account of the Gallic Wars: 'Gallia est omnis divisa in partes tres', ('All Gaul is divided into three parts').

So it has been with my life. My youth and adolescence were very different from what came later; my involvement in the GAA bore no resemblance to my working life in either business or public service. The first two parts – my youth and my GAA activities – are described in this book. But, in several ways, they were probably neither the most important nor the most valuable parts of my life and career.

As I look back over my life, it was what I did outside the reach of the public spotlight, in a variety of spheres, which has given me the greatest satisfaction, although I derived wonderful gratification from the Croke Park development. In most instances, the pleasure came from being provided with the opportunity to contribute, without interference, to the social, political and economic progress of one's country.

Following my period as Uachtarán, Cumann Lúthchleas Gael, I spent a total of eleven years as chairman of various bodies on behalf of the Irish government – from the National Minerals Policy Review Group to the imaginative and highly successful Social Finance

Foundation, with its immense potential to contribute to economic progress, to TG4 as it left the RTÉ nest and created its own positive and constructive niche in Irish broadcasting. Those were very rewarding and, thankfully, successful experiences with my time at TG4 being particularly satisfying.

On my return to the North, I spent eight years acting as 'facilitator' in the Drumcree negotiations and then as a member of the Parades Commission. Those years brought totally different challenges, huge frustration and great pressures including intimidation, death threats and the need to live behind bullet-proof glass. I shared much of the pain of that period with the late Reverend Roy Magee, a man for whom I had immense respect and one of the greatest peacemakers I ever met. Roy, wherever you are, I still miss you.

I also held the Chairmanship of the Irish Language Broadcast Fund and membership of the Board of the Northern Ireland Film and Television Commission (now Screen Northern Ireland) for a short period.

The last two decades have been marred by the life-changing tragedy which struck our eldest daughter. It was the largest negative in a predominantly happy, past half-century. As a result, I have tried to make some small difference to the lives of such people, through my involvement with a charity which aims to assist victims of acquired brain injury and their families.

I would not want to write the only part of my life story which will ever be written without acknowledging the people with whom I worked on those different initiatives, or without recognising their contribution to my life's work. They know who they are and both they and I realise that I owe them a lot – they made life after Croke Park very fulfilling and exciting.

Later, there were the lower profile activities, such as spear-heading the campaign for a new acute hospital in Enniskillen and acting as chairman of two local social economy projects when both were in serious financial difficulties and had to be rescued. They, too, were challenging experiences.

And then there were the business ventures. Fortunately, most were successful though some failed. Sometimes the failures were spectacular but, when they occurred, they had to be taken on the chin. That's life in the world of business and commerce and in the effort to create jobs and value. But not many people know that, because not enough have tried it or experienced the problems. Better to have tried and failed than never to have tried at all.

This book is about selected parts of my life only and is not, therefore, a proper autobiography. It is just part of the story. But, throughout all parts of my life, my family has been and continues to be the most important component though most of them were, and still are, vigorously opposed to my writing this story.

In this foreword, I want publicly to thank my wife, who has been a wonderful support to me for more than four decades, our five children who have given us virtually no trouble since the day they were born, my three siblings who shared some of my pain, and our two grandchildren, who still have their lives before them. But most of all, I want to thank my late father from whom I have drawn immense inspiration in times of trouble; his unequivocal support in times of difficulty and his wonderful philosophy, as enshrined in that memorable phrase, 'You'll never learn younger – now', have helped me throughout my life.

Finally, I wish to thank Liam Hayes, who first suggested this project to me, Kevin MacDermot who has done all the work involved in getting it published, including converting my overly precise grammar into a more modern and, apparently, a more readable format, and Irish Sports Publishing for taking the risk in publishing it.

Peter Quinn,
November 2013.

1

Death's Door

At six years old, I did not understand death. I awoke to find my mother and Mrs Coleman talking in hushed tones, as if they were scared, and there was a discernible atmosphere of concern. They were talking about my dying!

From the gist of their conversation, my death was both imminent and certain: I had no idea why and I was confused about the 'death' thing. Mrs Coleman was predicting that I would probably come out of it OK. My mother was adamant (my mother was always adamant!) that the doctor had said that unless something changed dramatically, I was not going to make it, or words to that effect.

I knew I'd been sick. I'd been in hospital and the doctor had given me penicillin injections after I came home. The nurse had arrived early the following morning to give me some more, and I had staged a 'stand-up-in-the-bed' protest, but it had ultimately been in vain and I got another needle-full of antibiotic.

As I discovered later, my 'sleep' had lasted more than thirty-six hours and had created panic in the family. I asked no questions. Eventually, Mrs Coleman noticed that I was awake. I have a vague memory of receiving an unusually warm welcome.

When I awoke that afternoon, I could not have known that that week was to have a defining impact on much of the rest of my life – especially on the following twenty years. It was to have a particularly negative effect on my health and my sporting career.

I had gone into hospital for an operation on Easter Sunday – I'd been prone to sore throats and the doctor saw the removal of my tonsils and adenoids as the only solution to my problem.

I remember nothing about either the operation itself or the preparation for it. When she arrived on the Wednesday to take me home and was told that I would have to stay for another day, we were both unhappy. In those days, farmers had no telephones, so the hospital had no way of advising her not to come to collect me, although the decision not to release me had already been taken. Some combination of my crying and my mother's insistence that she could not afford another taxi fare, forced the staff to release me.

It's impossible to say whether my life would have turned out differently, if I had stayed in hospital for another day or two, or if my welfare over that week had been managed better, and it no longer matters. I discovered later that while I was in hospital, I'd shown symptoms of some problem. There was a measles outbreak in the children's ward of the hospital and everyone had assumed that I had contracted that disease. While they would have preferred to keep me there for a day or two, going home appeared not to be a major problem.

Unfortunately, I hadn't got the measles; that was to happen several years later. As soon as I arrived home I insisted on going out to where my father was ploughing, less than a hundred yards from our front door. Normally, my mother was very protective of her children's health, but I was allowed out on this occasion. Despite being wrapped up in warm clothes, it seems that I became quite ill later that evening. My mother blamed herself for letting me out and getting cold, and blamed my father for not sending me back in again. But getting cold was not the real issue and the illness was much more sinister than measles. I had fallen victim to a poorly conducted hospital procedure, undertaken by a surgeon who had apparently celebrated Easter well, but not very wisely.

It seems that the tonsillectomy operation had somehow gone wrong. Somewhere in the process, I'd contracted septicaemia or blood poisoning as it was more commonly known then.

Slowness in detection led to slowness in reacting, and by the time my local doctor started to pump penicillin into my hips and arms, my problem had advanced to the critical stage. The poison had spread throughout my body, and I had gone into some sort of coma.

Fortunately, I wasn't aware of the problem, nor worried about it, apart from when the doctor or nurse came to administer the injections. But it seems that the family was devastated. My chances of recovery were deemed to be minimal, but for some reason I survived. My recovery was prolonged. It was about six months before I could go back to school, and even then my health was deemed to be a bit fragile.

The most significant result of my illness was that, for the next twenty years, some residual effects of the problem remained in my body and made occasional reappearances. I lived with regular courses of penicillin injections, anything from six to ten times a year, for about a week at a time. I grew to hate surgical needles.

The local GP, the late Dr Sam McQuade, had an unquenchable confidence in penicillin and streptomycin. Dr Sam and I were to become very closely acquainted over the next decade and more. Despite the several decades of difference in our ages and his penchant for sticking needles into me, we actually became quite good friends. He encouraged me towards a career in medicine and eventually offered to pay my fees at medical school, but by then I'd had enough of medicine.

He even put me on a sort of diet, for several weeks. It consisted of two bottles of Guinness and a pint of milk every day, in addition to whatever solid food I was given. I have since been told that Guinness is 'an acquired taste'. Although I have been a life-long Pioneer, I still recall that I had no difficulty acquiring the taste, and while I haven't sampled it in the past sixty years, I remember clearly that I liked it and even preferred it to the milk.

More than six decades later, what continues to annoy me is the realisation that, with better diagnosis and better management, the problem could easily have been rectified. I don't blame the GP for that – he had enough to do to keep me alive. But others should have identified the problem and dealt with it. Had they done so, I would have been spared many years of failure to achieve my full potential in a number of ways – not least in my sporting career.

2

In the Beginning

World War II was moving towards its conclusion when I was born. Ours was a farming family, as were virtually all the neighbouring families. But in several ways, we were different. Nowadays, sociologists would probably define ours as a dysfunctional family.

My late father, Hugh, was only a year old when his father died suddenly, in 1904. I have never discovered the real cause of his death, but apparently his illness was not perceived as life-threatening and his death was a shock to both my grandmother and the neighbours.

With only one sister, who was two years older, my father became 'the man of the house' at a very young age. His sister, my Aunt Cissie, was a wonderful woman – a genuinely nice person with a wonderfully warm, quiet personality and great empathy with young people. She raised an outstanding family of two sons and four daughters, and those cousins became an important part of my young life, although they were much older than I was.

There was also a physically disabled bachelor, my father's Uncle John, who supported my father and grandmother with farming advice, but with minimal capacity to contribute to the actual running of the farm. So, instead of attending school, my father became a fully-fledged farmer at seven years of age.

The farm was an 'upland farm' with more hills than flat fields. Most of our land was dry, being largely gravel-based, but it was not great for growing crops, because the soil was generally quite shallow.

My father operated a 'mixed farm' with a combination of milk production, which generated a small monthly cheque, beef cattle, which was the main activity, pig rearing, and tillage – virtually all of the latter being designed for 'home consumption'. We grew all our own vegetables and what was not used for human consumption was fed to the different animals. It was subsistence farming in the real meaning of that expression, with my mother adding to the family income by rearing chickens and selling the bulk of the eggs. I grew to dislike eggs, having been forced to eat far too many of them, in my youth, and I haven't ordered chicken in a restaurant for as long as I can remember.

In the pre-partition days of the early twentieth century, the Fermanagh-Cavan border area was just another deprived part of rural Ireland. Farm productivity in those years was abysmally low, and farming practices owed more to tradition than to profitability or efficiency. Consequently, living standards were low in both absolute and relative terms.

In common with most other local farmers, my father, who was perceived as a reasonably good farmer, continued to use very traditional approaches. As I was growing up, he regularly resented anyone's questioning the wisdom of certain established farming practices – I was normally the person who asked those questions. He could be described as conservative, and, in terms of farming practices, he certainly was. But in many other ways, he was quite liberal and even progressive. He had a very strong sense of the rights of the individual, was a great believer in equality and justice, and had no time for right-wing ideology – though he might not have understood the term itself.

Despite the low levels of income and wealth, no one in that community appeared to consider that he, or she, was particularly deprived, either socially or economically. Apart from teachers and shop owners, everyone had reasonably similar levels of comfort and income.

There was no basis for the sort of begrudgery which has blighted more recent Irish society. It was also virtually a crime-free society, apart from the odd politically motivated 'crime', which was not considered 'real' crime by local people.

The biggest socio-economic difference between then and now was undoubtedly in housing. I was reared in a small two-roomed thatched cottage with a very cramped loft space. It had no running water, no electricity, light being provided by an oil lamp and later by a 'Tilley' lamp, no internal toilet and no bathroom. We washed in a galvanised iron bath, initially in the kitchen in front of the open fire and later, as we grew older and modesty demanded a change, we moved to the scullery.

There was no phone and no television. We had to rely on a 'wet battery' radio, which always seemed to run out of power at some stage during the most important event of the day or the week. I vividly remember the whole family listening to the broadcast of Billy 'Spider' Kelly's unsuccessful attempt to win the European featherweight title in Dublin, against Ray Famechon, when the battery died. It did that during several important football games, too, when Michael O'Hehir's voice would just fade away and we would be left to wonder who had won. But Michael whetted our appetites for both the games and the strange places from which he was broadcasting – places where every game, whether hurling or football, was a thriller.

While Daddy had no interest in sport of any kind, O'Hehir ignited our youthful imaginations and transported us to faraway places, where giants of men played Ireland's native games. All-Ireland winners like TP O'Reilly, 'Sonny' Magee, whose sister was our next door neighbour, and the Gallant John Joe were well known in the area; others were known only by repute or by those who had played against them. But in later years, O'Hehir 'introduced' us to Seán Purcell and Frank Stockwell, to Paudie Sheehy and Tadghie Lyne, to Kevin Heffernan and Ollie Freaney, and to dozens of others whose skills and achievements we hoped to replicate one day.

Even though we had never seen hurling, it was still one of 'our' games and we imagined that, some day, we might see it being played. In the meantime, we settled for being regaled by the exploits of Christy Ring and Nicky Rackard, Tony Reddan and Eddie Keher and many more. And we wondered just how great Mick Mackey had been in his hey-day.

We had no car and the family had no tradition of Gaelic games. Travelling to faraway venues for a football game, much less for a hurling game, was a completely unrealistic expectation, but that did not hinder our dreaming. Young people now have the opportunity to see the national games, either live or on television; I was at university before I saw my first hurling game, even though it is now my favourite sport – by a long distance.

*****

As a result of becoming the family farmer at such an early age, my father never went to school, never learned to read or write and became both an example and a disciple of 'action learning'. He was clearly quite intelligent because, as I grew older, I discovered that he was exceptionally good at mental arithmetic – much better than the vast majority of other residents of the area. Later as I accompanied him to fairs, and then to marts, I discovered that if I told him that an animal weighed 8¾ hundredweight and we were getting £7.15.0 per cwt., he could work out the price in his head faster than most people could compute it with pen and paper. Learning by doing was a different sort of education, but one that was to stand him in good stead for the duration of his life.

Subsequently, in my own life I came to understand that education is a less-than-perfect mechanism for learning and a very unreliable substitute for either intelligence or common sense. Life's experiences have taught me that there is, at best, minimal correlation between literacy and intelligence, an even lower correlation between education and common sense, and that many of the most competent people I met in my life had less than average education. The late John Vallelly's witty comment about a certain player having been '*educated to be an idiot*' is still not without considerable merit. After years in the academic world I came to realise that, more than anything one might learn from books, learning through doing and by practise is real education for survival in a sometimes harsh world.

We were all lucky enough to inherit Daddy's ability with numbers. For three of us, at least, mathematics was our best subject at school, and we all have a facility with figures which not everyone could match.

I believe my father had a relatively happy childhood, though I have no doubt that growing up without his father was less than ideal. I never heard him complain about problems in his early years, although it was clear that life hadn't been easy and wealth did not exist. His mother was clearly a strong character and there appears to have been a tremendously strong and loyal bond between mother and son. As the only son and the heir-to-very-little, he was likely to have been a big favourite.

When Daddy was in his late teens, his only maternal uncle died from some form of lingering illness. His wife, who was also a distant relative of our family, was much younger than he was, so it was not surprising that she was widowed when she was still quite young. She subsequently re-married, reared a second family and lived long enough for me to remember her as an old woman, who invariably dressed in black.

There were two children from her first marriage. When the widow decided to re-marry, her daughter came to live with my grandmother, effectively becoming part of the family and replacing my father's Uncle John as the unpaid farm help, when he passed away. A few years later, when my father was in his early-twenties and still single, he went to visit a first cousin, who was in very poor health following the birth of her seventh child; in fact, she proved to be terminally ill. Her husband had already been in very bad health for some time and was unlikely to live for long either. So it was clear that the family would have to be split up and reared by relatives or friends. My father offered to take the baby, only to be told that she had already been taken by one of her paternal grandmothers. He took the second youngest instead.

He arrived home, having ridden his bicycle for six or seven miles, with a fifteen-month old baby in a cot strapped to the bar of the bicycle, as a 'present' for his mother to rear. That baby, later called Mina (short for Philomena), became the equivalent of my older sister; she is fifteen years older than I am. Although she left to work in Downpatrick shortly after I was born, she became a crucially important part of my young life and she is someone who still has a special place in my affections to this day. She is now widowed and lives in one of the most scenic parts of the United States, to which she emigrated in the early 1950s.

Over the succeeding months, most of the other members of that family were similarly placed with relatives or friends. In those days, there were no formalities associated with that kind of adoption. Each case was just another example of family, friends or neighbours showing the strength of their support, as a caring community, for a family in trouble. Unlike in what I have seen in media reports, those who were adopted through the informal processes applied in the rural communities of South Fermanagh and West Cavan, rarely lost contact with their siblings and most of them grew up having two families, with whom they continued to maintain close links.

That sense of community is still strong in the Cavan-Fermanagh border area and in much of the rest of rural Ireland today; it may not be as strong as it was eighty or a hundred years ago, but it is still there. Even though their roles may have diminished to some extent, in the intervening decades, community, family connections and a strong sense of identity are still hugely cohesive factors in rural society, even in modern, materialistic Ireland.

At least twice, but normally three times every year, Mina came back to Teemore on week-long holidays and those were consistently the most joyous times in our house in my early years. My father was always very animated both before she arrived and when Mina was 'at home'. When I became ill, she came home on special leave, though I remember nothing about her visit, since I spent most of my time sleeping. In 2005, during a short, family reunion in her adopted country, she told me of an incident which occurred when my post-tonsillectomy survival was still in doubt. She was both a wonderful worker and very gifted with her hands and one day, during that visit, she was knitting in the kitchen when my father came in.

"What are you doing, Mina?" he asked.

"I'm knitting a pair of mittens," she replied.

"Who are you knitting them for?" he enquired.

"For Peter," she replied.

"Aargh, for Christ's sake, don't be wasting your time; sure he'll never live to wear them," he said, as he turned to go back outside.

Mina still believes that he was starting to cry as he left to recommence whatever he had been doing and that caused her to start crying too. But I lived to wear the mittens.

* * * * *

My parents had been born and reared less than half a mile apart in linear distance and more than a decade apart in time. My maternal grandfather, Arthur Clarke, was an only son, who emigrated to the United States as a young man. His father had died when he was ten or eleven, and he too was reared by his mother. As a teenager, he was not enamoured of farming. Like many of his era, he envisaged the streets of New York as being paved with gold – an attraction which the small family farm in South Fermanagh could not match.

I never heard what he did in New York, but he met and married Ellen Keane, from Dunamon in Roscommon, who was about a decade his senior. They were married in St Patrick's Cathedral in Manhattan and some years later, for some unknown reason, they returned to Ireland, where he inherited the modest family farm.

My grandmother's seniority proved to be a wonderful advantage. Arthur was a difficult man, but one person had his measure and combined it with an outstanding capacity to avoid any form of strife. When he would suggest a trip back to the pub for 'a hair of the dog' after he had had a few drinks on the previous day, his wife would always find something urgent to do, until his thirst had eased and the need for a drink had been forgotten. Ellen Keane, one of the quietest and nicest people I met in my entire life, could control her husband's moods and manage his innate aggression without creating conflict.

From my later experiences, I now understand that she was a superb man-manager, with many of the personnel skills needed to be a successful entrepreneur or business woman. There have been many times in my own life, when I would have given anything for her dispute-resolution talents and her 'way with people', but I haven't.

A son, Patrick, died at a very young age, leaving my mother, Mary, and her sister, Eileen, as the surviving children; my mother was the older of the two. They were both born when my grandmother was in her early forties and grew up with quite abrasive personalities.

Because they lived so near to one another, my parents would have known each other from a very early age. Their farms had operated in tandem over many years, following my grandparents' return from New York.

Throughout the first five or six decades of the twentieth century, the traditional Irish concept of the 'meitheal' was widespread in our area and throughout most of rural Ireland; so too was the idea of working in 'comhair'. When crops were being harvested, especially when the oats crop was being cut and the potatoes were being dug, the meitheal assembled, often summoned by the sound of the machinery or the shouts of the horsemen. All the machinery was powered by horses, at that time.

It was common enough for two or three men to start the reaping, as soon as the horses could be harnessed after the morning milking, but by mid-morning that same field could have ten or twelve men in it and it took that many to keep the horses and the machine going steadily. These arrangements were generally informal, but they worked very well, with no distinctions on the basis of political or religious affiliations, or of social status, in that area.

This entire process contributed greatly to community cohesion and a feeling of togetherness. The day was not always wholly restricted to the main task; many a local dispute was sorted out over the dinner, lunch as it is now called, for the meitheal and, with so many witnesses, all such agreements were binding and no one could renege on them. The court of communal approbation became the ultimate judicial arbiter for such cases.

My father and my maternal grandfather worked in partnership – 'i gcomhair', pronounced locally as 'in core' – for many years. Apparently, the two had developed some sort of friendship shortly after my grandparents' return from America, when my father was still a 'pre-teen' farmer. Later on, from his mid-teens, my father appeared to act as Arthur's minder when the older man got drunk and started rows, which was a regular occurrence.

My father was a tall, slim man who was always very fit and immensely strong. He had a reputation for being handy with his fists – a reputation which survived intact until his death – so Arthur could afford to indulge his contrariness in the full knowledge that he would be protected by my father.

On one occasion, when my mother was about fifteen or sixteen and had left school, she served the dinner to the meitheal. She was washing the dishes at the kitchen sink as the men were going back out to the field, when my father allegedly gave her a friendly slap on her bottom, saying "Mary, I'll marry you some day." Five years later, he did.

My mother was a very bright woman. When she was about to leave school, her teacher came to her parents and tried to persuade them to send her for further education to become a teacher, because others with less ability were pursuing that path. But my grandparents had no funds to support such a career choice and rejected the suggestion. They probably accepted the reality that people of their status and background did not proceed to higher education, that was for children of the better-off classes, before the introduction of 'free education'.

In later years, she became what would be described locally as widely read and her ability to retain information was phenomenal. She was very articulate both in speech and on paper, and could be equally caustic through both media. At her funeral, the priest indicated in his homily that, being relatively new to the parish, he hadn't known my mother until the last six months of her life. However, he continued by saying that, from what he had heard of her, '… she could have trimmed hedges with her tongue.' We thought that his comment was entirely apt and though some of the congregation came to us afterwards to express their concern that we would, or should, have been insulted by it, we weren't.

The new husband-wife relationship encountered considerable turbulence. My mother had dreams and ambitions, and saw a world full of opportunities and potential. My father was a farmer, who was widely known and respected for his skills with horses, in particular, but he was also good at buying and selling, and looked after his cattle very well. He was entirely satisfied with his lot, had no ambition to explore or to expand his horizon, and just wanted peace and contentment. His laid-back, conservative approach frustrated my mother, who had just come into a house in which three women had already established their positions: her mother-in-law, who had a clear vision of herself as the boss and the head of the household, irrespective of who lived under its roof, and she was not prepared to relinquish her role easily; a young woman, Mary, who was almost as old as the new arrival (there was a difference of just over five years), even if she did not have the same ambitions and aspirations; and a young girl of six or seven, Mina, who was still a child in my mother's eyes.

The relationship between my mother and her mother-in-law had all the explosive potential of a keg of gelignite and it duly exploded. The result was that our parents' marriage did not really commence until after our grandmother died. I was born just over a year later and over the next six years my arrival was followed by two sisters, Miriam and Bernadette, separated by a brother, Seán.

Years later, I came to realise that my mother had long suffered from recurring, mild depression, which occasionally created problems for both her and the rest of the family. I suspect that some of my siblings may have realised that before I did. Today, she would probably be prescribed a mild anti-depressant and would have lived a much different and less disturbed life. To us, she was just a very cross mammy.

It was always clear to me that, in their own very different and not very obvious ways, both of my parents loved me, though neither of them would have displayed such emotions. Expressions of love or affection did not come easily to either of them. Consequently, as I grew older, I began to realise that I had no role model to follow when it came to developing close interpersonal relationships, though I was not then aware of how significant that was to young people, and I certainly never guessed how great an impact it was having on my life.

Better than most, I now understand those who complain about the way in which a lack of social and interpersonal skills affects one's sense of self-respect and erodes one's confidence, probably more than any form of physical abuse could ever do.

My father might have given us the odd 'cuff around the ear' (he used to call them 'lug-setters') or even an occasional relatively mild kick up the backside, but he was very moderate in his punishment, which was a rarity and never involved much pain. The threat of a lug-setter was normally enough to put us in our place, without any explicit action on his part.

Despite his impressive physical strength, I could not say that I was ever really afraid of my father, but I knew that he had absolutely no understanding of the world of education, which I had started to inhabit from a relatively young age. He saw it as an unnecessary intrusion into the world of farm work which was, for all practical purposes, his entire world and in those days he was probably right – education was not needed to plant potatoes or reap corn, to use a spade or pitchfork, to milk cows or harness a horse, to feed and fodder, or even to apply common sense and make a real effort to succeed.

However, as I got older, I began to realise that he would support any of us in anything we did, provided it was legal, reasonably morally acceptable and not completely stupid. That view was shared by my mother and they both did support us regularly. For my father, morality was a particularly important issue, though not everyone would accept all aspects of his definition of that trait. Sexual morality, honesty and truthfulness were particularly important to him, as was respect for family and loyalty to neighbours, friends and relatives; it was good, old-fashioned morality, and none the worse for that.

Overall, it would be an understatement to say that I didn't have a particularly happy childhood. In reality, growing up was for me a somewhat painful experience – physically and psychologically, with poor health making the former difficult and my psychological make-up and the family environment combining to render the latter very difficult.

Nevertheless, those issues never turned me against my family. I often felt that I was a bit of an outsider and I probably became somewhat of a loner. From an early age, I understood that I was not handling my problems particularly well, but I did not know how to handle them any better. I had no idea whether it was my own personality, or my domestic environment, which was responsible, though I now accept that it was probably a combination of several factors and that I was not blameless in the misery which I endured. I felt lost in a world which I could barely handle.

But all that never made me dislike the Mountain Road or the community there. They were and are wonderful people, welcoming but wary, warm though vigilant, loyal but careful, and respectful but not obsequious. I loved my home place then and I still do. Born and reared less than a mile from the border, that little bit of boundary area was, and for me still is, the most important place on earth and the place 'I love best of all'. Apart from my own house, with my wife and children, there is nowhere else I feel more relaxed or more 'at home'. Though I have not lived there for the best part of fifty years I'm there at least once a week. The place and its people continue to be, for me, the centre of the world.

3

Living with the Border

When my parents were born, the division between the 'Free State' and the 'North' did not exist but, by the time they were married, the 'border' was well established and meaningful in a legal sense though not universally accepted. Even though he was not politically minded, my father never really accepted the validity of the border. He felt, as did most of his nationalist neighbours, that Fermanagh should have been part of the Free State and that, had the infamous Boundary Commission done its work properly, it would have been.

For him and later for us, too, the introduction of the border had several consequences. For a start, my grandparents had always attended Mass in Ballyconnell, just over the border in Cavan. Until the early-1860s the old Ballyconnell and Tomeregan parish had extended into Fermanagh for just over a mile, which was enough to include our house; consequently, Ballyconnell was where those who lived along the Mountain Road went to Mass. There was another chapel for those who lived in the eastern part of what is now the Teemore area and it was subsequently replaced by the current St Mary's Church, in Teemore.

On every dimension Ballyconnell was our local village, or 'town' as it was normally called in the area, until external constitutional and political changes with little local support decreed that it ought no longer to be so. It was where groceries were bought, where cattle, sheep, pigs, donkeys and horses were bought and sold on the monthly fair day, where pints and half-ones were consumed and men got drunk, where politics was discussed and, most importantly of all, where most of those who lived along the Mountain Road, expected to be buried. My paternal grandparents are buried there, as are most of my other relatives of that generation and, indeed, of the subsequent generation.

Those relationships with Ballyconnell and West Cavan applied equally to the local Protestant population on the Fermanagh side of the county boundary, along the Mountain Road. Most of them were members of the Church of Ireland who also went to Ballyconnell for their Sunday Service and Sunday School. They too were mainly buried there, even post-partition and, indeed, right up to the present time. While revisions to parish boundaries and a programme of building new churches, involving the creation of new parishes within the Diocese of Kilmore, were implemented from the 1860s, they made very little difference to traditional loyalties or social links and had little impact on commercial and economic activity.

Regardless of being in a different county, Ballyconnell was much closer than either Derrylin or Teemore, with the result that Ballyconnell, which ultimately became part of a different political jurisdiction, was where people from our townland tended to socialise and the village with which they identified most closely. The creation of an international boundary could not break that link, in the short term at least. Indeed, in many ways, it has still not been broken.

So we grew up with a sort of bipolar perspective. We were in Teemore, but we socialised in Ballyconnell; we were in Fermanagh, but we were aligned economically and socially with Cavan; we knew west Cavan much better than we knew most of the rest of Fermanagh – in fact, we barely knew anyone in north or west Fermanagh at all. We lived in the newly established 'North' but we thought and acted as if we were in the Free State, as it continued to be called in South Fermanagh. We were happy going to buy cattle in Cavan, Leitrim, Roscommon or even

Mayo, but it would never have occurred to us to go to Kesh, Belleek, Irvinestown, or Tempo, all of which are in our own county. We had relatives in various parts of Cavan, but very few in Fermanagh, beyond the boundaries of our own parish. In fact, most of the older people from South Fermanagh had more relations in New York and other parts of the United States, than they had in other parts of Fermanagh, that was certainly true in the case of Catholic families, because the dreaded emigration did not apply as an equally consistent imperative to those of other religions.

In other ways, the border was an asset to be exploited. During the Second World War, when rationing of food and other items was introduced by the British government, those living along the border could get supplies of certain rationed commodities in the Free State. Various types of food including tea, butter, white bread, sugar, dried fruit (which was essential for making Christmas cakes), anything with preservatives, most brands of alcoholic drink, anything involving certain metals or rubber, clothing and much, much more, were rationed and available only on production of the appropriate coupons. But most of these products were widely available across the border and that was where virtually all the local families did their shopping and spent their money.

As a trade-off, fertilisers, in particular, were in short supply on the other side of the border, so smuggling and bartering became an accepted way of life. I learned about those practices from my earliest years. It was not uncommon for a donkey to be loaded with a couple of hundred-weight bags of fertiliser for the first half of the journey and return with a few rolls of 'suit-lengths' or other clothing material, later that night. Overall, the balance of economic advantage tended to favour those on the northern side. That may not have been what those who imposed partition had expected, but that was the reality.

Since partition was not really accepted by the vast majority in South Fermanagh, including by many Protestants, no one had any great scruples about depriving the British government of duty or import taxes, or any other form of tax. So, smuggling became a way of life for some and an essential part of their existence for others.

My parents were no different. They bought their allocation of butter under the rationing provisions and supplemented it with additional purchases across the border – Killeshandra butter was a staple in our house – and they did exactly the same with anything else which was in short supply on one side but available on the other. It is fair to say that smuggling saved many of our neighbours from the emigrant ship, but unfortunately it could not save them all.

Smuggling was not seen as a political statement in our area, as it was to become in later decades, nor was it perceived as any type of crime and it was equally common in both communities. While there were clear differences in some respects, Catholics and Protestants invariably mixed very well, socialised together, worked in harmony and smuggled in equal proportions. They went to different schools and different churches – in the days when everyone went to church – but they were still at peace with one another. To this day, people from outside that area have major difficulty accepting that reality, particularly in the aftermath of almost four decades of so-called 'Troubles' which undoubtedly caused an increase in suspicion. But on a daily basis, harmony continued, even in the aftermath of various atrocities, some of which served to increase suspicions – and understandably so.

As I was growing up, nobody objected to the annual celebrations of each community – the 'Twelfth' and Black Saturday for Protestants and St Patrick's Day or August 15th for Catholics. To this day they are not a source of significant problems in the area. Whether that was out of respect or apathy is hard to say, but it avoided the sort of problems which later affected other parts of the North.

For nationalists, there were virtually no jobs in the area in those years, apart from farm labouring and about half-a-dozen in local quarries. The vast majority of the young men who were not going to inherit the family farm were forced to emigrate though some remained in the family home – at least until they got married which an unusually high proportion never did. In many cases, they just remained as either unpaid, or under-paid, farmhands. It was not uncommon to have three or four brothers, sometimes with a sister or two, scraping a very poor living from a small hillside farm of poor land. I could count up to fifty houses within a one-mile radius which became desolate after the last of the unmarried residents died, within my first thirty years on this earth.

Many of those who emigrated, especially the men-folk, waited until they were in their twenties before they left, unlike in other parts of Ireland, where they tended to leave at a younger age. Whether the spirit of adventure was weaker in the border area, or the opportunities for smuggling provided an opportunity for economic survival is unclear, but one thing was sure, there were no jobs and there would be no jobs for those from our community. We all grew up knowing that emigration was almost a certainty for any of us who were not going to inherit a farm.

Four Quinn brothers, first cousins of my father and around the same age as he was, all left for America in the same way, but at different times. They told their parents that they were going to a local house dance on a Sunday evening but, when the dance was over, instead of coming back home to help with the milking or to do their share of field work on the farm, they walked about eight miles to Belturbet and boarded the narrow gauge train for Dublin. From there, they went to Cobh, then known as Queenstown, and took the boat to the United States without ever saying goodbye to either their parents or their siblings. None of them ever returned to Ireland, neither on holiday nor for family funerals. The method of their leaving I could understand, but the fact that none of them ever returned I still find depressing.

In that era in South Fermanagh, nobody in the nationalist community with a farming background went to secondary school, never mind to university. The only real choice for most people was between the spade and shovel at home, or the spade and shovel in London or New York – the farm in Ireland or the building site overseas – or, for the really adventurous, a farm in Australia's outback.

Most of these things I did not understand until much later in life. As I lay in bed, listening to the conversation about my imminent death, I was entirely unaware of a wider world. Like many others of my age in that area, I had no frame of reference by which to interpret our lives. That would come later – and slowly.

4

Born and Reared
to be a Farmer

It's a sad reflection on our scant understanding of life and death as we grew up that, when my father had a very serious thrombosis, always called a heart attack in South Fermanagh, at the age of 49, we four children saw no reason to be worried. I was only seven and the youngest of my siblings, Bernadette, was only two. Death had no meaning for us at that time and the fact that, under normal circumstances, or for a normal person, he should not have survived it (according to his GP and the other doctors who subsequently examined his case) did not upset us in the least. Daddy was rarely sick and virtually never confined to bed, so this was different, but we didn't appreciate how different.

Even though that first attack had occurred during the night, we were simply rushed out to school on the following morning as if nothing had happened. I think we all had an inkling that something was not right, but I did not really know much about it until I came home from school that afternoon and the doctor was just leaving. By then I could discern an atmosphere of panic and fear and an increase in visitor numbers.

Generally, visitors caused no raised eyebrows in our house, which was widely known as a 'céiliing house'. Every night of the week, we had visitors from about 8.30pm to anywhere between 10.30pm and 1.00am, depending on who arrived on any particular night. I grew up expecting such visitors, they brightened the mood of a house which often needed brightening. There were local musicians, footballers and ex-footballers, neighbours and relatives, as well as some non-locals who happened to be working on local farms.

In the early 1950s, it was assumed that those who had suffered a heart attack could never work again, it being accepted that they were, in the local terminology, finished. But Daddy had other ideas. Within a couple of weeks, he was back on his feet and, contrary to doctor's orders, he resumed his role on the farm almost immediately. Heavy work and light work were all the same to him. Even though he was tall at well over six foot, and comparatively thin, he was an immensely strong man, without fear of either life or death, and saw no reason to change his lifestyle just because he'd suffered a heart attack. He was alive and, for him, that meant business as usual. He would never have felt that he should do some of the less physical work and leave the heavy lifting to others – that was just not his style.

I've often wondered what would have happened to us as a family if he'd died as a result of that first attack and to what extent our lives would have turned out differently, but that is idle speculation. Nevertheless, I suspect that emigration would have had to be considered. I would probably never have gone to secondary school but even if I had, I would certainly not have finished my period there, never mind go on to third level. What that would have meant for the rest of my life, I shudder to think. But Daddy solved the problem by continuing as if nothing had happened, farming in his own way, living life and having more heart attacks over the next sixteen years. He was, and still is, a wonderful example for us and great consolation to all of us when times are tough.

We learned a lot more about heart attacks, or pulmonary thromboses, over the next sixteen years, because he had an average of one per annum until he eventually died at the age of 65. In some years he had none and in other years he would have a couple, but it was the seventeenth which eventually killed him. In fact we grew blasé about such events, though we understood that my mother considered them to be very serious. Still, however blasé we became, it was still a bit of a shock when we actually saw him collapse or when we arrived home after one of his attacks.

*****

A year before his first heart attack, my father had purchased a second farm, on the Cavan side of the border, a mile outside Ballyconnell and less than three miles from Gortmullen. With two sons he needed two farms, because it had never occurred to him that either of his sons would make his livelihood in any other way. I was to become the owner and farmer of the new land, when I was ready to start farming on my own account.

The farm being sold had once been part of the local Church of Ireland estate. No one had anticipated that it would be sold to a Catholic. Nevertheless, since Daddy knew the vendor, who was a member of the Protestant community and a very fair-minded man, he decided to bid for it and his was the highest offer. His offer amounted to less than £30 per acre.

The decision to sell was deferred and, eventually, he was told that the sale would be finalised, one way or another, on the day of Ballyconnell fair. The monthly fair day was always one of the highlights of life in the farming community – a day when all kinds of animals could be bought or sold, often for smuggling and always for cash.

In common with most of his neighbours, Daddy attended most fairs in Ballyconnell, unless there was something else of major importance happening on that day. So, it was nothing new for him to be going to this one. Nevertheless, I vividly remember the sense of anticipation that morning as he was preparing for the fair and we were leaving for school; we were told not to talk about what was happening when we went to school and, truth to tell, we did not really understand the significance of what we were hearing. However, I remember his suggesting that 'they' would probably not sell it to him anyway and Mammy insisting that he should bring with him all the money they had – just in case.

Subsequently, I learned that sometime in the late morning the deal was agreed, and Daddy and the vendor went to the solicitor's office to sign the contract of sale. The price was £2,250 for seventy-six acres and there would have been the traditional 'luck penny' out of that. The sale, when it became known, caused consternation in certain quarters and, by early afternoon, there was a small meeting in a local hall to see if the sale could be overturned. For a small minority, such property should not have been sold to a nationalist but at the meeting one of our Protestant neighbours suggested that as 'Quinn was the highest bidder, it should be left with him'.

About a month after he acquired the land my father bought a few animals, early in the day, at Derrylin fair – marts had not reached the South Fermanagh or West Cavan areas at that point. The best store animals were invariably sold early at those fairs and he knew the difference between good cattle and the not so good. Later in the day, his first cousin, Terry Curry, noticed that he was no longer trying to buy and asked him why.

"Sure, you'll need a good few more cattle to stock that farm in Cranaghan, why are you not buying a few more?" he asked

"I have no money to buy any more," Daddy replied truthfully.

"Buy away," said Terry "and I'll pay for them. You can pay me back when you sell them."

And that is how the new farm was stocked – Terry was repaid when the cattle were sold, with no interest and no disagreement. That meant everything was in place for me to become a Cavan farmer, with my brother, Seán, inheriting the home place along the Mountain Road. The result is that, even to this day, I have a huge grá for Cavan and its people. I would never support another county, apart from Fermanagh, against Cavan in any form of competition.

When asked about what he feared most, the British politician, Harold Macmillan, is credited with the memorable response: 'Events, dear boy, events.' Events or 'fate' were to dictate that farming would not be my choice of career.

It was not easy to make a living from the land in those days. However, along the border the low profitability was often partially offset by the margin that could be generated through smuggling.

Having land on both sides of the border meant that, occasionally, we had to smuggle the cattle in both directions. Over a two-year period, any given animal might have made this journey up to half a dozen times depending on where grass was most available. I was regularly involved in driving the cattle across the border: I was a good, fast runner, could tune into what an animal intended to do very quickly and was entirely comfortable with cattle especially – less so with pigs. I developed a minor reputation as being useful in that sort of activity.

While I would always have preferred reading or other forms of learning to most kinds of farm work, I was always interested in cattle farming, at ease with the animals and athletic enough to avoid problems even with cross animals, though I was always wary of bulls. Even though smuggling was slightly risky and, therefore attended by a degree of temporary excitement, it was seen as just a normal part of farming near the border in the 1940s and 1950s.

Oddly enough, I was also good with horses, which could be temperamental too. I'd clearly inherited some of my father's gifts and, occasionally, I could manage a horse which others, apart from my father, had difficulty in controlling.

While farm horses are not nearly as difficult to manage as thoroughbreds or even sport horses, a minority can be difficult enough. I seemed to have had some sort of knack with them from early in my teenage years, though I remember being dumped into a dung-hill by a horse which was stretching himself as I was removing the harness from him after a day's farming. It was not a pleasant experience but I suffered no injuries, apart from a damaged ego and an urgent need for a change of clothes and a wash – deodorants were unknown about the Mountain Road, at that time.

For me, the most difficult part of working with horses was in ploughing. I cannot claim to have done much of that work, but I stood in for Daddy enough times to recall how hard it was. To manipulate the plough, one had to walk between the two iron handles and I still recall, only too well, the pain when the sock hit a stone. On those occasions I wasn't strong enough to hold the plough steady with the result that, as the horses kept moving, the entire plough would jump around like a jack-rabbit. The handles would drive into one side of my thinly-covered ribs, and then the other, as I struggled to manage the combination of horse and machine. The land was dry, gravel based and stony along the Mountain Road and, after a few hours ploughing these uneven, rocky fields, my body would be covered in black marks from just above the hip to about the level of my elbow. Years later, to the relief of my ribs, we bought a tractor.

I learned as much about farming pigs and cattle from my cousins on our weekly Sunday visits to my aunt's as I learned at home, though my father (for whom his nephews had tremendous respect) was not a bad teacher of those subjects either. When it came to the matter of horses – working horses, since he had no interest in others – Daddy was in a league of his own, with a knowledge and understanding of equine animals that was immensely surprising for someone who could neither read nor write.

To his nephews and to him, farming was a vocation. They loved what they did and took a pride in it. They respected their animals and cared about their welfare and were happy to impart their knowledge to any willing listener. I loved watching and learning from them on those Sunday visits.

Best of all, my cousins would recount what had transpired at recent fairs, about cattle prices and their own and others' smuggling escapades. They would talk about who was dating whom, discuss politics and the state of the economy, especially the agricultural and rural economy. It made us feel mature and wise beyond our years – in reality we weren't, but the illusion made us happy.

Unfortunately, we visited our cousins on the maternal side of the family much more rarely. That was probably predictable, in light of the frequently poor relations between Mammy and her sister. Family was very important in our house – as it still is – but clearly it was a much stronger force on my father's side of the tree than on my mother's. I never really understood why the two sides of the family were so different in that respect and I have long regretted the reality that it was, because my cousins on my mother's side are wonderful people, with whom we should have had so much in common.

The problems created by the disagreements between my mother and her sister, and I have no idea what caused the 'bad blood' between them, taught me that one generation should never pass its prejudices or its disagreements on to any other generation, because it causes so much unnecessary division and ultimately creates regrets and heartbreak. Family rows should have no place in life.

Daddy consistently emphasised the importance of maintaining links with relatives and always acknowledged even remote relationships, when we met distant cousins. He would never have missed the funeral of one of those relatives, however inconvenient it was. Whatever the advances of recent times may have delivered for modern society, the family, however defined, is still the ultimate source of support and moral sustenance – at least in rural society.

5

Farming Interrupted

My mother was reasonably keen on education, though not in a pushy way and none of us ever felt under any pressure to do well in examinations. Unlike many of the other local mothers, she did not send me to school until after my fifth birthday. I now realise that I'd always been prone to sickness and that Mammy was protecting me by keeping me at home.

I started after Easter, presumably so that I would have my orientation completed before the summer holidays. Ours was a small two-room, two-teacher, primary school at Garvary, which was a little bit more than halfway to Teemore. Putting it mildly, every aspect of its facilities was very poor – especially its sanitary facilities. The fact that we did not contract all sorts of disease was a miracle.

The schoolyard in which we played in our bare feet had just an ordinary hard-core surface, but come sun, rain or snow, that was where we spent our lunch break. It was not a good place to fall, so one quickly learned the art of balancing and swerving, which was very useful on the football field later. As a consequence, bleeding toes and cut feet were common but, over time, we learned to accept them without whingeing.

Virtually all the pupils walked to school in their bare feet from about

St Patrick's Day until the end of September. For us, it was over a mile and a half each way. The outward journey was normally completed fairly quickly, in order to be in time for school. The return journey took longer. If there was a good reason to get home quickly, we would do it in about three quarters of an hour, if not, it took more than an hour – much more if there was an opportunity to play a bit of football on the way or when we ran races against one another. Such late returns often led to a scolding from my mother about not being available for work, whether inside in the house or outside on the farm. Most times there was no reason to hurry, so we dallied, accepted the scolding and hoped it would go no further than that. Generally it didn't, but occasionally we called it wrong and suffered the consequences. If things were particularly bad at home, we were often happy to accept whatever came our way as a result of being late.

Schoolwork came easily to me. My first teacher, Miss Cassidy, was a confirmed spinster but a very kind person who seemed to like me and I was very happy with her. Halfway through my first year, I was promoted from 'low infants' as it was called, to 'high infants'. A year later I went out to the 'big room' to be taught by the principal, Mrs Dunne. She and her husband, who was the chairman of the local Teemore Shamrocks club and a former county chairman and inter-county referee, lived in the same townland as us. Master Dunne (Jim to his footballing colleagues) taught in the other end of the parish, in Derrylin. For some reason, not necessarily her fault, I never seemed to get along with Mrs Dunne in the same way as I had with Miss Cassidy.

Eighteen months later, I was promoted to fourth class. So, in less than four years, I'd climbed six steps of the academic ladder. Despite frequent periods of absence, over the two years following my illness, I was in the 11-plus class (5th class, as it was then called, but now called P7 in the Northern system) by the time I was nine, having skipped a couple of classes. Later that year, because three of my new classmates – all at least a year older than me – were sitting the examination and my teacher, anticipating my turn the following year, decided that the experience would be good for me. So, I was enrolled for the exam as well, even though I'd absolutely no idea of what the implications were, or even why I was sitting it. Talk about being naïve!

Only one other person from the Mountain Road had ever passed this exam and she was the teacher's daughter, so I had no role model to follow and I felt no pressure to succeed.

There were four papers: two 'intelligence tests' followed by a two-part test covering English and Mathematics, which had always been my favourite subject. They were taken at monthly intervals over a three-month period. I estimated that between forty and fifty aspiring academics took the first two papers, but I noticed that there were fewer candidates at the third session. My tenth birthday occurred between the second and third sessions.

The examination hall was in Derrylin, which served as the centre for about a dozen primary schools – both Catholic and Protestant – in the South Fermanagh region. I knew none of the other candidates, apart from my three classmates. Of the four from our school who sat that examination, two passed and I was one them.

There had been no pressure on me to pass the examination. My father had already decided that both of his sons were going to be farmers. He never envisaged any other future for his male children and the 11-plus was of absolutely no interest to him. Though he never said so, I am convinced that he thought this entire 'exam thing' was a waste of time and totally unnecessary for a prospective farmer – though that was before the arrival of the bureaucracy now associated with a career on the land.

The result came in the post which normally arrived between 11am and 1pm each day. But when I arrived home from school, I was told that my grandfather had died from a heart attack a couple of hours earlier. That was more important than any 11-plus result. All the excitement related to my grandfather's death so I was immediately dispatched to the bog to tell those who were cutting that year's turf to come home. The bog was up near the top of the mountain at the back of our house and involved a very steep climb. For some reason, not now obvious to me, I ran the entire two miles there and then ran back again, though the return journey was much easier. Presumably, to quote Steve McQueen in The Magnificent Seven, it: '... seemed to be a good idea at the time.'

As things transpired, I only found out I'd passed the exam some time after I returned from the mountain. The 11-plus exam was very good for young people from the nationalist community but it was particularly good for me. It was a central element of the opening up of access to higher education following the Beveridge Report in England, and the delay in its adoption in the North was seen by nationalists as being purely politically motivated. That Act made secondary level education and ultimately tertiary education available to the minority population and those of little means in the North. Later in life, I realised how important it was to the entire nationalist community of the North; it had the effect of contributing to their liberation and their development as a coherent economic, social and political force.

More than anything else, it influenced the social and political developments which have occurred in the North, over the past half-century. It's immensely regrettable that those changes could not have been secured in a more civilised manner, with no loss of life.

Although I'd no idea what to expect, I was happy enough to leave Garvary and Mrs Dunne. I became the youngest pupil in St Michael's Grammar School by about nine months, with Cormac McConnell, of the nationally and internationally known musical and journalism family, one of Fermanagh's greatest families, being the second youngest. I sat at the same desk as Cormac for the first year. He was the first person I ever met who could do speed-reading and – predictably given his background and his and other family members' subsequent choices of career – he was always a wonderful story-teller. But then so were both of his parents so, as they say in Fermanagh, 'he didn't pick it off the road'. His father, Sandy, was a stalwart of the Bellanaleck Art Macmurrough's GAA club. Alongside Hugh D'Arcy, the father of another national personality, Fr Brian D'Arcy, Sandy managed the club's affairs for many years.

Cormac left to enter journalism before completing his education at

St Michael's and was followed into that career by his brothers, the late Seán – a gentleman and a great journalist – and Michael. Apart from achieving great recognition in journalism, two of the trio have also made a name as songwriters, while Cathal, of *Boys of the Lough* fame, has made a name for himself as a talented musician who can play a variety of instruments.

At that time, St Michael's was a small secondary school compared to the norm. Total enrolment was about one hundred pupils across five classes, with almost 80 per cent of those being in the first three classes. There was a steady drop-off in class size, starting from the end of first year, when more than 10 per cent normally failed to return for a second year, with only a minority of about one-third staying on after Junior Certificate (the then Northern equivalent of the 'inter cert' in the South).

By modern standards, it was what they would call in South Fermanagh, a 'rum joint'. There was none of the formality associated with other secondary schools of the time: no morning assembly; little or no deference to teachers; no organised physical education. Advice on careers or further education was conspicuous by its absence as was sex education and any great emphasis on results. To cap it all, there was almost no real discipline and certainly no co-ordination of disciplinary procedures. We regarded the modified version of caning which we called 'slapping' was harsh enough until we later discovered what happened in other schools. Only then did we realise that ours had been a particularly benign regime.

No other school with which I ever came in contact offered similar freedom to students or similar opportunities to waste talent, and yet none provided the same opportunities for personal development geared towards the realities of a harsh world. It was a most unusual academy and, while I am very conscious of its inadequacies, I also recognise that it created a much more entrepreneurial spirit than was engendered in most similar schools of that era. That was reflected in the fact that an unusually large proportion of its output finished up in self-employment within a decade or so of leaving the place.

It was a great place in many ways. Unusually, for reasons I have never fully understood, there was virtually no bullying. Horseplay was common enough, but it rarely, if ever, descended into sustained bullying. With my very thin frame, my younger age, my capacity to absorb information with comparative ease and my dysfunctional background, which fortunately most of my colleagues never discovered, I should have been an obvious candidate for bullying, but I can honestly say that it never happened to me – why, I am not entirely sure.

Perhaps it was, in part at least, down to the very strong culture in the school of standing-up for the underdog. That culture was fuelled largely by some of the more authoritative and more politically aware personalities in the school. Chief among those figures was Frank McManus who, within a decade of leaving the place, became our representative in Westminster. In St Michael's, Frank, as he continued to be later in his political and professional life, was a huge defender of those who were most vulnerable. That empathy with the underdog was, and to some extent still is, a feature of life in rural South Fermanagh. While everyone was expected to stand up for himself and most inter-personal disputes were sorted out by a hastily organised bout of fisticuffs, there were always enough bystanders to ensure that no one got badly beaten and to stop the fight when one of the combatants was gaining clear supremacy. For me, that was just as well because I had not inherited my father's skills with his fists, nor his physical strength.

In his autobiography, Darragh O'Shea, one of the great midfielders of the modern era, refers repeatedly to the need to stand up to the opposition and put down a marker in the physical stakes. His comments related mainly to playing football, but they have wider application, too, in most aspects of social intercourse. Darragh would have been disappointed in me. I simply did not have the physique or the strength to 'mix it' with most of my opponents.

I now realise that, in its own way, St Michael's provided a wonderful education for later life in an imperfect society. But it was not quite so good on the academic front – in fact, it was outrageously deficient in that realm. The syllabus was exceptionally narrow and did not allow for the teaching of any foreign language, though Latin and Irish were mandatory. It didn't include subjects like physics, or biology, or any practically-based or technologically-based subjects, or physical education or anything related to civics or citizenship, or to business and the economy. In fact, apart from the Latin and Irish, the syllabus was not much broader than that of a good primary school, though clearly the depth to which subjects were taught was immeasurably greater. Equally, there was no formal structure for pupil assessment, the assessment of progress, careers advice or career planning, which probably contributed to the exceptionally small number, anything between zero and two per annum, who proceeded to further education.

In this new life, instead of walking to Garvary, I was collected by a local school bus outside our front door at 7.20 every morning and transported to Derrylin, three miles away. Another bus then took us to Enniskillen, a further thirteen miles away where we had time for a quick, disorganised game of football, until class started after 9am. The bigger lads dominated the football with the rest of us just hoping that the ball would break in our direction often enough to keep us interested. Despite the tarmac surface, there were hardly any injuries beyond the odd scraped knee or elbow. Unfortunately, I couldn't dodge my health problems off the pitch.

I was not long at St Michael's when my personal bogeyman reappeared. I became quite ill and was subjected to another episode of penicillin injections. When it recurred a few weeks later, the doctor decided that I should be taken from St Michael's and returned to the primary school at Garvary. According to the doctor, the travel and the long day followed by homework were affecting my health. I was 'not fit for it', he claimed; it was too long a day for a ten year old. Goodness knows what he'd have said if he'd known I had to help with the milking as well.

I objected vehemently because I did not want to go back to primary school, under any circumstance. I guess I perceived such a return as some form of loss of face, rather than arguing on either a health or an educational basis. With hindsight, I realise that my mother was not keen on the idea either though, over the next few years, she often used it as a threat when she was in bad form and I happened to be the butt of her anger. This time, she was on my side and argued her case forcefully, as was her wont. A compromise was reached – the doctor would allow me to continue at St Michael's, but only on the explicit condition that I was exempt from homework.

My mother was mandated to negotiate the doctor's new demand and travelled to Enniskillen on the bus to meet Brother Alfred, our wonderfully kind Principal from Tipperary, who favoured hurling over football and sprinkled his speech with phrases *as Gaeilge*. Obviously, I wasn't present at that meeting but I understand that Br Alfred accepted the doctor's argument and agreed to speak to the other teachers and get me an exemption from homework. When I returned, the exemption had been put in place, though some of the teachers clearly did not approve.

That exemption was never withdrawn and, for the remaining six and a half years of my time at St Michael's, I was excused from homework whenever I did not feel like doing it – which was most of the time. It made school life much easier for me, than for my colleagues.

But my recurring bouts of sickness made life difficult in other respects. From an early age, I'd been a sports fanatic. I read sports books and magazines whenever I could get my hands on them and was particularly interested in football – of the Gaelic kind, other football games were known as soccer and rugby, but 'football' was always Gaelic – athletics and sport generally. I read Fear Ciuin's column on Gaelic Games in the *Sunday Press*, the only national paper to come into our house in my youth, and the GAA pages of *The Anglo-Celt*, as soon as I was able to read. Strangely, we never bought any of the 'Northern' papers and my knowledge of Cavan football far exceeded anything I knew about Fermanagh, as did my appreciation of Cavan's sporting pedigree.

The Celt, as it was known was, and still is, produced in Cavan and provided tremendous coverage of Gaelic games, in particular football. From it, I learned about the exploits and successes of those who played for Cavan in the 1930s, the 1940s and the early 1950s, especially the heroes of the Polo Grounds final. I also learned how Cavan had been 'robbed' of an All-Ireland title by a bad refereeing decision, when even the commentator believed the result to be different from that produced in the official report, about how good scores were disallowed and faulty ones allowed when Cavan played teams from outside Ulster in major Championship games, and about how there was an anti-Ulster bias among referees and in sections of the national media. It was much later that I realised that sport is not always fair and that supporters are sometimes slightly blinkered in their interpretation of events, not to mention their view of reality.

I had a good supply of reading material. A relative in London, the son of one of Mammy's cousins, used to send me second-hand comics and books on subjects like cricket, which I had never seen and did not understand, though I was to play it later in life. Mina sent me books from America, and from these I first became acquainted with American football and baseball. Like cricket, I couldn't understand them and would have to wait many years before I saw either of them in real life, but I read everything I was sent.

Part of the doctor's deal with my mother was that I would not play football or any other sport as, given my poor health, he alleged it was too risky for me. Initially, he argued that I would never live to see fourteen years of age if I insisted on playing football. Over the years, that prognosis changed to eighteen and then twenty. In fact, it kept getting revised upwards as I survived successive 'death deadlines'. I kept on playing. For some odd reason, the doctor never seemed to have similar reservations about athletics, which was my second sport – indeed, my first sport for a while. I suspect that his real concern was that my obvious physical frailty made me especially susceptible to injury and that football provided much greater potential for such calamities.

What Dr McQuade could never have understood was that I had a totally different view of the world from his, and that my greatest ambition was not about getting into university or succeeding academically. It was to play for Teemore Shamrocks and, hopefully, for Fermanagh. The fact that neither was particularly successful at that time was irrelevant – I still wanted to play for them, more than almost anything else.

To play football, I had two human hurdles to clear. The doctor was bad enough, but had she acted on her many threats, my mother's opposition would have been far worse. There were regular warnings and I would often fret about whether I would be allowed to play in some upcoming underage game – not ideal mental preparation for sporting encounters at any level. Fortunately, she rarely prohibited me, though I received frequent admonitions to avoid getting wet, and not to 'overdo it'. Since she never attended the games, I could 'overdo it' as much as I liked once I got away from the house, though there might be a price to be paid when I returned.

Teemore had no underage teams at that time. In fact, in the early 1950s, the club's representative on the County Board announced to County Convention that Teemore Shamrocks would not be registering any team for that year, nor fielding a team for the foreseeable future. Teemore had been the kingpins of Fermanagh football, boasting 15 senior Championships and the only eight-in-a-row in the county's or – before Crossmaglen's great run – the province's history. But the club had been decimated by emigration and could not field thirteen players – the required number for junior football in the county at the time. Thankfully, the then secretary of the Board, the late Tom Fee, and its chairman, the late Gerry Magee, persuaded the outgoing club officers to try and keep the club alive and it survived throughout that decade, albeit with difficulty, before ultimately recovering to achieve senior Championship success again in later decades.

But the result of Teemore's mid-century troubles was that I played all my under-age football with Derrylin – our arch-rivals, who represented the other part of the parish and could select their adult team from about two-thirds of the parish's population. We cycled the three or more miles to Derrylin for home games or got a lift to away games but, even then, being collected from home was never an option, so the choice was cycle or walk, neither of which was optimal preparation for a competitive game.

Our mentors – there were no trainers in those days and no organised training either – were the late Paddy 'Slates' Maguire, Johnny Maguire and Benny McBrien. Slates was a former inter-county player of the forties and early fifties, whose career was interrupted by a broken leg and later ended by a serious knee injury which plagued him for many years afterwards. Thankfully, he survived until relatively recently, maintaining his interest in Fermanagh's fortunes and playing a weekly card game with my brother, Seán, over several decades.

Although he was a very committed Derrylin man, no manager I ever had subsequently gave me more support and encouragement than Paddy, and he was ecstatic when, later in life, I was accorded different honours. He had a great capacity for concentrating on a player's strengths and for praising rather than criticising. Given my low self-esteem and lack of confidence, that was particularly valuable to me. The contribution of such men to our country and to their own communities has never been properly recognised, but of course they don't do it for recognition – they do it out of a sense of duty, commitment and patriotism.

When I was twelve, I was asked to join the Derrylin under-16 squad. For me, it was a bit like winning the lottery. With hindsight, I realise that I was not good enough to be next nor near the team, but for some unknown reason they selected me and we reached the county final.

Our team, was principally built around one outstanding player, John Cassidy, who was one of the finest players it was my privilege to see play Gaelic football in my county. With support from a couple of others – especially Pat Flanagan and the late Joe Shannon – he carried us to that final and very nearly won it for us. Having played for Fermanagh minors for a couple of years he, together with the great PT Treacy, was seen as a core part of the future of Fermanagh football. By the time he left St Michael's and Ireland for a job with the British Civil Service in London, John was already on the county senior panel.

A few years later, I was privileged to play in Breffni Park on a Fermanagh U-21 team captained by John. We were playing in the unofficial competition in that grade, organised by the Ulster Council, several years before the GAA accepted it as an official, national competition. Again, I suspect that I was not good enough for that team either and probably should have been substituted, though I wasn't. John was immense on the night, too, and it was not his fault that we lost again to Cavan, as Fermanagh teams had been doing for more than sixty years.

Unfortunately, while playing for his club in a tournament game during his holidays in Fermanagh a year later, he suffered a serious knee injury. His career had ended almost before it had started properly. He was an immense loss to the game and to Fermanagh in particular. Like most other good footballers, he was also a gentleman on and off the field, who never felt a need to abuse an opponent either verbally or physically.

That so-called 'mouthing' appears to have become more prevalent in our games over recent years. I detest it and I have absolutely no respect for those who indulge in it, however good their football skills – in fact I dislike such players intensely. I also believe that referees are failing the Association in not taking stronger action against the perpetrators of such activity; they do not deserve to be allowed to play Gaelic games. Thankfully, it seems to be somewhat less prevalent in our national game of hurling, though it seems to exist in virtually all sports at present.

We lost that under-16 final by four points and I would have to wait a few more years before I secured a county medal of any kind. Still, I was one of the lucky ones – I was one of only two members of that team to win a County Senior Championship. Though most of the others were better footballers than I was, I was luckier. They say it's better to be born lucky than born rich, and they're right.

*****

Back at St Michael's, things were progressing naturally and successfully. I was hardly ever the focus of attention, for either favourable or unfavourable reasons, other than when a new teacher arrived and my exemption from homework had to be negotiated anew. One or two of the teachers would hardly have known my name.

The normal pattern in second level was three years to Junior Certificate, or four for those who were less academic. This was followed by two years to Senior Certificate, following which a minority proceeded to A-Level, through a one-year programme. That minority tended to aim for either teacher training or university, but it was a very small minority – never more than one or two in any year and in the vast majority of years, no one at all.

So I arrived in the Junior Certificate class ready to face the examinations in the summer, only to be told after Easter that the Department had a rule that no one could sit the examination until they'd reached the age of fourteen. I was only thirteen, so I had to repeat the year.

That was the year, too, when St Michael's started the process of change, which was to lead to the replacement of the Presentation Brothers by Diocesan Priests. We later discovered that this was a somewhat acrimonious transfer but, at the time, we knew nothing of the clerical or pedagogical politics involved – and cared less.

We now had a priest on the staff. Dr John McElroy was from outside Fivemiletown, on the Fermanagh-Tyrone border. With an academic background in mathematics, he taught English, geography, Latin and religion in St Michael's, and demonstrated outstanding teaching talent in each of them. I benefitted enormously from being taught by him and from knowing him then and later.

So, I spent a year repeating what I'd already done. I'd no need to make any great effort to understand what was being taught and, with no homework, it was essentially a wasted year. That was as much my fault as any systemic failure – I just 'dossed' for the year and got into the habit of attending the mart in Enniskillen, two mornings a week before school, to keep abreast of cattle prices. When I arrived home, the cattle prices were much more important to my father than any classes I'd missed and, anyway, I was very interested in cattle farming at that time.

Since Daddy believed that one learned by doing – and *only* by doing – he decided that I needed to learn how to buy and sell, or 'deal' as it was called in the farming community. That was fine, except he never told me what he had in mind.

One Friday afternoon, he arrived home with a heifer which he had bought from one of the farmers with land adjoining the farm in Cranaghan. He called me to help him to get her into the byre and we tied her in a stall next to one of the mature cows. Naturally, I asked him how much he had paid for the heifer and he told me: £14.15.00 – £14.75, in modern terminology. I thought he had bought well and told him so, without realising how cheeky it was of a 13-year-old to comment on the trade of someone with years of experience.

As we were walking out from the byre, he continued our conversation: 'He had another one, you know.'

"Why didn't you buy her?" I asked, "sure, you know we need another one or two."

"Ah, no," came the reply, "I was leaving her for you."

"How would I buy her? I have no money to buy a heifer."

"If you want to buy her, don't let money stop you," he replied. "You'll always be able to get the money, if you're sure the value's right."

"Well," I responded, "You seem to have got good enough value. Is the other one as good?"

"That's hard to know. She's half-Friesian and she's there for you, if you want her," he answered.

I'd no idea how to respond, so I said nothing, though I wondered why he had not bought the half-breed, since I knew he was keen on Friesians – they produced more milk.

After dinner on the following day, he brought up the conversation again.

"Are you going to buy that heifer from Magee?"

"I can't buy her, I have no money," I answered.

"I told you we'd get the money, if you want to buy her," came the reply.

"Do you want me to buy her?" I asked.

"It's not up to me," he continued, "it's up to you. Do you want to buy her, or not?"

"Well, we need another one or two anyway," I offered, playing safe.

"If you want her, then go and buy her," he finished with unassailable logic.

One last time, I tried to sound him out: "How much should I give for her?"

"It's you who's buying her, not me," came his conclusion, ending the conversation and making it very clear that he expected me to take the decision. I would have been happier if he had given me some indication of the likely price. On a couple of previous occasions he had sent me to sell cattle at the mart, which was relatively easy, without indicating a minimum price, but buying was a different matter altogether.

I hopped on my bicycle and headed off to Magee's. I'd been in the house often before and always received a warm welcome. They were a lovely, hospitable couple though his language tended to be liberally littered with swear words. When I arrived, Lyndon's wife offered me tea and some homemade bread, which I accepted –it would have been an insult to refuse. I have no doubt that the man himself was cute enough to realise that I was nervous about being there at all. Eventually, I decided to raise the objective of my visit.

"Daddy said you had another heifer," I said tentatively.

"Be Jaysus, I have, too," he replied, adding "and she's better than the one your father bought the day before yesterday! You wouldn't be interested in her, would you?" he asked, while getting in the first blow in the process of consummating a deal.

I was somewhat nonplussed, but I stumbled on regardless: "I suppose we should have a look at her, before we decide that."

We went out and viewed the heifer and, after about half an hour of haggling, we agreed a price of £14.10.00 – five shillings less than Daddy had paid the previous day; Lyndon made it clear that he had been easy on me because I was only a 'young cub', and he was probably telling the truth, partially at least!

Two days later we put the heifer into the byre beside her comrade and, as we were coming out, my father asked me: "Now, which of us got the best deal?" betraying his lack of appreciation of the difference between comparative and superlative.

"I don't know; who do you think got the best deal?" I answered, echoing his grammatical error.

"Well, damn me, I don't know either," he replied, "but, sure, we'll both know in a year's time." 'Damn me' was one of his favourite expressions, though he pronounced it 'dammy'.

It was years later before I realised that this man, with no education, was using his own experience of 'learning by doing' to prepare me for the world of buying and selling, in farming or any other business, in which I might become involved. It was around that time, too, that I began to understand what he meant when he said, as he did frequently when one of us claimed that we could not do something because we didn't know how to do it, "You'll never learn younger now".

For a 13-year-old, that sort of experience was a much better way of learning than reading books or anything I did at university later. And his philosophy that 'now' is always the best time to learn what one does not already know, is still valid. He may have been illiterate, but he was also wise in the ways of the world and intelligent enough to know that experience teaches even the greatest fools.

He did the same with my brother, when his time came to learn the art, or science, of trading, and I have to admit that, despite a few mistakes, he made much better use of the lesson, in his business dealings in subsequent years.

At the end of that wasted year, I sat the Junior and did reasonably well – well enough that three days into my Senior 1 year, the science teacher, Tim Keneally, arrived into the classroom, asked ask if there was a Peter Quinn present.

When I raised my hand, Tim boomed: "You! Sure, I thought you were called Murphy. Anyway, you had better gather up your books for you are being transferred to Senior 2."

And that was it. I was to leave my classmates of the previous year and return to the group which had sat the 'Junior' a year earlier and most of whom had been my classmates for the previous three years. Despite his not knowing my name after four years teaching me, Tim and I became firm friends over the next three years. I loved chemistry, especially the experimental aspects of the subject, which Tim taught with a level of enthusiasm which bordered on fanaticism. His attitude to the subject was rivalled only by his support for Cork hurling and his adoration of Christy Ring. He was a great teacher for those who displayed an aptitude and a willingness to learn, though those who had no such interest saw him as a bit of a tyrant.

Occasionally irascible when things went awry, Tim was an absolute gentleman with those who were prepared to work with him. For me, he was on a par with Dr McElroy as a teacher, with a massive enthusiasm for his subject and an unquenchable optimism for the future of his better students. During my two A-level years, I spent most of the free classes I had in the chemistry laboratory – apart from those spent playing football on the tennis courts – either as a sort of unofficial classroom assistant or messing around doing experiments, not all of which were on the prescribed syllabus. Half a century later, I still remember Tim with huge affection.

By this stage, student numbers had increased to something like 120-130 and space was scarce. The building of a new school, to be run by the priests, had already commenced on a site about a mile from the town centre and the bus terminus. The primary school had already begun the relocation process and there was spare space in the basement of their old building. Known as the St Michael's Reading Rooms, this space was a dark, largely underground room, capable of holding just over a dozen pupils. Many years later, in November 1987, that building was to gain notoriety as the site of the infamous 'poppy day' bomb, when eleven people were killed, including Marie Wilson, whose father became a symbol of forgiveness and reconciliation with his description of how she had held his hand and talked to him as she lay dying.

After my transfer, I had a bit of catching up to do, but the subject range was restricted so it wasn't too hard to make up the lost ground. Despite some teachers' misgivings, the homework exemption was never revoked and the regular mock exams which we sat weren't taken too seriously by most of us. I figured that I'd generally done well in them, but the whole process was so haphazard that we never knew exactly how we'd done, nor did we really care. So, when the process became more formal it came as a bit of a shock. In the Easter tests that year, we faced a much more rigorously formal report on progress, with marks in each subject, a comment on each student's progress in each subject and a place in class. Though I hadn't worked as hard as I should have, my latent competitive instinct resulted in me doing well, even though I might not have deserved to.

Some of the results were announced prior to the Easter holidays but not mine, and though I waited for the arrival of my report card with anticipation, by the time I returned to school, there was still no sign of it. At school, it became clear that the reports were still being collated formally – a process echoed informally by the students themselves. As a result of feverish classroom speculation and amateur educational punditry, I concluded that I was certain to be in second place at least, out of a class of 13 students.

As the days ticked by, it became clear that all of the school reports had been circulated to pupils' homes, but there was still no sign of mine. Every evening I asked about it and got the same response from Mammy: "It hasn't arrived."

After a week, I got fed up and finally announced to her, as we were out in the byre finishing the milking, that I would raise the issue with the Principal when I arrived at school the following morning. She advised me to forget about it but, when she realised that I was determined to raise the subject at school one way or another, she eventually admitted that it had arrived.

"What did you do with it?," I asked.

"I burned it," she replied.

Flabbergasted, I asked, "Why?"

"It was very bad," she said, "I was afraid you would be very disappointed, so I burned it. How many are in your class anyway?"

"Thirteen," I replied.

"Well," she said, "that's what I thought. You came thirteenth."

"I was definitely in the first two," I retorted, with a combination of annoyance, lack of comprehension and concern.

"No, you didn't," she argued. "You came last."

This time, my response was full of frustration: "I have seen all the marks and first place is between Finn McCann and myself."

"Well," she eventually countered, "I have the evidence. I didn't burn it, but I hid it because I didn't intend to show it to you. I knew you expected better and I wanted to spare you the disappointment."

The 'squirrel' element of her character was still alive and well – she never disposed of anything

"Let me see it," I begged.

She went into the house and came out with the document. "There you are," she said, almost triumphantly handing the letter to me, "… and it says Number in Class: Thirteen; and Place in Class: Thirteenth."

I looked at it and saw a very badly scribbled entry in the Principal's handwriting. The number in class was thirteen all right, but the place said 1st, though given the way it had been written I could see immediately how my mother had construed it as 13. I don't think I ever saw Mammy more relieved or more excited than that evening, and I was somewhat pleased myself, too.

At the end of that year I sat my Senior Certificate and did reasonably well, so it was back again for A-levels, with no idea of what I wanted to do in life, though farming was fast losing its attraction as a choice of career. By then, the combination of the new regime and a new school, with a new approach to education, had started creating initial progress towards an acceptable educational experience. So, instead of the one or two who normally returned to study for A-level, there were seven or eight of us, though the choice of subjects was still very limited – any three from mathematics, chemistry, English, Irish, Latin, history or geography. Clearly, any reasonable choice of career or any contribution towards career planning was not adequately reflected in the range of subjects available. Still, when the examination results came, I'd done well enough to get into Queen's University, Belfast, on a scholarship.

6

Play – Whatever the Price

During all those years, I continued to suffer regular bouts of illness. On more than one occasion the new school Principal and future Bishop of Clogher, Fr. Patrick Mulligan, had to drive me the seventeen miles home from school, because I had become so violently sick that the school authorities decided that I couldn't wait for the normal evening bus.

Generally, I got no warning of these attacks. I might not have been feeling on top of the world but neither would I be feeling particularly unwell when, over a period of an hour or less, I would run a temperature, start to tremble, feel cold, have serious headaches and become almost incapable of doing anything physical.

Normally, I was fit, happier running than walking, full of energy and then, suddenly, I could barely do anything requiring physical effort. A week in bed, with daily penicillin injections and the slow trek back to normality would begin again. Fortunately, I've always had a capacity to recover quickly – usually within a week, or so – though my energy levels could take another week, or longer, before they returned to anything close to their former levels.

It was enormously frustrating. For a start, I had a very slight build and could not put on weight. My wrists and hands were more like those of a girl – indeed, I still have small hands and wrists that are thinner than those of many women. At an eventual five foot ten and half inches tall, I was only eight stone in weight. Despite wanting to play football more than anything else, I was too light to play the game with any degree of physicality or any capacity to take abuse. I was fast enough and skilful enough, but there were always doubts about whether I was strong enough and I harboured those doubts more than anyone else.

As if my 'normal' illness was not enough, one Saturday afternoon that year I suddenly became violently ill. In some way, I discerned that this was different from my other episodes and Dr McQuade was called urgently. He always responded quickly when he received a message. "It looks very like meningitis," he opined, and he was right. Again, he reacted in the normal way: a couple of penicillin injections. It was a good choice, because, as we now know, that was the very best response he could have made. Once again, Dr McQuade had been my 'life-saver'. I still remember the severity of the pain – the worst I have ever experienced – and I recall the need to eliminate all light from the bedroom. The diagnosis was confirmed by a visiting specialist from Belfast, who diverted from his visit to the hospital in Enniskillen, to see me on the Monday morning and announce that I was going to be fine. Another storm weathered!

*****

I'd been called into the Teemore senior team when I was just fourteen and a half years old. The club was reduced to a position which could euphemistically be described as 'in transition', having lost most of its players of the previous two or three years to emigration. The team was built around one exceptional player, James Cassidy, Jim to his inter-county colleagues, but always James around home. His father had been an outstanding club and county player in the club's early years – considered to be one of the classiest players of his era in the South Ulster area – and James went on to play at senior level for his county for fourteen seasons, including wearing the pivotal number six jersey in Fermanagh's march to All-Ireland junior glory in 1959.

The Shamrocks' reduced status was a sad reflection on the club which had dominated Fermanagh football in the first three to four decades of the twentieth century. Lack of job opportunities led to emigration and population decline, and Teemore was becoming marginalised in every respect. There was no public housing in the area and no new private houses were being built either. Over a period of approximately two decades, the number of occupied houses in one part of the locale reduced from thirty-odd to about five, and virtually all other parts of the area declined. too, though not quite so spectacularly. That trend has been largely reversed since then.

Despite that serious decline in the club's fortunes, James stayed loyal to his own place and carried his team though victory and defeat, without a word of complaint, and heedless of the many stronger clubs which sought his services. For such an outstanding player, it must have been frustrating, but he never displayed any such attitudes. He was a wonderful role model for all of us in the Teemore area. More than anyone else, he was the role model for those who answered the call, when the decision to start fielding and developing young talent and building a new team was made.

Two players, Petie Fitzpatrick and Brian McCaffrey, who were older than me by fifteen and six months, respectively, were already on the team, when I was approached. Petie had played a year earlier and Brian was called up just a week earlier.

I'd never even seen the Shamrocks play away from home though I knew they were scheduled to play away against Bellanaleck, a strong senior outfit at that time. After Sunday dinner, I was out on our front street kicking a ball against a wall and practising my catching when a local taxi pulled up and the driver called out: "I was asked to collect you and bring you to Bellanaleck, you may get your boots."

I didn't hesitate – I was delighted. I ran into the house and was collecting my boots from the cupboard under the stairs, when my mother came in through the back door.

"What are you doing?" she asked.

"I'm going with the team to Bellanaleck," I said.

"Well you can go, but you're not playing, leave the boots there. I'll have a word with the driver."

At least I was being allowed to go.

Out she went to 'interview' the driver who would have known of her reputation. As she went out the front door, I exited via the back door and deposited the boots in one of the sheds. My father just smiled and remained in his chair. Though he'd only develop an interest in football in later years, it was clear that he had no desire to stop me playing.

I went out via the front door to hear Mammy telling the driver, in no uncertain terms, that I could go to the match but I was not to play – I was far too young, not strong enough and could easily get hurt. When she went back into the house, I nipped round the corner and retrieved the boots. I hadn't heard the entire conversation but I gleaned from the expressions and comments of my new teammates as I got into the car, that she had put her views quite forcefully and that no one was greatly surprised by her directness. When the taxi finally pulled away, with me and my boots safely inside, everybody breathed a sigh of relief – no one more so than myself.

I was selected at right half-forward and scored one of our points in a 0-6 to 0-5 defeat, though my score was a gift from the opposing full-back who, despite a terrible reputation, showed enough sense not to end a young player's career on his first outing. It was probably the team's best performance of a year in which we won no games. We lost all of our matches in both the League and Championship but at least one Teemore player was very happy with his year's achievements. Oddly enough, when I arrived home, I could see that Mammy was very proud to discover that I'd played, though she did her best to hide it.

We returned to Bellanaleck for the first round of the senior Championship two weeks later. James came to me before the game to tell me that the opposition (not Bellanaleck) had a particularly infamous corner back, a former county player, who would probably not stand aside to let a young lad get the ball, and it might be safer if I was not selected. Since I already knew of the player's reputation, I accepted his view – in fact, I was relieved.

Thereafter, I was selected for most games in the second half of that season, at the end of which we were relegated to junior. That created a problem for me in that junior was only thirteen a side and I'd major concerns about whether I could retain my place on the reduced team. Teemore had only sixteen players in total then, but one of them was teaching in England and available only in holiday time, so I played in most of that second year's games, too. We performed poorly in the League, but we played and won two Championship games which was enough to get us to the County junior final.

From a playing perspective, the Association in Fermanagh was very weak in those years, with a total of fifteen or sixteen adult teams, split approximately equally between senior and junior. There was no intermediate grade for another few years and each club fielded only one team, apart from Lisnaskea – then the dominant club in the county – which frequently fielded in both grades. At under-age level there were fewer than a dozen clubs, so if a team failed to reach the semi-final its players had, at most, four games in the year and probably no coaching.

Teemore Shamrocks had been to the forefront in the re-establishment of the GAA in Fermanagh, just over fifty years earlier. It had dominated the sport in the county for several decades but, by 1959, it was in very poor shape. The club was already in decline prior to Jim Dunne's early death, but it went downhill even more rapidly after that.

Nobody gave Teemore much chance of winning the final, least of all our opponents who appeared to underestimate us. Even our own players, who were long on determination, were short on confidence. In any event, we were reduced to two substitutes for the final, of which I was one. I'd have loved to be playing but, at the age of fifteen, I knew only too well that the strongest thirteen had been selected and I had no grounds for complaint.

As it turned out, the game was played on a wet, heavy pitch and no place for weaklings of less than eight stone. Despite conceding a rather soft own goal in the final minutes of the game, our defence performed particularly well in the last ten minutes and held out for a narrow win. I was very happy to receive my medal for having been a substitute. Though I'd won a couple of races in underage athletics – I was a better runner than a footballer – this was my first football medal and I was delighted.

Despite playing senior and junior club football (admittedly at a very low level), I had difficulty getting my place on the school team. Clearly my lack of physique was a problem, but I was disappointed – success as an athlete was no compensation for failing to make the school football team. I eventually made my debut on my sixteenth birthday, when I came on as a substitute against my own diocesan college, St Patrick's Cavan, in the McRory Cup. We drew a match in which my contribution was negligible and I was dropped for the last game in the competition, in which our sole success was that draw. A year later, I made the team easily enough and, within eighteen months, I was on the county minor team, playing at midfield, although I'd still not managed to get my weight up to nine stone.

My brief inter-county career got off to a bad start. Fermanagh minors were due to play Monaghan on Easter Sunday in a challenge match, but I'd been off school and didn't know about the game. I'd been sick from the previous weekend and had just finished a seven-day course of penicillin injections when I was told I'd be starting at full-forward for the county team. In fact, my appearance in the No.14 shirt for my county owed much to the previous year's county minor final, where I had started at full-forward and scored an early goal en route to our first win at that age level.

My elevation to the county minor team to play Monaghan was strongly opposed by my mother who, realistically, pointed to the fact that I'd been receiving injections for the week leading up to the game. But I'd reached the age of disobedience and was determined to play, seeing it as my passport to becoming a county player, so I hid my illness from the team manager, John James Treacy. As things transpired, I played poorly and John James showed tremendous patience in leaving me on the pitch for so long. But eventually, for the only time in my comparatively short inter-county career, I was called ashore with less than ten minutes to go in my very first game. I returned home desolate, fearing that I had just played my only game in a Fermanagh jersey.

We were off school the following week and I'd spent the Wednesday ploughing in a field a bit away from the house. By that time we owned a tractor, so ploughing was not the problem it had been some years earlier. At almost 7pm, I finished and headed home to help with the milking. As I approached home, which was just across the road from the club's pitch, I saw several cars and a number of people, most of whom I did not recognise. As I drove through the mini-assembly, John James Treacy stepped out in front of the tractor and demanded, very sharply, to know what the hell I was doing on a tractor, when I was supposed to be playing at midfield against Cavan in ten minutes. That was news to me, but it was also music to my ears because it meant that I'd not burned all bridges on the previous Sunday. I parked the tractor in the back yard, raced into the house to collect my boots and informed whoever was there that I would not be available for the milking.

If Sunday in Clones had been a disaster, Wednesday in Teemore was a triumph. I played well, won a lot of breaking ball and scored exactly half of Fermanagh's scores from play, and from midfield. To cap it all, we won. I'd established my credentials and was selected for every match for the rest of the year, even managing to score a last-minute, match-winning point from a superb pass from Gerry Magee, against Antrim in our Ulster Championship first-round game. I well remember our neighbour and friend, Paddy Drumm, running onto the pitch and giving me the biggest hug of my life; he was delighted with my success.

Unfortunately, I reserved one of my worst performances of the year for the Ulster semi-final in Dungannon a few weeks later where I lined out at right half-forward, or right three-quarters as it was known in Teemore. My performance in that semi had more in common with my first outing in Clones, though for some reason I wasn't substituted.

But overall, I had the kind of footballing year I could only have dreamed of, and my lack of physique proved less of a problem than I, and my mother, had feared. Truth to tell, my midfield partner, the late Hugh O'Connor, was responsible for most of my success. Hugh was physically strong, full of courage and, in football terms, very intelligent so he did the 'donkey work', breaking the ball for me to collect and making me appear a much better player than I actually was. In fact, playing at midfield and without taking the frees, I finished the year as the team's top scorer, but at least 90 per cent of the credit was due to my partner.

As things turned out, I ended my minor career with a flourish. Again, without playing particularly well, I scored all Fermanagh's scores in the Ulster Minor League final against Down, who literally hammered us on one of my favourite grounds, Ballybay, which had a wonderful sod and was then seen as one of the best pitches in Ulster – I loved the spring in the ground and generally played well there.

In that final, I notched up our only two points and can still claim to be the only Fermanagh man to get all his team's scores in an Ulster final! As I left the pitch our goalkeeper, Tommy Moohan, who unfortunately died a couple of years later while still a member of our under-21 team, put his hand on my shoulder and told me that if the other fourteen had each scored as much as I did, we would have won. They didn't and we didn't. But it was the nearest I came to winning a provincial medal.

7

Student Life
and Disenchantment

I arrived at Queen's University, Belfast, in October 1961, as a gauche seventeen-year-old with no idea of what I wanted to do in life and no idea of what being at university meant. It was my first time in that city, or any city for that matter, apart from two trips to Croke Park to see Down play in All-Ireland semi-finals – unsuccessfully, against Galway in 1959 and successfully against Kerry in 1961. My arrival coincided with the first major intake of students from the nationalist community, an influx based on almost universal grant-support for students who qualified for admission on the basis of their A-level results. Prior to that, admission did not necessarily result in the awarding of a grant and access to third level education was largely restricted to those with money or influence, or normally both.

My A-level results were hardly spectacular by more recent standards, though they were more than adequate for admission to Queen's and they were the best from St Michael's in that year. Because of my age, I'd two bites at those examinations and didn't have to study for them on the second occasion, as I'd already achieved the qualifying standard for a university scholarship on the basis of my previous year's results. So, I spent two half-days per week at the mart in Enniskillen, regularly arriving at school after the roll call had been taken and I'd been marked absent. The Department of Education's attendance officer was not impressed and threatened to demand the payback of my scholarship because of my poor attendance, until he had received some form of confirmation from the school that I'd indeed attended all my mandatory classes and that I normally arrived late on Mondays and Thursdays, after being 'about my father's business' on those mornings. Someone at the school must have convinced him that I'd met the minimum attendance requirement.

Daddy decided that, if I was not going to be a farmer, there was no point in retaining the farm in Cavan. He was already in his sixties, his health was a source of concern (though not to him) and Seán was to inherit the home farm – all twenty-one acres of it. Ten days before I started at Queen's, the farm outside Ballyconnell was sold for £3,700, or less than £50 per acre. Later, he attempted to buy another farm in the Teemore area to create a more viable enterprise for Seán, but even though he was the highest bidder – by quite a margin and he was prepared to offer even more – he did not get it. Someone had learned the lesson from a decade earlier and 'the mistake' was not going to be repeated.

✱✱✱✱✱

The student grant back in 1961 was £320 per annum, a considerable sum and more than enough to keep any student well-fed, fully supplied with books and other materials, and leave a sufficient residue to maintain a reasonable social life. I'd enrolled for a BA degree on the back of no careers advice and no specific career ambition: Latin and mathematics were to be my main subjects, selected entirely on the basis that I'd secured reasonable marks in them at school.

Ten days after I enrolled, I was selected to play for Queen's against the famous St John's in Corrigan Park. Apparently, playing midfield for Fermanagh minors was taken as an indication that I might have something to offer. I was told to catch the bus at the foot of the Donegall Road, beside the infamous Sandy Row, and given directions as to how to get to Corrigan Park from the Falls Road. As I stood waiting for the bus, totally unaware that Gaelic footballers would not be welcomed by some of the residents of Sandy Row, I was approached by another student who asked me if I was one of the freshers who had been selected for the League game against St John's. His name was Peter Harte (his brother Mickey is now better known) and that was to be the start of a friendship which was to last for the next forty-nine years, until his death at far too young an age.

In the early 1960s, Corrigan Park was a totally different ground from the magnificent facility which now exists there. A fine pitch in the summer, it became sticky and heavy in the latter months of the year and in wet weather. I had been used to playing on Teemore's sand-based pitch where the ball actually bounced and one of the first tactics one learned was to 'kill' the ball as it bounced otherwise it went over one's head. In Corrigan, the ball did not bounce. Instead, it 'died' once it hit the ground and one was forced to go down in front of one's marker, to pick it up. At just nine stone weight and totally dependent on my speed, I was not particularly well-suited to such conditions. I was selected at right corner-forward – never my favourite position – and my immediate opponent was one of the Gallagher family – uncles of Gerry Armstrong, the former Northern Ireland soccer player, and part of the backbone of that great club over the past sixty years. There were five brothers playing on my Queen's debut and, unfortunately, one of them was marking me.

It is probably just an excuse, but I still blame the ground conditions for contributing to my poor performance that day. Deeper down, however, I know full well my lack of strength was at least as significant.

Early on, I was caught flatfooted a few times and could not get out of the way of some very hard, but totally legal and absolutely fair tackles, and my appetite for the game evaporated rapidly. I wasn't subjected to a single dirty tackle that day, just tackles which were too physical for me. Peter Harte, who was playing at centre half-forward sent a few passes in my direction, obviously with the intention of bringing me into the game, but I wasted them. Not surprisingly, that supply line soon dried up and I was left a virtual spectator for the last twenty minutes. It was a harsh lesson, especially as I was used to being one of the main scorers for Teemore, for whom I would normally have scored more often than I touched the ball on that day.

*****

I'd succeeded at school by listening to the teacher and absorbing as much as I could, without supplementing it with homework or extra study. I assumed that I could do the same at university; why should it be different? So, I attended the vast bulk of my scheduled lectures, took copious notes, by and large tried to absorb the content, did no extra reading or study and hoped to pass the examinations in the same way as I'd done at school. I hardly ever visited the library. In fact, I was a student for at least two terms there before I discovered how to gain admission. I never read the prescribed texts nor did any research. Instead, every Tuesday night I played in an all-night poker school and then went directly to Wednesday morning's lectures from the poker game – hardly the best preparation for absorbing the content of the lectures. I would never have succeeded, or even survived, had there been the sort of continuous assessment, which currently obtains.

During the first half of the spring term, we had to meet our respective advisors of study in order to get an interim evaluation of progress to date (though success or failure would ultimately depend entirely on the outcome of the examinations). My advisor was not very complimentary about my performance to that point and told me, in no uncertain terms, that I had no chance of passing my first year examinations. In fact, I discovered in discussions with my peers that mine was one of the worst evaluations in my year. Even that did not provoke me into a more rational or more responsible approach to the tremendous educational opportunity being made available to me. I continued to attend lectures but neglected all other forms of study, though that was still much more than some of my colleagues were doing. It was inevitable that the casualty count would be high when the exams results were published – and it was.

Fortunately, I managed to pass all three subjects, probably scraping through a couple of them and I was sure I had nothing to spare in one of them. But a pass is a pass and I proceeded to second year, adding economics to my subject portfolio which sounded interesting, though I had little or no understanding of what it involved. Most of my colleagues opted for politics or scholastic philosophy, or archaeology, or similar subjects, none of which seemed very attractive to me. The decision to choose economics proved to be one of my better decisions from those years, though it was another several years before I began to understand the reality of the subject and how a 'theory of markets' could be converted to practical use. Odd as it must seem, I subsequently went on to teach this subject at post-graduate level in England.

Years later, I also realised that, like me, the majority of those who took economics as their main subject, finished up knowing very little about the reality of economics either – certainly about micro-economics and its expected implications for business. That's because micro-economics is not even remotely related to business practice, notwithstanding contrary claims by some of its adherents. But it does provide a good grounding in some related issues.

A few days after I received the results, I left to spend the summer in London, working in an Irish pub owned by a neighbour from home, who was also a very distant relative. I'd decided not to stay at home to work on the farm, where I might have been marginally useful. London was an interesting experience and I made reasonably good money while I was there. For the most part, I enjoyed my first real job, and it paid better than working at home on the farm.

I have never forgotten some of the lessons which I learned in those three months. I saw men and women, who had been forced to leave Ireland in the 1950s, living lives of utter misery in London, working very hard, many making good money and spending it all on drinking heavily to drown their sorrow at having to emigrate. Most of them carried a grudge of enormous proportions at their native country's inability to provide them with employment and a living in their own land.

I saw at first hand the real 'fighting Irish' in rows which started out of virtually nothing and finished up with good men being carried off to jail, in the infamous 'Paddy Wagon' which was never very far from the door of the pub after 10pm, to appear in Bow Street Magistrates' Court the following morning. There they'd face a choice between a £5 fine or a week in jail. They paid the £5 if they had it but, occasionally, someone with empty pockets would have to spend a week away from work and from the pub.

I experienced the terror of facing a customer, who was dissatisfied with something I'd done, breaking a glass and trying to stab me in the face. Fortunately, he was drunk and I was able to side-step his lunge, though I brought home a nasty scar on my hand where I'd warded off his attack. I never told my parents what had happened.

I also encountered the wrath of a customer who claimed that I'd left too much 'head' on his pint of Guinness, and deemed that I hadn't given him value for money. He waited, with two of his friends, for me to leave the bar after work and I am still thankful for the former Irish army boxing champion from Limerick who sorted out my problem in a most unconventional way. He saved me from a drubbing and allowed me to jump on the first bus which came along, even though it was going nowhere near where I wanted to go.

There were times when I was absolutely terrified, but I was never bored, apart from one occasion when I had a recurrence of my regular illness and was confined to bed for a couple of days.

I still recall the pathos and the misery, the loneliness and the repressed homesickness, which were clearly evident among the pub's regular customers. To some extent, but only partially, because when I emigrated in later life I did not have to leave Ireland, I understood their feelings of being rejected by their homeland and ignored by those who could afford to stay at home. I became capable of interpreting the heavy drinking and the shows of bravado which were unwittingly being used to disguise a sense of failure and low self-esteem. As captured so magnificently and so accurately, several years later, by Jimmy Murphy, in his play, The Kings of the Kilburn High Road, those traits were prominent among the clientele of the bar in which I worked.

I saw the tears of frustration and loss, from both men and women, after too much gin, with its apparently depressive side effects, had been consumed. At eighteen, I was too young to appreciate the entirety of the social and societal implications of what I was seeing but, almost half a century later, the memories are still vivid and still disconcerting. In a way, many of those people were, and are, part of another of Ireland's 'lost generations', who felt that they had been denied their birthright and were rightfully resentful of the inheritance they had missed.

More than a decade later I too was an emigrant but, crucially, a voluntary emigrant and there is a massive difference. It was then that I realised how enormous the difference was between those who left Ireland in the 1950s and earlier, and those who left in the 1970s and since then. A much greater proportion of the latter cohort had left voluntarily and did not have quite the same feelings of rejection and defeatism – but in particular of inferiority and second-class citizenship.

Most of all, I remember a man from a neighbouring county to my own who did heavy manual work during the day and drank equally heavily in the pub every night of the week. Though we had little in common in terms of either background or prospects, he was a very affable man, quiet and inoffensive, never contrary as many became with a few drinks and, over the three months or so, we became reasonably friendly.

At least a couple of times every week, especially at weekends, the alcohol would induce a state of maudlin depression, during which he would confide in me that he would be going home to visit his mother for Christmas and how much both she and he were looking forward to that. I was amazed when another customer (the brother of a then well-known inter-county and interprovincial footballer from Clontibret), told me to pass no remarks on my acquaintance, because he would never go home. When I asked why, he told me that 'yer man' had been in London for nearly a decade and had always talked about going home, but had never gone and would never go, because he would never have the money to pay his fare. I was taken aback and highly dubious – surely, he would go back to see his mother in her new home at Christmas?

Although we had the best part of a couple of thousand semi-regular customers, only a few made a lasting impression on me, but many times subsequently, I remembered him and I often wondered what had happened to him.

One Sunday night, almost forty-five years later, when my mother was moving rapidly towards the end of her life and her children were ensuring that one of us was with her every evening, it was my turn to sit with her, and boredom enticed me to read one of the local papers, as a sort of respite from her repeated asking of the same question.

As I flicked through the pages towards the sports pages, I saw a heading which, for no reason that I can recall, caused me to read the full article. It described how a man who was less than a decade older than me had died in London, having lived there since the mid-1950s. This man had never returned to Ireland in all those years and the article recounted how the patrons of the pub in which I'd worked had collected the money to send his remains back for burial in his native place. There was no photograph with the story but I didn't need one – I recognised the name and the place where he had been buried a week earlier, and I knew that I would no longer have to wonder about what befell one of the more memorable of my pub's patrons.

Ultimately however, I knew then, and became even more conscious of it as I aged, that I was in the presence of men and women to whom I could relate and with whom I could empathise far better than many others from my own country.

While there, I met a few relatives, a couple of former Teemore teammates and many more others from the border areas of South Fermanagh and West Cavan. But the majority of people I encountered were from parts of Ireland which I'd never seen and about which I knew very little.

Nevertheless, my abiding memory is that the vast majority of them were great people. Most of them were wary of someone who was attending university and that was understandable, because it was so far removed from their backgrounds. But on the whole, they were friendly, hospitable and supportive – salt of the earth. The majority were a credit to our country though they have never received the recognition and support to which they were, and are, entitled. The reality is that they have no vote so, in the eyes of many of our decision-makers and administrators, they are irrelevant.

Inevitably, there was a minority who allowed their frustration and feelings of rejection to draw them towards trouble and wrong-doing and fighting, which damaged the image of our entire nation. But who are we, who have never been exposed to their frustrations or their loneliness, to condemn them? Though we are entitled to be disappointed by their actions and the image they portray, it's neither our place nor our right to condemn them.

In the years since, I've visited the Irish community in London on a number of occasions. Much had changed since the 1960s, and yet some of the same feelings are discernible among the older cohort. But the majority are now much more successful and their children are amongst the best educated of the many nationalities who now populate Britain. At last, the Irish are now 'making it' in Britain in the same way as we like to think they have long been making it in America – though that view, too, may contain less reality than we would like to believe. I have huge respect for our emigrants and I understand their frustrations, their loss and their sometimes 'erratic' behaviour.

Apparently, I was reasonably good at what I did over that summer. It's relatively easy to be good at something one enjoys and bar tending was definitely easier than farming. I was approached, a number of times, by the owners of other pubs, who offered me a job. Just before I left, I was also offered the opportunity to manage a new amenity which was being developed in a part of London with a large Irish population. Though it would have meant a steep learning curve, I was seriously tempted to accept it. But I was slightly homesick and missed the football so, eventually, I decided to go back and finish my education. By the time my three months were up, I'd determined that I would never drink alcohol and that three-month period is the main reason I've continued to be a Pioneer all my life.

Although I did not fully appreciate it at the time, nor for long afterwards, those three or four months provided me with a first-class insight into the Irish emigrant experience – a tragedy of failed hopes and expectations, and of unfulfilled aspirations. I have never forgotten the negative realities I learned in those months.

Not only did I have a wonderfully different experience, but I'd enjoyed London much more than I could reasonably have expected. Unlike most of those with whom I was associating, I could go home at any time, with a reasonable prospect of finding some form of non-manual employment – and that was a very important distinction.

In tandem with that enjoyment, the naïveté which had been a feature of my earlier life had been trimmed somewhat – though not entirely eliminated. I'd begun to learn about life outside the confines of my native border area and the campus in Belfast, and I'd a few quid in my pocket, too.

*****

I've never worked out whether my 'London experience' made me restless, or whether I'd already become frustrated with academic life, but returning to university proved a massive anti-climax. I was studying subjects in which I no longer had any interest, least of all in Latin, which was my main subject. I hadn't played football for more than six months and had begun to lose interest in the game which, I discovered, was much rougher in London than in Fermanagh and I'd even decided to stop playing poker, which had been a major social outlet in my first year. But, worst of all, I had no career plan and no ambition for the rest of my life, apart from not wanting to be a farmer, even though I enjoyed many aspects of that business. The most – and the least –that could be said about me was that I was confused about life and my future.

I was unhappy and irritable during that first term as my roommate, Paddy Heaney (brother of the late Nobel Laureate, Seamus) often reminded me. Though I attended lectures I continued to avoid any form of supplementary study. Three weeks before the term was due to end, I decided to go back to Fermanagh, but deferred doing so for a week so that I could claim to my mother that the lecture programme was effectively over. With over four decades of hindsight, I now realise that I was suffering from mild depression and potentially heading for a nervous breakdown. What I still cannot understand is why. My life was not that difficult. I was under no particular pressure and had no reason to be depressed or unhappy. I wasn't worrying about my future and I was free from the turmoil that sometimes pervaded our home. I should have been happy and carefree, but clearly I wasn't.

Over Christmas, I decided that I would leave Queen's and return to London, because I believed that, if I left university, I could not stay in Ireland.

As happened on farms in those days, work restarted on St Stephen's Day and, a day later, John Coleman our club's goalkeeper and I were working in meadows on the mountain, digging drains and laying pipes to improve the drainage system and the future growth potential of the meadow. It was bitterly cold and we were working while wearing our overcoats – something that rarely happened on farms, since shirtsleeves were more common. The pipes were made of clay which had been heated to very high temperatures and that meant they were brittle and chipped easily. Fitting them individually by hand, so as to minimise leakages, was tedious and regularly resulted in fingers getting nipped, ensuring that, by the end of the day, most knuckles were skinned and bleeding. Soaking them in warm water, to which some kind of cleansing or sterilising agent had been added, was the only realistic source of pain relief. And yet for me, that manual work, near the top of a mountain in the cold of winter, provided a freedom and a release from pressure, which made me happier than I'd been for months.

John and I always had a good relationship, so I told him of my plans to pack in university and go back to London, knowing that there was no chance that he would tell my mother. He listened carefully, but said nothing. He didn't even ask me why.

Later that day, while we were sitting down on the wet grass to drink cold tea from a bottle and eat soggy sandwiches – they were always soggy in winter, but tasted much better in the meadow during the sunny days of June and July – he raised the issue again, asking me if I wanted to spend the rest of my life laying pipes and watching blood running from my knuckles, whether in tunnels in London or on a farm in Ireland. My father had often told us that good manners was 'an easy burden to carry' and John advised me that 'education is an easy load to bear' and that if I packed in university, I might regret it for the rest of my life. The entire conversation probably lasted no more than five minutes but, in some ways, it was the most important five minutes of my life. It was the sort of injection of realism that I needed – from a man with no education, no background in psychology and no course in counselling, but someone who cared about what was best for me and my future.

By the end of the week, I'd decided to go back and finish my degree. It proved to be a good decision.

8

A New Impetus

It might seem surprising, but I hardly remember anything about the next eighteen months at Queen's. I played the odd bit of football with Teemore and won another county junior medal, this time as a player who got a few scores and probably made a small difference. I even managed, as a nineteen year old, to get selected to play at corner-forward (a position I hated) for Fermanagh seniors in the Lagan Cup, which was then the Northern division of the National League. I did not have a great campaign and, by the time the Championship came round in June of the following year, I had suffered a relatively minor knee injury and had lost my place on the panel. That was hardly surprising given that I weighed between nine and a half and ten stone at the time, which must make me one of the lightest players ever to play senior, inter-county competitive football. I continued to be selected for the county under-21 team for the next three years and played for the county juniors, but I was never again selected to play senior for Fermanagh, apart from a few challenge games when they were short of players.

Back at Queen's I continued to attend the majority of my lectures, though most of the lecturers would hardly have known who I was. I had no great interest in the subjects I was taking and so I studied very little. I failed to get selected for the Sigerson team having annoyed the trainer, Paddy O'Hara, by failing to turn up for the previous year's game against the newcomers to Sigerson football, Trinity College, Dublin. Though Paddy and I eventually went on to become friends, I'd blotted my copy book with him by getting involved in an all-night poker game, which had started as a social game but progressed to something much more serious as the night went on. I had lost a fair bit at the start and felt that I had to keep going until I recovered it, which I eventually did, but that was long after I should have been in bed resting for that Sigerson match. No wonder then that I slept through the alarm and missed the bus to the game. Paddy had selected me to start at midfield so when I failed to appear, it was little wonder that he got annoyed. I was slated to line out against the late Kevin Coffey, who had won two All-Ireland medals with Kerry, so maybe it was just as well that I slept in – I could have been even more embarrassed if I had played.

Examinations never worried me enough to make me study much for them as I always passed, sometimes on the back of a couple of weeks' cramming. Even when I was cramming, I never opened a textbook after 9.30 at night. Many of my colleagues studied late into the night and early morning using various stimulants to keep themselves awake, but I never did. Instead, frequently Paddy Heaney and I would go to a cinema called 'News and Cartoons', on the evening prior to an examination, to relax and get ready for the pressures of the following morning. That might sound an unusual form of preparation but it worked for me, though, unsurprisingly, very few of my colleagues followed my example.

However, one thing did change – I stopped playing serious poker, though I continued with the occasional 'social' game with my housemates, in so far as any card game can be deemed 'social' when there is money involved, however small the stakes. I probably became the most 'unstudent-like' student at the university and I was certainly the least studious of those who consistently passed their exams. With the great 20:20 vision of hindsight, I was wasting my time in a most irresponsible way: I'd lost interest in my studies and in most other things, too. I needed some stimulus to inject a bit of energy and interest into my life, and it came in a most unexpected way.

About a month before the finals were due I was sitting in the students' union, watching a snooker game – the semi-final of the university's competition – when Philip McLoughlin from Derry parked himself beside me. I remember, almost verbatim, the conversation which followed.

"What are you going to do next year, Quinn?" he asked.

"I have no idea," I replied.

"Are you going to do the DipEd?" he queried, that being the principal passport to teaching at the time and the northern equivalent of the HDip.

"No," I replied. "I haven't even applied for it and, whatever I do, I have no intention of teaching," I added.

"Have you applied for any jobs?" he asked.

"No," I responded again. In reality, I'd given virtually no thought to my future. The possibility of going back to London and getting involved in managing a pub or club was still foremost in my mind, and jobs around South Fermanagh were not an option.

"Tell me," he said, "would you think about doing accountancy?"

"What the f***'s accountancy?" I asked, genuinely not having the foggiest notion of what it was.

"Ah Jaysus, Quinn, do you know nothing?" he asked, with some degree of justification. "They're guys who do your tax returns and things like that."

"Would you ever wise up, McLoughlin." I responded. "There's no need for eejits like that about South Fermanagh. Sure, no one pays tax down there." And that was almost true, at the time – though not entirely so.

"Well," he said, "I'm told they make good money."

Even that did not pique my interest. Running a pub in London still seemed a better option, but Philip was not going to be deterred.

"The main accountancy organisation in Ireland is an outfit called the Institute of Chartered Accountants and they have an office down in the city centre. I'm going down to see about it. Will you come down with me?"

Seeing that I was about to demur, he added, "Sure, you're doing nothing anyway. Come on. We'll only be half an hour and this game is a foregone conclusion already."

Reluctantly, I agreed, but with absolutely no enthusiasm for a trip down town and even less interest in the possibility of a career in accountancy. But then, as the politician said: "Events, dear boy!"

The office was on the first floor of a building in Callender Street where we were greeted by a lady who seemed very old to me, though she was probably many years younger than I am today. Courteously and calmly, she explained the structure of the profession, the need to sign-up for 'articles' – a form of apprenticeship – the different mode of entry for graduates as compared with that for school leavers, the prospects for those who qualified and even the ridiculously high failure rates in the examinations. I found the whole thing boring: I wasn't even remotely interested, especially when she quoted pass rates in the 11 to 20 per cent range as being the norm – there had been a particularly low pass rate of 11 per cent in the previous session's final examination, in those days called the Part V.

Nevertheless, when she told Philip that seven firms in the Belfast area had indicated that they would take graduates as 'articled clerks' at the start of the new recruitment year that September and handed him a list of those firms, she gave me a copy, too. I headed for the door with every intention of putting the list in the first bin I met. I, literally, had my hand on the door handle and was in the process of opening it, when she asked:

"By the way, what religion are you?"

I was somewhat taken aback. With all the disrespect of a bad-mannered twenty-year-old, I turned and asked, much too sharply, "What the hell difference does that make?"

"Oh," she said, "I'm sorry. I didn't mean any offence. It's just that I thought by your names that you might be Catholics and I wanted to warn you that, if you are interested in accountancy, you should get your applications in early because most of the offices in this town don't take Catholics."

Oh dear! I was absolutely and totally stunned by her comment, and embarrassed and annoyed with myself for having been so aggressive with her. I apologised for my sharpness and thanked her for her advice and she was most gracious in her response – much better than I deserved. As we walked down the stairs, I folded my copy of the list of firms, without thinking. It didn't go in the first bin, nor into the second, it went into my pocket. As we sat on the bus going up Great Victoria Street, towards Shaftesbury Square, I mulled over what I'd just heard. Eventually, I turned to Philip and announced: "Philip, I'm going to do accountancy."

"For f***'s sake Quinn, what's got into you? Half an hour ago, you didn't even know what it was and you showed no interest when we were in that office. Why the sudden change?" he demanded to know.

"If those bastards have this thing all sewn up, it must be a good racket. And if it is, I want a bit of it." It was as honest an answer as I have ever given to anyone. Events!

Within a week, I'd written to four or five of the practices on the list provided by the lady in the Institute's Belfast office. Only one of them replied to invite me for an interview, which I accepted. During that process, my future Principal explained the legal implications of signing articles, especially the consequences of signing and not completing the three years, which would result in a breach of contract, leading to significant financial penalties.

Only a couple of years previous to that, all accountancy students were expected to pay a premium to secure articles and that sum of money was refunded over the period of the articles, becoming, effectively, the nearest thing there was to remuneration. There was no other form of payment, so it was small wonder that it was a minority activity and, almost exclusively, a non-graduate profession. All those aspects have changed dramatically since then.

He also told me about the options likely to be open to newly qualified accountants and queried whether I was likely to pass my finals. When I responded that I hoped to pass them, he indicated I should communicate with him as soon as the results were published. Rightly or wrongly, I had the impression that he was not entirely convinced about my academic credentials but when I'd received the last of my results, I contacted him and he offered me a contract, starting in September. As usual, I'd been lucky and passed all three subjects. I'd no idea whether I did well or badly, but I'd passed and that was all that mattered.

9

Escape from Accountancy

I was probably the most stupid articled clerk ever to enter an accountancy office in Belfast, or anywhere else. I'd come from a background where we paid for everything we bought in cash. We had no bank accounts, other than the deposit account, which I'd used to lodge my grant cheque. Invoices and statements meant nothing to me – we had no use for them around Teemore. Credit notes, delivery dockets and all the other documentation, with which auditors and accountants have to wrestle, were totally foreign to me.

I spent the first week adding columns of figures for one of the senior staff – those were the days before computers or calculators. It must have been clear that I found the whole thing boring because, at the end of that first week, the Principal came in and told me he would defer the commencement of my articles until October 1st, in order to give me an opportunity to change my mind without any financial penalty, should I so decide. After that, if I withdrew, the full rigour of the appropriate penalty would be applied.

Primarily because I'd nothing else to do, I signed my contract at the end of that month. My pay was to be £4 per week, out of which eight shillings and four pence, around 42p, was deducted for my contribution to National Insurance stamp, the equivalent of PRSI today in the Republic.

I was paying £4 per week for my digs in a house owned by a wonderful landlady from Castlederg, who was married to a man who became one of the most unfortunate of the many innocent people to lose their lives in the so-called Troubles. He was one of the casualties in the bombing of a pub on the Ormeau Road, having entered the premises just seconds before someone rolled a barrel filled with explosives through the front door. He died instantly.

The £4 did not cover lunch so I had negative cash flow. Fortunately, I still had some of the money from my London income and I could survive without badgering my parents for money, for the first year at least. That would do for a start because I was not in the habit of looking too far ahead in those days.

Early on, I discovered that most students enrolled for a correspondence course, but some attended lectures provided by the Institute. I decided to follow both paths in tandem, though, since I never had any intention of returning the assignments associated with the correspondence course, I registered on a 'read only' basis for which the fee was reduced.

Within a couple of weeks, I was seriously considering looking for another career. I could not get to grips with the documentation, the terminology, the adding of vast columns of figures without a calculator to help me, or the regimentation – particularly the regimentation! Eventually, it was my first class on the Institute course that helped convince me to persevere. Without it, I would almost certainly have changed my mind and left.

Because of a lack of money for the bus fares, twice weekly I'd walk the five-mile return journey from the Ormeau Road to Roden Street, where the accountancy courses were delivered. At least it was good for the fitness.

My first lecture was supposed to be on accounts and was to be delivered by a man who was closely aligned to one of the most successful 'foreign games' clubs in Belfast. It was an experience which stiffened my resolve to succeed in this career which hadn't been attracting my interest until then. My attitude to such work has not changed in the interim – I still hate accountancy.

On that first night, I walked into a room where seventeen or eighteen young men were already seated. There was not a single female in the class. As I looked around, I realised that I knew no one there, though there was one lad I recognised from the Union at Queen's. He was sitting on his own so I sat beside him. He told me that he had played in goals for his own club which had won the Antrim senior football Championship a year or two earlier. So he had two advantages over me – he'd studied economics and had some knowledge of accountancy, and he'd won a senior Championship medal.

When the lecturer came in, he spoke to most of the other students by name. He had taught them on the Part I course, from which graduates were exempt, and he had developed a good relationship with many of them. He then turned to us and, addressing us in a manner which was very clearly both condescending and aggressive, he asked us where we had done our Part I study. We told him that we were exempt.

The next hour was a revelation! It turned from an education into a challenge. It provided a motivation for both of us, which was in directly inverse proportion to what our lecturer had hoped. It was one of the best things to happen to me in my early career in accountancy – probably the single most important factor in determining my future career path.

He began with a denunciation of graduates as a whole, claiming that all graduates had an exaggerated view of their ability, their intelligence and their importance: they had inflated egos and were arrogant and incompetent. He then turned to graduates who entered accountancy and advised us that we were not nearly as smart as we thought we were, that graduates had a very poor track record in the accountancy examinations – that may well have been true, but I doubted it then and I still do. He warned us that if we thought we could pass Part II without doing Part I first, we were in for a huge shock. He concluded by telling us that we were effectively beneath contempt, by comparison with the good, honest lads who entered the profession directly from school.

As his tirade continued, I began to realise that not only did he dislike graduates (he had made that very obvious), but there was little chance of us winning him over however we performed. We were both seething, but managed to maintain our cool.

As we exited the class, I turned to my co-graduate and announced that, whatever it took, I was not going to fail my Part II examination. My core sentiment was reinforced by a few expletively decorated additions, designed to underline my conviction to succeed, and was met by an equal display of non-parliamentary determination by my new friend. I was beginning to get motivated for a career in accountancy.

My Principal was, and is, a fine man. Bigotry was not part of his nature and he was extraordinarily fair and flexible with his articled clerks – the remuneration scale was a city-wide one, so he could not be blamed for the poor rates on offer. I had the utmost respect for him then and I still do, but I soon realised that I'd a choice between working to pass my examinations or working to add to the profitability of the practice which had offered me articles. I chose the former. For the first time in my life, I really studied. I left for the library at Queen's immediately after my tea and stayed there until about 9.30pm at least three evenings a week. My productivity during office hours was not anything like as good as most others but the efforts I invested in the evenings was much higher than average. I was determined to pass those exams, whatever price I might have to pay.

Within a couple of weeks of starting work in the office, I was handed a cardboard box full of all sorts of documentation – bank statements, invoices, hire purchase agreements etc., together with a file containing the accounts and working papers for several years past. I was told to prepare the accounts but I'd absolutely no idea how to go about it. I'd never even produced a bank reconciliation at the time – in fact, I'd no idea what it was. So I plagued my colleagues with questions, of which the most common was, "What do I do now?" normally followed by, "How do I do that?" They were remarkably patient and, indirectly, they finally produced a set of accounts because I still had virtually no understanding of what I was doing, or even of what I'd just done.

Nevertheless, it was a tremendous learning experience, proving again that Daddy had been right about 'learning by doing'. The second assignment was slightly easier – but only slightly.

Nevertheless, by Christmas I was still floundering with debit and credit, debtors and creditors, farmers and pharmacists, linen companies and lingerie shops. I did not seem to be getting to grips with the subject and my first lecturer's assessment of graduates' performances in this profession was beginning to appear well-founded.

But then in late February, suddenly and without warning, the 'fog' just lifted. This stuff was simple! It was just basic mathematics; debit and credit still had a place in the system, but ultimately it was simple arithmetic. By Easter, I was confident that I'd every chance of passing the exams in July. A year earlier, that would have meant taking things easy, but this was different – I wasn't going to take any chances with the prospect of stuffing my lecturer friend's tirade firmly down his throat. So, I continued to study most evenings, putting most of my effort into passing the exam instead of producing work in the office.

The examinations proved easy enough. In each of the four papers, I was finished early and was first to leave the examination hall, apart from one guy who made it before me in the first paper, but never re-appeared. I suspect he concluded that he had not done too well in that first paper and that he should not bother continuing.

The final paper was a half hour shorter than the others and I was finished well before the end of the scheduled time so, again, I just got up and left. The invigilator started to laugh openly when I was leaving – not in a nasty way, in fact she was very friendly, but she clearly thought that this stuff was beyond me. I realised that she was convinced that I was just another failed statistic in the accountancy system. I was told afterwards that she sat down in the desk which I'd just vacated and looked through my paper, though I never found out what she thought of it. Many years later, when I worked for the Institute, I discovered that I'd passed the examination quite easily. My graduate friend and two others were the only ones from that class to pass the exam at the first attempt.

Part III of the then examination structure was open for graduates to take at any point in their articles. It consisted of a number of papers, in both company and commercial law, and in economics, and those with degrees in those areas tended to sit this part at the earliest convenient session, in order to get it out of the way. On that basis, I'd mentally committed myself to sitting it in the winter session, just over fourteen months after the commencement of my articles.

I was already beginning to prepare for it when, at the end of September and in common with every other student, I received a circular from the Institute. The core message was that, because of fundamental changes in the UK taxation system, namely the introduction of Corporation Tax and Capital Gains Tax, those from the North, who would normally be eligible to sit Part III in the forthcoming winter session, would, by special concession, be allowed to sit Part IV, in order to avoid having to study two different taxation systems. From the Institute's perspective it was an extremely generous concession. I subsequently discovered that no other student took advantage of it.

I thought about it for a day or so and decided that I would try to avoid studying two completely different tax systems. I approached my Principal, knowing full well that the dispensation was never designed for graduates in my position. He knew nothing about the circular and referred me to his partner who was then a member of the Institute's Education Committee. The latter rejected the idea out of hand, claiming that the concession was never designed for people in my position. Nevertheless I pressed him, pointing out that, according to the wording of the circular, since I would be entitled to sit Part III, I should now be eligible to sit Part IV, in the following December. I had to tread a fine line between annoying him and getting what I felt was my due.

Eventually, he reluctantly agreed to seek a direction from the Institute's headquarters as to whether, having worded the circular in such an ambiguous way, it would allow me to sit the examination. Two weeks later I was advised that I could avail of the 'loop-hole' but was told, in no uncertain terms, that if I failed, I would not be allowed any study leave for the re-sit which they all assumed I would be taking.

I studied like hell for the next six weeks – I've never studied harder in my life. Clearly, and surprisingly, I was beginning to get the hang of this study thing. But ten days before the examination, I started to lose faith in my capacity to pass it. I knew that I'd put in a great effort over the short period available to me but that was the point – the available time was just too short.

The Sigerson Cup was being played in Dublin on the weekend before I was due to make a fool of myself by failing an examination for the first time in my life. I decided that I'd go to Dublin and abandon hope of passing the exam. So, with me as driver, five of us headed for the capital, with the intention of having a good weekend.

We arrived back in Belfast very late on the Sunday night and, after only a few short hours sleep, I entered the examination hall. For the only time in my life, I faced an examination with little confidence that I would pass it, though I was determined to do my best. In those years, Part IV was considered by most students to be the most practical of all the accountancy examinations – the one most rooted in the traditional accountancy disciplines of accounting, auditing and taxation. Normally, graduates had to have been a minimum of twenty-one months under articles before they could sit it, and non-graduates who were then very much in the majority, had to wait for three years. I had only slightly over fourteen months under my belt. To pass, one needed to get at least 40 per cent in each paper and an overall average of at least 50 per cent – a tall order for someone with so little practical experience.

The first paper appeared to me to be fairly easy and I was confident I'd secured the necessary 50 per cent. The second one went reasonably well, too – probably over 50 per cent again – but I was not entirely sure. I was beginning to think that, if I'd done just a little bit more on the other two subjects, I might have passed the entire thing, but my third paper, Taxation, was a bit of a disaster – most of it was beyond my comprehension. After it, I estimated that if I secured 100 per cent in all the questions I'd answered, which was highly unlikely, I would still be well below the 50 per cent needed to meet the average – my estimate was 47 per cent, but realistically I was unlikely to get even the 40 per cent minimum. The final paper, in Management Accounting, was not much better: I would certainly not get 50 per cent in it.

I concluded I'd certainly failed one paper, probably failed two and had definitely not achieved the overall average.

Immediately on my return after Christmas, I started to study for the re-sits – a new experience for me. I was determined not to fail it a second time. It was a Saturday morning in late February when the results arrived. I recognised the envelope and, to avoid my housemates asking how I'd done, I stuffed it into my pocket unopened so that I could examine it later, on my own, with no embarrassment. It looked bulky, suggesting that the application form for the re-sits was included. That's life, I thought to myself.

Walking up to the Union at Queen's about an hour later, I felt the envelope in my pocket and opened it to see what sort of grades I had achieved. I'd passed! Later on, when I worked for the Institute, I discovered how little I had to spare – in fact, I secured only one mark above the cut-off, and my highest estimate of the outcome in the third paper was out by only a couple of marks.

But a pass is a pass and, against all the odds, I'd done it. In the process, I became the only articled clerk in the history of the Irish Institute to pass Part IV after less than fifteen months in articles and, since the system has now changed completely, no one can ever emulate that achievement. On the Monday, I took great satisfaction from the fact that nobody, including my Principal, believed me when I said that I had passed. My Principal had to check with his partner who was on the Examination Committee who duly contacted the Institute, which confirmed the result.

Part III was taken in the following summer, with no drama, leaving me an entire year to prepare for Part V, which I also passed without any problems. At the time, I was the youngest graduate in the North of Ireland, who had also qualified as a Chartered Accountant. It was a long way from an Arts degree, which I didn't deserve, in subjects in which I had no interest and with, at best, only one alternative calling in life – the prospect of managing a pub in London.

Even though I thrived on the challenges of the examinations, I never graduated to liking accountancy and I absolutely hated audit work – stultifying to the imagination, lacking any element of stimulation or adventure, and completely devoid of innovation or autonomy. On many issues, my views have changed over time – sometimes dramatically – but over the best part of half a century, my dislike of professional accountancy and auditing hasn't shifted one iota.

I've huge respect for the majority of Chartered Accountants, who go into business and broaden their experience, expertise and knowledge-base in 'the real world' but I've little respect for those in professional audit firms, who know nothing about manufacturing, or the hospitality sector, or most tradable or other services, but who still purport to having expertise in all of them.

For many years, I could not understand how people, with no experience of the real world of business, were used by the banks and government agencies to act as receivers and administrators. Now, too late, I know the reason … bankers and civil servants know nothing about business either, not even enough to understand that professional auditors are not capable of running businesses.

Those who remain as professional accountants and auditors are primarily balance sheet managers, with a wonderful understanding of control systems and compliance, which are important in economic life. But they do not have the entrepreneurship, the understanding of market dynamics, the people-management skills or the risk-taking capacity, to run a dynamic business successfully. Neither do they have the skills to save a business which is in difficulty. They have none of the skills needed to manage the profit and loss account, which is ultimately the driver of success in business.

Hence, I view liquidators, administrators, receivers and restructuring specialists with huge scepticism, bordering on contempt – however acceptable, or likeable, I might find them individually. Incidentally, being totally consistent, I harbour many of the same reservations about bankers and certain other financiers too – they haven't a bloody clue, either.

At no point did I ever envisage myself as an auditor. Therefore, when my articles expired on September 30, which happened to fall on a Saturday in that year, I left on the Friday evening and never returned. I suspect, there were dry eyes in the partners' offices, but I didn't wait to see. No leaving party, no goodbyes, I just walked out and never returned.

About a fortnight before I left, someone asked me what I proposed to do in the future. I'd very little idea, but answered that business held significant attraction for me and that, one day, I wanted to run my own business. He mentioned that Queen's had started a new, one-year diploma programme in Business Studies, which could lead to a Master's in Business Administration. I expressed some doubts about going back to university, but he suggested that, at least, I should go up and talk to the professor and find out what it was all about. So, that is precisely what I did. I met Professor Jim Bates, discussed the programme with him and was sufficiently impressed to decide to undertake another year's study. It turned out to be one of the best decisions I ever made. When I went home on that Friday evening and announced that I was going back to university, there was a deafening lack of response. It was clearly not what my parents had expected. At that time, when I came home on Friday evening, the milking had normally been done before I arrived and I was happy enough about that – milking was not my favourite hobby. On the morning after my announcement, my father arrived up to my bedroom, while my mother was preparing his breakfast, rested his elbow on one knee as he teased the tobacco and declared:"Dammy, Peter, I think that any young lad who wants to go back to school when he's nearly twenty-four must be mad. But if that's what you want to do, I'll try and help you, though there's not much money about at the minute."

I told him that I hoped to get a scholarship, but appreciated his offer of support. I could not have known then that, within a few weeks, my world and his would be turned upside down.

In those times, scholarships for post-graduate study were dispensed at the whim of the local education authority, rather than by the

Department. Fermanagh County Education Committee and its workings were a mystery to people of my background but, nonetheless, I went to Enniskillen with the intention of speaking to the chief executive. There were no mobile phones in those days; so I was acting on impulse and had not made an appointment. It really was a most unmannerly way of doing things.

I arrived at the office and asked if I could speak to the County's Chief Education Officer. Not surprisingly, I was told that I would have to make an appointment and that he might be in a position to see me the following week or some time thereafter. But I was due to enrol on the course on the following Monday, so a week's delay was not really an option for me. The receptionist was somewhat less than polite and that stiffened my resolve not to be beaten without a fight. Cheekily, I indicated that I would wait until he had a spare minute, since I could not come back the following week. My cheekiness was met with the contempt it deserved.

But when I parked myself in the waiting room and announced that I was not leaving until he met me, the main man eventually arrived out to the waiting area, having left me sitting for almost two hours. In fairness, I was invited into his office and he was quite polite, though he made it obvious that he was not impressed by my approach to seeking an interview.

On placing my request, I was brusquely advised that applications had closed in the previous March and, even after I'd explained why I could not have applied by that date, I was advised, with a combination of aggression and dismissive condescension, that the matter could not be reconsidered since all the scholarships had been awarded.

Taking a chance, because I'd no idea whether it was true or not, I claimed to be aware that there was still some funding available because not all of the allocated scholarships had been accepted. From his reaction, I knew immediately that my intuition had been accurate though, for obvious reasons, I could not tell him where I'd got my 'information' when he raised that query. But the chance had been worth taking as, clearly, there was some funding left. Eventually, he conceded to considering my case, though without much encouragement that I might be successful.

I started my new course a week later with no idea of how I would fund the fees if my ham-fisted attempt to secure a scholarship was unsuccessful. I felt that, with family support, I could manage the living expenses, but the fees would be problematic and, in those days, banks did not lend to mere students.

For the first time since I'd left school, I really enjoyed academic life. The course was interesting and the student numbers were small enough that we became almost a unit (similar to a football team). The staff members were approachable, tuition was as much by case studies as by lectures and I really enjoyed the experience. In early December, I received a letter to say that my application for a grant had been successful. Things looked good.

I still played cards – mostly poker – three or four nights a week, but I'd developed a routine whereby I joined the game only after I'd spent a couple of hours in the library studying, normally after 9pm. My undergraduate approach of eschewing study, effectively wasting my time and the value of my scholarship, had been replaced by a much more disciplined approach and a continuation of the determination to do well which had driven me to succeed in my accountancy course. I even went to the library first thing in the morning and, if our lectures did not start until 10am, which was the case on two or three days per week, I did an hour's work before going into my classes.

I knew that I had a bit of a reputation for playing cards instead of studying, and I realised that my colleagues continued to hold that perception. Regularly, I overheard comments of, 'Quinn must have been playing cards last night,' and others in the same vein, when I arrived for my lectures at the last minute. Technically, they were right, I probably had played for a while on the previous night, but I'd spent a much longer time studying and they were not aware of that.

By far the biggest lesson I'd learned during my accountancy days was that wasting time was, as they say along the border, 'the road to no town'. When I went back to university, I was there to learn and I found most of the content interesting and potentially valuable.

On the morning the letter arrived to advise me that my late application for a scholarship had been approved and that it covered both fees and living expenses, I was delighted. Later that day, I learned that one of my father's first cousins had died very suddenly. A day later, being the nearest male relatives apart from his brothers and a nephew, Daddy and I were asked to carry his coffin on the evening of the removal to the local church. To a large extent, that was because both of the brothers were the worse for wear, having over-indulged in poitín during the wake, and were incapable of carrying anything.

At the burial ceremony the next morning, Daddy and I were on opposite sides of the grave, having acted as the front pall-bearers. I looked across at him and had a most unusual and vivid premonition. He was a fine-looking man when he was well dressed, despite having, by then, already had sixteen heart attacks. On that day, he looked particularly well – fit and happy with life.

For the only time in my life, I experienced a sort of supernatural premonition. I thought to myself: "I've not seen him looking so well for a long time – he's going to die soon." That evening, I told my mother about my *gestalt* but, predictably, she dismissed it out of hand. Still, I could not get the thought out of my mind. In fact, it became a conviction and I could not get rid of the idea for some days. Eventually, it almost faded from my consciousness – but not entirely.

Exactly two weeks later, on the Sunday before Christmas, I decided to go back to Belfast to do a few days' extra work on my project, which would count for 25 per cent of the overall marks in the final course assessment. I knew there would be very few there and that I would get a fair bit of work done, with no distractions. As I left home, Daddy was leaving to go to the removal of the Teemore football club's chairman, who had died a day earlier.

By the time I arrived in Belfast, a very dense fog had started to descend. It was still there when I got up the following morning. In those days, Belfast was prone to 'real pea-soupers', largely because of the widespread use of coal and anthracite in a built-up area. The

The Greatest Honour – addressing the crowd at Croke Park.

Left, Graduation photo, July 1964. Bottom, the Quinn family! Left to right, my father Hugh, myself, Seán, Bernadette, Miriam and my mother, Mary.

Blessed Among Women – with Mary, Niamh, Claire and Miriam (1990) and, below, a family photograph; from left, Oisin, Mary, Claire, Peter and Niamh with Miriam kneeling to my right.

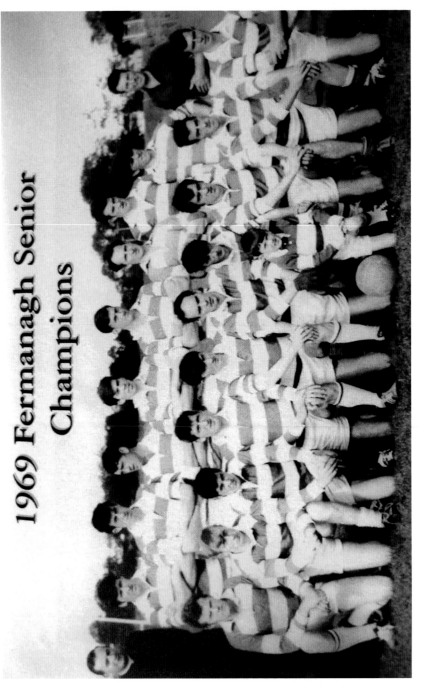

1969 Fermanagh Senior Champions

The 1969 Teemore Shamrocks team which won the Fermanagh senior Championship. I captained the side and anything I achieved afterwards, pales into insignificance.

In Croke Park with the photos of previous Presidents as the backdrop and, below, in 1992 with members of Coiste Bainistí. From left: Micheál Maher (one of Tipperary's infamous 'Hell's Kitchen' full-back line, but by then Chairman of the Munster Council) (Waterford), John Dowling (RIP), Seamus O'Brien (RIP) (Waterford) and Fr. Dan Gallogly (President of Comhairle Uladh).

Teemore locals and members of Fermanagh GAA Club in New York at their Annual Dinner, in 1991. Top photo, Mary is on the extreme left, and third from left is Matt Reilly who played for Teemore in the late 1950s with me.

Seamus Horish (Tyrone) representing Bass Ireland, making a presentation to Jim Nelson (then Antrim hurling manager), with Adrian Logan of UTV; being presented with a commemorative plaque by the Chairman of Cavan County Council at a civic reception, in 1991; at the launch of the London County Board Draw (1993) with Pat Griffin, Eugene Hickey and Tommy Harrell.

Top, Presenting the Fermanagh Hall of Fame Award to the late Tommy Durnien (Lisnaskea), the first Fermanagh man to win a Railway Cup medal, in 1942, when Ulster won it for the first time. Standing, left to right, are Frank McManus, Des Crudden and the late Paddy Donnelly.

Middle, With Fintan Ginnity, the Meath County Board Chairman.

Bottom, At the launch of the Patrick Sarsfields Club's Pitch Development project. On my immediate right, the late Jack Rooney, former Chairman and Treasurer of Antrim County Board and loyal friend from Ulster Council days, with Seamus McGrattan, Ulster Council's Hurling Development Officer, to his right.

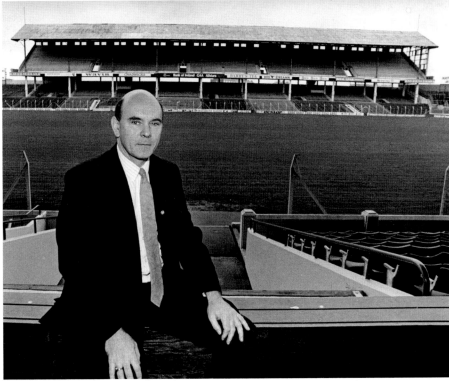

Top, with former President, Mary Robinson, in Croke Park, presenting the 1993 Liam McCarthy Cup to Kilkenny's Eddie O'Connor and, bottom, overlooking the Croke Park pitch shortly before the demolition of the old Cusack Stand.

Top, Croke Park in 1991 as it was before the redevelopment and, bottom, the task of demolishing the Cusack Stand began on the evening of the 1993 All-Ireland Football final, after Derry's win over Cork.

What a difference a year makes ... by 1994 the new Cusack Stand was already taking magnificent shape.

Top, by 1999 we were beginning the demolition and reconstruction of the Hogan Stand and the Canal End, and within a few years the demolition, bottom, of the iconic Hill 16 was underway.

Croke Park, top, before the redevelopment of Hill 16 and, bottom, the final stadium shines as a beacon for Gaelic Games across the globe.

Pitch-side with Croke Park stadium manager, Peter McKenna, before the Ulster minor football final of 2005.

Top, as Chairman of the GAA Strategic Review Committee it was my pleasure to work with, middle, Sean McCague, one of the GAA's greatest Presidents, and, right, Brendan Waters. Meanwhile, bottom, at home in Fermanagh in my office.

library was almost deserted when I arrived just after 9am.

I'd agreed to meet one of my former colleagues from the accountancy firm, Gerry French, for lunch – my first contact with any member of that firm's staff since I'd left about ten weeks earlier. So, shortly after 12.30, I gathered my books and was walking down by the side of the university when I saw a neighbour walking towards me. I assumed that he'd been in Belfast on business, probably getting one of his lorries serviced, until I realised that he was not in working clothes. We exchanged greetings but, before I could initiate any form of conversation, he stunned my by saying, "Peter, your father died last night after you left."

I'd often heard expressions like 'hammer-blow', or 'hit by a sledge' or 'a blow to the solar plexus'. It was just like I had imagined such occurrences. I could feel my legs getting weak. In fact, I had to rest against the wall to maintain my balance. Lots of good and lots of bad things have happened to me since but hearing of my father's death was one of the worst experiences of my life. I was absolutely devastated. I was told that my mother had refused to allow other family members to contact the police station at Donegall Pass because she realised I'd almost certainly have tried to drive home and the fog was just too bad.

I will never forget the memory of entering my parents' bedroom, with my father lying in a coffin, never again to speak to me, or advise me, or support me, or just be there for me. It had been his seventeenth heart attack.

For the first time in my life, I really understood both the finality of death and how tremendously important my father had been in my life. Many of my interests were different to his, though we shared an interest in cattle and cattle farming, but his death created a void which I found difficult to handle, partly because we had only begun to get really close to one another after I left home. Over that Christmas, I finally realised that I was alone in determining how my career would proceed – it was now entirely up to me.

When I returned to Queen's, I was determined to do my best and settle down to real work, as soon as possible. I even thought about applying for jobs.

Before the end of January, one of the teaching staff in the Department overtook me as I walked across the quad towards the departmental building. We were on first-name terms with our lecturers, an informality which didn't apply in most other departments. He was aware of my father's death and had sympathised with me earlier. Now as we walked back, he casually asked me what I intended to do after the course ended. I replied that I hadn't yet decided and hadn't applied for any jobs.

"You wouldn't like a job here, would you?" he asked, again apparently casually.

"What sort of job? In administration?" I responded, assuming that that was what he had in mind, because he had worked in the university's administration department before getting a lectureship. I wouldn't have been interested in an administrative position.

"No," he said, "a teaching job – teaching finance."

"Come on," I retorted. "There's not a chance in hell of someone like me getting a job lecturing here."

As I saw it, that was a statement of fact. I realised that it carried a political implication because he was reasonably prominent in Unionist circles, though he would have been on the most moderate wing of Unionism.

"I wouldn't agree with that," he answered. "We've been watching your performance so far and we think you could do a good job for us. There's a new full-time post becoming available next year, and we'll be trying to recruit for it over the summer."

There was another qualified accountant on the course and he had far more experience than I had. I mentioned his name and continued: "Sure, he has far more experience than me, he would be a better choice."

"We don't think so," came the answer.

As we climbed the stairs towards the department, I was still not sure what was being proposed or if a real proposition was being made at all.

"I'd be interested," I said, without much confidence in the prospect, and confirmed I'd have no problem with his relaying my interest to Professor Bates.

Two or three days later, I was walking up the same stairs, when I met the Professor coming down, heading for his afternoon tea in the staff common room. Professor James 'Jim' A Bates had been appointed to head-up the newly established Department of Business Studies at Queen's a year earlier. He was a larger-than-life Englishman with a great sense of humour, a hearty laugh and an easy-going manner. He had a great way with people and was very popular with the students.

"Peter, have you a minute or two?" he asked and steered me back up the stairs and into his office where he raised the subject of my earlier conversation with the member of the department's teaching staff.

"I believe you'd be interested in a job here," he said.

"I would, but I'm not sure if I'd be capable of doing it," I said reflecting a fundamental absence of self-confidence.

"We think you would," he responded. "But you'd have to prove it."

"What do you mean by that?" I queried.

"Well, for a start, you'll have to come in the first three in the year. Do you think you can achieve that?"

"I'll give it one hell of a try," I answered, as much to myself as to him.

Two minutes later, I was leaving his room, absolutely determined not just to finish in the first three, but to finish first. It was a completely different motivation, but it begot a similar ambition to that which had helped me pass my accountancy examinations. Events, again!

I'd put in a reasonable effort, before Christmas. Now, I increased that effort substantially though I was careful not to show any signs of such a change. I continued to play cards at night – after all, I'd an image to sustain and it would have not have looked good to be seen as a 'swot' – but now I started to find excuses not to participate in any all-night games.

Some weeks before the formal examinations, I learned that I'd produced a good project, getting the highest mark in the year by some distance, which was a great start. That project had involved analysing the published accounts of a number of the public companies quoted on the Belfast Stock Exchange, other than banks and financial institutions

– there were twenty-six of them, in total.

My report raised a number of queries which, in tandem, suggested the possibility that the published accounts of one of Northern Ireland's 'blue chip' manufacturers might have been 'massaged' to show steady growth in profit instead of the violent fluctuations, including losses in some years, which I assessed as being closer to reality and I produced some regression-based data to support my conclusion. I also suggested that this was a particularly risky business, which was overtrading and could not sustain a significant market down-turn. While my analyses were considered very good, my conclusions caused considerable concern within the department. The idea of having a student suggesting that a high profile company, with very strong political connections, might be 'fiddling' its accounts was seen as potentially so explosive that my report was the only one of that year to be filed, where nobody but a member of departmental staff could have access to it. Within a year, the company had gone into liquidation and my report formed the basis of an authoritative article in one of the main British Sunday broadsheets.

The examinations stretched over a week with one paper each morning and a couple of afternoon papers. Our second paper was in 'Operations Research and Statistics', my favourite subject. I tackled the OR first and did three questions in which I thought I'd done quite well; I then did two 'statistics' questions and was reasonably confident at the end. Not for the first time, I left the examination hall before the allotted time had expired.

As I left the hall, I met the OR lecturer, who was probably waiting to find out our reaction to his component of the paper which I'd thought was relatively easy. I'd developed a good relationship with him and that was to survive for several years, until I left Ireland and our paths ceased to cross. He asked me how many of the questions from his section I'd done and seemed pleased when I said three.

"What answer did you get to the first one?" he asked. I told him and he looked at a sheet he had in front of him. I immediately noticed a frown.

"That's wrong," he said; "It's not even close." I was dumbfounded.

"What other one did you do?" he asked, and I told him.

"And what answer did you get?" he continued.

Again I told him and again I saw the frown; this was not what I'd been expecting.

"It's wrong, too," he said.

Now I was rattled. I'd heard of guys misreading papers and 'losing it' in other ways during examinations but I never saw myself as being in the category of collapsing under pressure.

"What was your third one?" he asked, followed by a cautious "... and what was your answer to that one?"

Again, I told him.

This time, it was not a frown – it was sheer disbelief.

"That's wrong, too," he said. I was in a state of shock, and he seemed to be in shock, too.

I went off to the Union for lunch, sat in a corner on my own, and proceeded to redo the three OR questions: I got the same answers. I checked the methodology in a textbook and it appeared as if my approach had been right. I was close to panic – I could see a potential lectureship disappearing over some distant horizon and I'd made no alternative arrangements for earning a living when the course ended.

That afternoon, I sat the Finance and Accounting paper, but I was badly distracted. While it would be an exaggeration to say that I did badly in it, I certainly did not do nearly as well as I should have in my own area of expertise.

Before the fourth paper, on the Wednesday morning, I was hanging around the examination hall, still distracted, but hiding my worries as best I could, when the OR lecturer walked in.

"Is Peter Quinn about?" he asked.

I'd neither seen him enter, nor heard his enquiry, but someone called me and told me that the lecturer wanted to speak to me. He asked if he could speak to me privately, so I walked outside with him.

"Peter," he said, "I'm really sorry. I corrected your script last night. You did very well. In fact you got 60 out of 60 in my section. When I told you that you had the wrong answers yesterday, I was looking at the answers to another examination paper. My apologies! I hope it didn't upset you overnight."

Was I relieved? You bet I was! I didn't have the heart to tell him that not only had he caused me a sleepless night, but that I'd been distracted during the previous afternoon's paper and probably had not done as well in it as I should have. However, I knew that, when the statistics marks were added, I'd have another high score – which I did.

Following the final paper, a group of us were hanging around in one of the lecture rooms and the subject of ;student of the year' came up. About ten different names were mentioned, but mine was not one of them. I sat there thinking to myself, "surely I have to be in there with a shout", but no one else seemed to share my unspoken view.

Before we left that evening, I was approached by the Professor who asked me to make myself available for a research project, on which he wanted me to start work as soon as possible – preferably on the following Monday. I took that as a signal I'd done reasonably well in the examinations though I'd no idea how well, or whether it would be enough to get me the promised post. So, I started my new job as a researcher on the following Monday, sharing an office with the man who'd first mentioned the possibility of a job to me. In reality, it was my first job because my accountancy training was, technically, not real employment.

Being offered my first job, instead of having to apply for it, set a pattern which was to last for the rest of my life. I eventually retired last year without ever holding a paid position for which I applied.

Information-leaks occur in all organisations. I became aware that the faculty was holding a meeting to ratify the Economics and the Business Studies examination results, before their official publication. When my new roommate returned to his desk, he never mentioned the outcome and I never asked, but, later on, he confided in me, telling me that I'd done well, had secured first place and was being recommended for the Sir Charles Harvey Award as the best student in the department in that year. He warned me not to tell anyone until I'd received official confirmation.

Later on that week, the Professor confirmed that I'd been appointed as the new Teaching Fellow, on a scholarship provided by the Foundation for Management Education. He wanted me to start immediately, so that I would have a chance to have lectures prepared for the start of term but agreed immediately to let me take three weeks holidays as I'd already bought a ticket to go see Mina in Chicago. I landed in New York and visited two of my father's first cousins, neither of whom was married but who provided me with most comfortable accommodation and showed me around the Big Apple. I was taken to see the sights of New York, to a Broadway show, to the military academy at West Point and to several places of which I'd never heard previously. He also took me to visit other family relatives. It was a wonderful, whirlwind week.

The flight to Chicago still ranks as one of the most uncomfortable flights of my life – certainly among the three worst I have ever experienced, and given the amount of flying I did in subsequent years, that says something. Still, it was brilliant to see Mina and her family again. There she was known as Phil or Philomena, but she was still Mina to me.

One evening during my second week there, I received a phone call from a friend who had been on the course in Queen's. He was head of a department in a college in northern Chicago and was married to an Irish woman, from Crossmaglen, which was the main reason he had selected Queen's for his year's sabbatical – he was also a keen handballer and that helped to reinforce his selection. He asked if I'd like to spend a couple of days with him and his wife and, having asked Mina's permission after all, she was my hostess, I agreed. He collected me the next morning in a typical American gas-guzzler, the like of which I'd never seen in Ireland.

We had a great couple of days and I got to see more of Chicago. One morning he suggested that we'd go out to the campus of North-Western University, in Evanston, to see the American Football 'All Stars' in training. At the time, I'd no idea what the All Stars were and I'd never seen American Football, but I went along with the proposal anyway.

We arrived mid-morning and, though the training programme was in full swing, we were virtually the only onlookers. Within seconds, I could barely believe what I was seeing. There were massive men thundering forward to hit and push very heavy steel structures, moving them yards at a time – this was new to me. But the real surprise was the equally large men who were running what seemed to be between 80- and 100-yard sprints in twelve or thirteen seconds or less. I could hardly believe what I was seeing – I'd won juvenile races in times like theirs. For big men, they could really shift. I'd spent years training under a variety of football managers, but I'd never experienced anything like this. It was a real eye-opener, which made me understand how far GAA players still had to go to match the training of professionals.

*****

When I returned to Ireland, the doubts and lack of confidence which I'd harboured from childhood started to fall away and I began to realise that I was capable of far higher achievements than I'd ever envisaged. It was time to start setting higher horizons for myself.

10

A Short Career

Like the majority of other university lecturers, I started lecturing at Queen's without any training or qualifications in teaching, without any help in course design or understanding of what it entailed, without any supervision of the content of the courses I was teaching and with no track record in either public speaking or debating. And while I was quite confident in my own ability, I wasn't so confident in front of a class, nor indeed in front of any group. Neither had I any experience of presenting material, of how to communicate effectively nor of how much content I would need for an hour's lecture. In reality, I was very much out of my depth and it probably showed – students are pretty quick to pick up on such shortcomings.

I had two different groups of students. There was the post-graduate group, studying business and largely comprising mature students who were committed and willing to work – they were all losing money by coming back to university and were not in the business of wasting their time.

Then there was the undergraduate cohort. The undergraduate programme was spread over two years, with no examinations at the end of the first year and correspondingly little incentive to take the subject particularly seriously over that year. The majority of the undergraduate students tended to treat the subject differently in the second year, but only marginally so. That group comprised students who were taking a degree in economics, which was the primary focus of their study, with accountancy being simply a subsidiary subject for them, though some had aspirations of taking articles with a view to becoming accountants, when they completed their degree.

Worse than that, each year of the undergraduate class contained a considerable proportion of mature students who were already in employment. Many of them were working in banking or the civil service and some were considerably older than me with more experience of book keeping and practical accounting than I had. The majority were very patient – even helpful – but, inevitably, there were some who wanted to show off their superior knowledge and were a pain in the arse for any new lecturer, but especially for one who was attempting to find his feet in the subject. The fact that I understood accounting in arithmetical terms rather than in 'debit' and 'credit' terms – I still have no idea how to deal with debit and credit, but then neither do computers and they're better than any humans – did not help my credibility with that latter group, one or two of whom proved quite disruptive, in my first year.

I knew what the post-graduate group needed – finance rather than accounting – and I was reasonably confident that I could deliver that syllabus with some conviction, though I was nervous enough at the prospect of moving to the other side of the lectern. However, I'd no real idea of what was appropriate for the undergraduate courses, since I'd never taken such a course myself and had no input into its design.

A comprehensive syllabus had already been agreed and published by the faculty but I suspect very few of the students had read it. Syllabi can be interpreted in many different ways and I was not sure how I should interpret this one. Eventually, I worked out what I thought might be most relevant and spent the remainder of that summer preparing enough lectures to keep me going for almost the entirety of that first term.

With hindsight, the content of my lectures, especially my lectures to the undergraduate students, must have been awful. They followed the syllabus directly, which was quite inappropriate for what, I later discovered, was really required – a basic grounding in the theory of accountancy, with some appreciation of how that theory could be applied in practice. I have no idea who prepared the syllabus but, in terms of sequencing, it was not very good and it contained far too much nonsense that neither business people nor accountants were ever likely to use in practice.

To make matters worse, my presentation was also terrible. I prepared my lectures from various textbooks and delivered them by reading them aloud, deviating from the script only to respond to direct questions from the students, and very few were interested enough to ask a question. As I realised later, the whole course was a disaster in both content and presentational terms. While I knew that at the time, I had neither enough experience nor confidence to make the necessary changes.

Within weeks, I realised that I enjoyed teaching finance on the post-graduate course but that teaching accounting was never going to be my forte. Still, I had no option but to do my best. With the benefit of many years' subsequent experience, I think I can say with some confidence that my best (and I gave it my best) was probably short of what those first students had a right to expect.

Right at the start of the new academic year, I'd tried to alert the students to the new reality – that standards would have to improve. I was under no illusion that the first appointment of a full-time lecturer in accountancy in what was still the only university in Northern Ireland, was designed to ensure that standards were raised to an acceptable academic level. However, as the year progressed, I could tell that, apart from the usual few consistently hard workers, no one else was putting much effort into this subject.

Most students were expecting me to follow the established practice, whereby the last three or four weeks would be devoted entirely to the revision of those areas, which were contained in the examination paper. That was how the subject had been taught until then – hence the 100 per cent pass rate. I had decided that I was not going to follow the established practice and that 'my' accountancy students would have to compete on an equal footing with those studying other subjects for their economics degree.

Following normal practice, I forwarded a copy of the paper together with my draft answers, to the external examiner, who was a dour, but very fair, Scotsman. While I never warmed to him, he combined practice with academia, and I recognised that he knew his subject through and through, and was not likely to accept low standards. That coincided with my own preference. He expressed satisfaction with the questions and with the emphases I expected in the answers – in fact, he made not a single recommendation for change.

Alea iacta est – the die had been cast. Those who had not put in enough effort were destined to fail and I would be under pressure, with my teaching standards almost certain to be questioned. I understood the implications only too well, but I also understood that, if I was to have any credibility in my new career, I had no choice. Much later, I realised just how risky that strategy had been.

The failure rate was just a few points short of 50 per cent. My professor came back to me, clearly on the instructions of the wider faculty board, and asked if I was satisfied with the outcome. Failure rates of 50 per cent were not normal in any university, at that time or any other time, and there was a palpable sense of shock, which was not restricted to the unsuccessful students. Obviously, I was not happy with the outcome either, but I had started on a path which was irreversible. So, I explained the issues involved and the implications of continuing with the previous practices, as I perceived them.

Professor Bates accepted my argument and committed himself to supporting me at the higher level. I was not a full member of the faculty, at that point, since I held only a teaching fellowship not a lectureship. As a result, I was not entitled to attend the Examination Committee's meetings. Consequently, I've always been appreciative of his support over that period, since I was dependent on his representations on my behalf at faculty meetings. Otherwise, mine could have become the shortest academic career in history.

Whatever happened at faculty level, my results were accepted, probably based on the fact that the external examiner had confirmed that the papers were fair, and that my marking scheme and its application met the standards applicable to degree level examinations. In any event, there were no negative repercussions for me.

Not all the students who failed would have been entitled to take the September re-sits but, among those who did, the pass rate showed a marked improvement. Clearly, the subject was being taken more seriously and much greater effort had been invested in studying for the repeats. The marker had been laid down and recognised and accountancy would no longer be the 'soft option' for economics students at Queen's.

As it turned out, there was a slight reduction in the numbers taking accountancy in the following year but it was only very slight. I'd expected a bigger effect from my decimation of the results and was thankful that the faculty could not point to my performance as the source of a significant reduction in student numbers.

The net result was that the attitudes of the students in that second year were significantly different and the pass rate, whilst still below the faculty average, was very much higher than it had been a year earlier. We were making progress and the message was getting through – the 'soft option' in the economics faculty at Queen's was a thing of the past.

Nevertheless, the lower-than-average pass rate prompted the head of another department within the faculty to query whether Queen's – specifically within its Economics and Social Sciences Faculty – should not, "… get rid of this dastardly subject". By that time, I had secured a proper lectureship and was in attendance when the comment was made. Other colleagues thought I should have felt insulted but I didn't – I was amused. I understood precisely where he was coming from and I knew that some of his chagrin was justified.

I was also doing my MBA thesis throughout this time. It involved a full master's level thesis, as opposed to the 'projects' which applied and still apply in other MBAs. I'd chosen to examine the implications of the changes in the taxation system introduced by the British Chancellor of the Exchequer, Jim Callaghan, for the dividend policy of quoted public companies in Northern Ireland. My thesis was heavily mathematical in content, involving advanced regression and correlation analyses, and the use of a variety of non-parametric statistical tests.

Such analyses necessitated the use of a computer which were in their infancy then. Compared with their modern counterparts 'real-time' data input, the practice of punching holes in a pre-prepared data sheet to record the information to be processed was laborious and time-consuming. I spent many an evening, after an hour's football training or a game of squash, preparing data for overnight analysis and was frustrated, more than once, when the results, specifically, my analyses of the 'residuals', indicated clearly that I must have made some mistake in the data entry. That meant that I had to re-do the entire data preparation for that part of the analysis from scratch, for submission for the following night's computer run. Nevertheless, the project proceeded successfully, if somewhat more slowly than would have been considered optimal.

Looking back, I realise that I was trying to keep too many balls in the air and I was lucky to get away with it – particularly since I was still learning how to manage a syllabus and improve my presentation of content, which was also developing less rapidly than I would have wanted.

When the new full-time lecturer's post was advertised at the end of my first year, I was persuaded by some faculty members to apply for it, even though my original appointment as a Teaching Fellow had been for two years. The reality was that the money from the Foundation for Management Education had been used to fund a pilot initiative in the subject and the university was now prepared to invest its own resources, despite the disastrous results in the first year of that experiment.

I had 'the inside track': I was already teaching the subject and hoped to do a better job in my second year. Some, but not all, of the selection committee knew me; I was able to research the sort of questions others had been asked in similar situations and my new colleagues gave me good guidance in that respect.

I knew that, despite the concerns about the failure rate, the new position was mine to lose – I just needed to avoid doing something stupid! I'd been asked to apply in a way which was tantamount to an offer and, effectively, I was in the post already. All the same, I prepared diligently for the inevitable interview, researching potential issues of interest and actually sitting down and preparing answers. It all worked out well – I got the job together with promotion and a pay rise. I was now destined for a career as an academic – or so it seemed – and, probably for the first time in my life, I was satisfied that I knew where I was going in life.

What I was not factoring into any calculations was the possibility that, once again, 'events' might change the course of the predicted graph.

11

Winning a Championship

By the time I returned from the United States to prepare for my new career at Queen's, the Shamrocks had already lost their Championship semi-final game to an up-and-coming team from Ederney, who had been our main rivals at junior and intermediate level for much of the previous decade. It might be an exaggeration to say that I was blamed for that loss through not being available, but my absence had certainly been noted. Anyway, Ederney won that game and went on to win their first and, so far, their only senior Championship though they deserved more. Despite the keen rivalry between the teams, we were happy for them and, of all our opponents in those years, the Ederney players are still among those for whom we have most respect and with whom we are friendliest. Games between us were always hard – sometimes very hard – but anything that happened on the field was forgotten as soon as the final whistle was blown.

That kind of camaraderie applied to most of our other opponents, too. We tended to have healthy rivalries with all the clubs in East Fermanagh, the local clubs and our other great opponents of those years, Devenish. Later, we came up against a strong Tempo team and a great Enniskillen squad and I honestly believe that, apart from the odd individual, we have retained good relations with all of them.

Despite my absence from the most important Championship game in the preceding year, I was selected as captain for the 1969 season – my selection was based on my seniority rather than for my performances on the field. The Shamrocks had not won the senior Championship since they collected their fifteenth title in 1935 and, though they had played in two finals in the interim, they hadn't really threatened to regain the position they had held for the first three decades of official competition in the county. For the new season, I was returned to the forward line, although I had played well at centre-half back over the previous year and had come to prefer that position. In fact, I was a better half-back than I ever was in the forward line.

We had been knocking on the door for a couple of years by then. Two years earlier, we'd reached the senior League final where we faced Devenish – the dominant team in Fermanagh during the sixties and one of the best Fermanagh has ever produced. Despite scoring more often than Devenish, their four goals, one or two of which were in the 'soft' category, made the difference; our scores were all points. But 'goals win games'.

I had started that game at centre-half forward, but was switched to midfield about ten minutes before half time. Coincidentally, exactly the same applied to the great PT Treacy, so we finished the first half playing directly in opposition to each other. PT was an exceptional player – possibly the best I ever saw wearing a Fermanagh jersey, though Peter McGinnity and our two more recent All Stars (my own club man, Barry Owens, who has two, and Marty McGrath) were also superb and would have to be considered for that accolade, too. I was fortunate enough to have played alongside PT on a couple of occasions and I recall very well the tremendous encouragement he gave to young players. He could win a game in seconds and often did, for both his county and his club, including against us on a couple of occasions. But most of all, PT was an outstanding club man, and, in my book, that is very much to his credit.

I vividly remember the aftermath of that match. We were hugely disappointed at failing to bring a senior trophy back to Teemore after so many years in the football wilderness. Brian McCaffrey and I were sitting in the corner of the dressing room, feeling sorry for ourselves and, to tell the truth, not far from tears, when James Cassidy, who had played corner back for us that day, came over to us.

"I don't know why the two of you are so sad," he said. "You'll win senior Championships and Leagues yet, but my chance is gone, I'll never win one now."

His comment was understandable, because he was almost forty years old and had 'carried' the club for almost twenty years, by that stage. We didn't know it at the time, but he was wrong in one of his predictions.

By 1969, we knew we were developing into a reasonably good team. We'd been holding our own in the senior League for a couple of years – something Teemore had not done for almost three decades – and had been beaten in the Championship in three successive years, by the eventual champions. But we had a very small panel of players, most of whom were quite young and no one outside the club expected us to be in contention for major honours for another few years, if at all.

Later on, I realised that we had no real idea of what it took to win a Championship, but we trained five or six nights a week, often without any manager or trainer, and sometimes on a concrete surface. Nowadays, we would be considered completely mad to be at such things, but facilities were poor in the late '60s so we had to use whatever was available – and we enjoyed it. Three of us, who had started playing adult football at 14, were now 25 or over, and considered the veterans of a panel dominated by players who were under 21.

The draw for the Championship pitted us against Ederney in the first round, which was also a quarter-final since there were, and still are, only ten senior teams in the county. Right from the start of the year, from when the Championship draws were made in January, that had been our target and the focus of all our attention and discussions.

In those days, the club never held a formal meeting, apart from the AGM. Instead, there were regular, informal meetings after training though most of our meetings were held outside the church gate, after second Mass every Sunday.

About three weeks before the Championship game, our manager, the late Fr. John Maguire who was curate in Teemore at the time, came out to join the post-Mass discussion, as he did every Sunday. He suggested that we would have a reasonable chance of winning the Championship, if we had a reliable goalkeeper. I wasn't present, but it was my brother who spoke up and said he knew, "the very man for that position".

"Who?" asked the curate.

"James," he replied. There was only one James in Teemore.

As a result of his work with cattle on the farm, James Cassidy had developed a problem, which led to his retirement from football more than a year earlier. He had already retired from county football about five years earlier as he approached his mid-thirties, having played for Fermanagh for fifteen years. James had no expectation of ever playing again; he had 'done his bit'. But he was naturally athletic and his farm work ensured that he continued to be fit.

"He won't come back," the team manager said.

"If he thought he could help us to win a Championship, he'd come back and there is no better man in the club to organise a defence. He would be a tremendous asset to our young backs, who need that sort of experience behind them," Seán argued.

Nobody disagreed that James would be the ideal solution to the team's problem position, but not many believed he'd agree to return.

"Sure, we'll only find out, if we ask him," Seán suggested.

Eventually, Seán and Fr. Maguire were deputised to approach James about making a comeback in goals, which they did immediately – in fact, he was just about to sit down to his Sunday dinner as the pair arrived on the street. When the proposition was put to him, the response was in keeping with the man – though hesitant about returning, he agreed to do so if the club members thought he could do anything for them.

"I doubt if I have anything to offer," he said, with predictable modesty, "but if you lads think I can do a job for you, I'll give it a try.

I won't be able to attend all the training sessions, but I'll play in goals and I'll try to make training at least one night a week, anyway."

For a man on the cusp of forty it was a generous offer and it was to make a huge difference before the year ended.

The game against Ederney was fixed for Tempo – a ground which had been good for us over the years. Predictably, it was tough and the old saw, 'no quarter given and no quarter taken', was particularly apt that evening.

Cassidy was magnificent. Right from the start he was called into action regularly but his reading of the angles and his innate footballing brain saved us several times. It is impossible to beat twenty-odd years' experience of football, especially when it includes fifteen at inter-county level.

We edged ahead of them with a goal midway through the second half and the last few minutes were particularly tense. Ederney tried for a goal. Kiltegan student and Sigerson Cup winner with UCC, Seán McGrath (now Fr. Seán, who is doing Trojan work with the disadvantaged in Sao Paulo), hit the crossbar with a rasper from a free, Tommy Farmer had his jersey tugged at just the right moment (or just the wrong moment for him!), but the referee did not see it and James saved the weakened shot, though he would probably have saved it anyway – at least, so we tell the Ederney lads, whenever they raise the subject. Still they kept cutting into our lead; it was nail-biting stuff until eventually they equalised. We were close to panic, but we held our nerve – just.

With only a few seconds to go and with the scores level, our midfielder, Seán O'Reilly, was fouled just short of forty yards out and to the right of the posts. I hit the resultant free reasonably well but, as it got close to the posts, it started to drop off to the left and seemed to lose impetus. In the end, it barely scraped inside the left post and only a few inches above the crossbar, but that was enough to persuade the umpire to raise the white flag. The kick-out was the second last kick of the game and we were in the semi-final.

That semi-final pitched us against Devenish who'd beaten us in two of the previous three years. It was a dour struggle in which I played poorly but Seán made the difference, driving his body through flying boots to score the game's only goal with his fist. If my life had depended on it, I could not have done that – I didn't have the physique, or the strength, or the courage. On that day, I was there simply to point the frees. We eventually wore them down and, while it wasn't pretty, it was our passport to Teemore's first senior Championship final in over a quarter of a century.

Paddy Drumm, who 'ceilied' in our house several nights each week, had always told me that I could never claim to be a footballer until I'd won a Championship. He had won two and had played at inter-county level for a number of years. In the early days, the comment had annoyed me, but as I got older I understood that this was his way of motivating me to put in more effort and to challenge harder for success. In an odd way, he was a wonderful mentor. Clearly, he had identified that this squad had some potential before the rest of us realised it. He laid out our chance of making history in stark terms: there would be only one winner and the losers would be forgotten. It registered with me.

The final was the main topic of conversation around the area for a couple of weeks in advance. Everyone was going to the game, which should have been played in Enniskillen but, because of on-going work, was switched to Irvinestown – the home ground of our opponents which was at the other end of the county. More importantly, we had only eighteen players to select from, having lost John McCaffrey to a broken foot a few months earlier. Clearly, we'd have to play at least one of our minors, a host of under-21s, and have two under-16s among our subs.

We got off to a great start. Seán, who was playing full forward, scored a point in the first minute and broke through a minute later to set up Brendan Reilly for a second. I have no doubt that, three or four years later, they would not have settled for points but, at that stage, we lacked the experience to make best use of our chances. We were totally dominant for the first fifteen minutes and, with more experience, would have built up a handsome lead before Irvinestown got into the game.

Meanwhile, I was having no impact from the centre half-forward position. So much for a captain leading by example! I didn't get my hands on the ball for about six or seven minutes. Then, about ten minutes into the game, Brian McCaffrey sent a perfect pass in my direction – just the sort of ball to bring a slow starter into the game. It was coming right on to my chest; I knew my marker was racing towards me and I turned to shoot before he arrived. Unfortunately, somehow the ball managed to squeeze its way between my elbow and my body, right into the hands of my immediate opponent, the Irvinestown captain, Gerry O'Donnell. He was, if anything, even more surprised than I was, but I was much more embarrassed – even ashamed. It was a silly mistake, but it was also a message for me; it was long past time for me to get into the game.

Concentrate! Keep your eye on the bloody ball, lad! Most of all, get into the rhythm of this game – it's passing you by! You're the captain – you're supposed to lead by example, for Christ's sake! Next one's mine.

Within a minute or two we got a free, which I pointed. It got me into the match. By half time I had added a couple more and, from there on, things started to go reasonably well for me, though I couldn't claim to have been dominating either the game, or even my own sector of the pitch.

Before half time, Cassidy made two tremendous saves – one from the late Stephen McGarrity and the other from Gerry Magee. In a game, which we had controlled for most of the half, we were lucky to go in at half time leading by a couple of points.

Still, we did not heed the warning. We were far too naïve to be successful but, fortunately, so too were our opponents and the result was a game which was recognised as probably the most open and most enjoyable final played in the County for decades. Naïveté has some advantages, though I would not recommend it as a recipe for success.

We extended our lead and, while they matched us score for score, we still had a cushion. I got my only score from play off a pass from Peter Hegarty out on the left wing, to put us three points ahead and

I could see the New York Gold Cup heading for South Fermanagh. Then, as we were mentally celebrating, Gerry Magee, Irvinestown's star forward of that era, raced through our defence to plant the ball firmly in the net. Game on! I switched with Seán, who went out to the half-forward line in order to help our midfield, which had started to lose the dominance it had enjoyed for the previous three quarters.

With less than ten minutes to go, our opponents went ahead we equalised they went ahead again. Time was running out. We got a free slightly more than 40 yards out and 15 yards from the left sideline. It was just about within my range and on the preferred side for a right-footed kicker. I hit it perfectly – easily the best free I hit that day – but probably nobody apart from myself remembers it. We were level again. Less than two minutes to go and Seán was fouled as he raced through the middle. Even though the whistle went, he soloed on and blasted the ball over the bar and out of the ground.

"What the hell did you do that for?" I asked, irritably, as I met him on my way out to take the free.

"Wasting time," he replied. "Can't you see it's level? It's up to you now. Point this and it's our Championship," he added, pointing to the scoreboard.

Though it was a tight game, I was unsure of the exact score and hadn't even noticed the scoreboard, but a quick glance down towards the Tyrone end of St Molaise Park confirmed his claim. I knew only too well what I had to do. Normally, the referee Ken Browne (one of my favourite referees) would hand the ball to the kicker. In those days, once the referee set the ball down, the free-taker was not allowed to replace it, so handing the ball to the kicker was a bonus. And, of course, all frees had to be taken from the ground, at that time. This time, he placed it.

"Can I place it again?" I asked. Had I placed it without asking him, I would have lost my free and possibly Teemore would have lost the Championship.

"No," he said. "This is too tight. Kick it from where I've placed it."

I didn't have time to get annoyed and, anyway, I liked Ken, both as a referee and as a person. Just over 40 yards out and straight in front of the posts – no angle. Not everyone would appreciate that straight in front of the posts is one of the worst places from which to take a free, for someone who hits the ball off the ground with the instep, a slight angle is a major help. Ten yards out and it was heading for the black spot five yards out it started to fade but it never looked like missing. We held out for the remaining two minutes, largely due to a great defensive interception by Seán.

In previous years, I'd attended several county finals in a number of different counties (Antrim, Cavan, Meath and Fermanagh especially), but I had never waited for the presentation of the trophy. Consequently, the only presentations I had ever witnessed were in Clones and Croke Park, and the captain had always started with a few words in Irish. So, not knowing that this was not the normal practice at Fermanagh county finals, I gave half of my acceptance speech as Gaeilge though probably not many understood it – possibly including some who were fluent Irish speakers!

Even yet, over forty years later, captaining Teemore Shamrocks to their sixteenth Championship success, thirty-four years after they had won their fifteenth, ranks as one of the proudest days of my life – easily the proudest of my sporting life. I know that for those who have won All-Irelands and captained All-Ireland winning teams such an achievement is of relatively little significance but, for me, it was and is immense. Anything that happened afterwards, as a result of that achievement, pales into insignificance by comparison.

I have so many memories of that evening. Meeting and being greeted with a big embrace from Paddy Drumm at the door of the dressing room, with tears streaming down his face after witnessing an end to a three-decade famine, presumably as he recalled his own wins of more than thirty years earlier; asking Terry Curry what he was thinking as I was taking that last free, to be told that he had turned his back to the pitch and started to pray; remembering Mrs Fitzpatrick, who prayed her way through all our games, saying a succession of Rosaries; recalling the sheer, understated but undiluted joy of James Cassidy, as he won the medal he had craved for more than two decades and would certainly have won, had he been prepared to play for another club. James was our 'man of the match' that day, even if others got the major credit. There are other memories, too, such as watching the unrestrained pleasure our win gave to former club players who had turned out, en masse, to support us. It was good to be a Teemore player that evening and it was an honour to be captain.

Only one negative cast a shadow over that 'day of days' for a Teemore footballer – my father was not there to witness it. Despite the reality that, in my younger days, we had often held very different views of the world, he had eventually accepted that I was not destined to be a farmer. We'd grown quite close in the later years of his life and, on the day, I missed him greatly. He had started to attend our games only a few years earlier and then only by chance, but, from then on, he had never missed a game. I can only guess how proud he would have been, though he'd never have shown it.

Our next game was in the Ulster Club Championship against the Donegal champions, on a wet, heavy pitch which did not suit me. I was playing against one of my favourite players from my youth, John Hannigan, a man who played in nearly every position for Donegal and was effective in all of them. He gave me a lesson in football that day. Even when I managed to get the ball, which was rare enough, he seemed to take it from me again, totally fairly and sportingly. He absolutely destroyed me and I could not even blame the pitch, because the conditions were the same for him. My confidence sank so low that I even missed an easy free and that didn't happen too often in those years. It was just one of those days and, while I was easily the worst of the lot, none of us played well.

I was to win three more Fermanagh senior Championships, in 1971, 1974 and 1975 and four senior League titles, but that first one gave me most pleasure and I never played as poorly again in the Ulster Club Championship, as I did in that first year. That first win was also the one which had the biggest impact on the rest of my life.

The late, great John Doyle is reputed to have said that 'Christy

Ring won eight All-Irelands for Cork, but the Tipperary team won eight All-Irelands for me'. I understand his sentiment completely. I may have been Teemore's top scorer in most of our victories, as a result of being the team's free-taker, but it was the others who won those frees and I was rarely the real match winner. As well as my brother, I had other great colleagues and wonderful friends. It was almost a team of families – four Fitzpatricks, four O'Reillys (all those eight played for Fermanagh at some time), two McCaffreys, as well as two of us. But there were about ten others on that 1969 panel who were equally important to the team and that number increased over the following seven years. The friendships created through wearing the jerseys with the green and white hoops have lasted long beyond the end of our playing days.

Since we had started as players together, played county minor together and played midfield together for the club for years, Brian McCaffrey and I had an almost telepathic relationship, which worked more to my advantage than to his, over those years; he was a big asset to my game.

Those were the men who 'made me' in GAA terms because, without them, I would never have been involved in administration or elected to any senior office within the Association.

12

Entering GAA Administration

Apart from being team captain, I was also assistant secretary of the club when we won that 1969 Championship, and the nomination papers for the 1969 county convention were sent to me. I filled them in and returned them, essentially re-nominating all the outgoing officers. In Teemore, in those days, we had very little interest in the operation of the County Board; our sole interest was in playing. Our lack of interest in County Board affairs was a reflection of how far our club had fallen from the days of the Clarke brothers and Jim Dunne and the many other great officers Teemore Shamrocks had provided to the Association in Fermanagh, and even in Ulster, in the early years of the twentieth century.

So, I was following a well-trodden path when I filled in the nomination forms for the 1969 County Convention, without making any new nominations. Interest in any aspect of the Association, apart from playing the game on Sunday afternoon, was gone completely around Teemore Cross and the Mountain Road. The Shamrocks had lost their former status, even if they had just had success at senior level, for the first time in thirty-five years.

Though I was selected as one of the club's delegates to County Convention, it came as a surprise to learn, a week prior to that gathering, that I'd been nominated to contest the position of 'Representative on Ulster Council'. Normally, a nomination would come from one's own club and I knew with certainty that this one had not. More surprisingly, no member of the club seemed to know which club had nominated me – not that many cared anyway!

At the Convention, held in Kinawley in January, 1970, there were three nominations for the two Ulster Council positions. Outgoing representative, Malachy Mahon, who was also County Secretary and one of the best GAA men in Ulster, was acceding to the position of Treasurer of the Council, an appointment which would ultimately lead to his becoming the first Fermanagh-man to be elected President of Comhairle Uladh. Other provinces used the expression 'Chairman', but Ulster always used 'President', and still does.

John Vesey, the other outgoing representative, had also been nominated. A native of Mayo, he would later become President of the Provincial Council (and Vice-President of the Association), Chairman of Fermanagh County Board for several years, a candidate for Trusteeship of the GAA, and one of the best GAA men Fermanagh ever had. The other nominee was the late Mickey Brewster, the former Fermanagh and Ulster midfielder who had played at full-back on Queen's University's first-ever Sigerson winning team.

I had no real interest in the role and would have withdrawn my nomination, had my club Secretary, Seán Martin, one of the men who had carried the club through some of its leanest years, and still a staunch Teemore man, not suggested: "Sure, you may as well run anyway, Teemore has not had a County Board officer since Jim Dunne."

At that point, I hadn't really begun to understand the dynamics of the GAA's electoral and administrative systems, so I allowed my nomination to go ahead.

Following the discussion on the Secretary's Report and the Chairman's address, the election of officers commenced. I noticed that the late Gerry Magee, a former Chairman and then President of the

Association in Fermanagh, went round the room speaking to each delegation in turn, but he never came to meet us. I asked Seán Martin what Gerry was doing and why he had not approached us, but he had no idea either.

When the first vote was taken for Ulster Council Representative, predictably John Vesey was elected on the first count. I was second, but had not reached the quota, so there was a second vote between Mickey Brewster, one of Fermanagh's best-ever and most successful players, and myself, who'd enjoyed only a very short spell on the Fermanagh senior team. I won by one vote – I think it was fifty-three to fifty-two.

I'd just been elected to the first rung of the GAA hierarchy, with absolutely no idea of where it would lead. It was not until several weeks later that I discovered that Gerry Magee had been canvassing for me at the Convention and that Malachy Mahon and he (two of the greatest GAA men Fermanagh ever produced) were responsible for my being nominated. Ultimately, they are to blame for some of what happened over the following thirty years!

13

Events Produce Change

Back at Queen's, I was settling into a comfortable routine, finishing my Master's degree and still finding the undergraduate teaching trying enough. My presentation of the lectures was improving slowly and so was the content, but both were still very far from a finished product. The post-graduate teaching was easier for me and far more interesting, but as the North's then only full-time lecturer in Accountancy and Finance, I had to teach both subjects. I was also writing an occasional newspaper article and, generally, I was beginning to settle into academic life; there was every likelihood that it would be my career. I was happy enough about that as it was secure and reasonably well paid. Running a pub in London was no longer under consideration.

But three years into the job, things were about to change. One day, I arrived back from an afternoon tea break in the staff common room, to find a message indicating that I had missed a call from Dublin and that I should return it. I contacted the number given to me and that call was to lead to an invitation to leave Queen's and take a somewhat similar, but much better paid, job in Dublin, from the start of the new academic year.

We agreed an arrangement whereby, with effect from October, I would spend two days (Monday and Tuesday) each week in Dublin and still deliver a full lecturing load at Queen's, over the remainder of the week, in order to avoid disruption for the university as it recruited my replacement. That arrangement was to run until the end of the academic year.

Leaving Queen's to move to Dublin turned out to be a mixed blessing – a bad mistake on one hand, but one which opened new doors of which I might otherwise never have become aware.

My time in Dublin was not particularly enjoyable. Though I like Dublin and am especially fond of Dubliners and the supporters of Dublin's football and hurling teams, I never felt comfortable following my move there. Had I had more time, I might have changed my view, but my time there was to be shorter than I had anticipated.

I was unfortunate in that I suffered an unexpected health scare only six months after I decided to move; apparently, the two jobs were too much for me. As a result, I was advised by the hospital, in no uncertain terms, that the double-jobbing had to stop and that I had to stop playing football, if I was not to run the risk of serious heart problems. The double-jobbing was almost over anyway, as I was about to take up a new post in Manchester, but I completely ignored the other part of the advice and played for Teemore ten days later.

I'd had very little time to get to know the ropes of my new place of employment in Dublin but I was already beginning to realise that I was not integrating well into that organisation's social structures. My subsequent experience of business has taught me how important the ability to integrate into an organisation's social structures is for any employee. Being different, whether socially or otherwise, is frequently a significant impediment. I wasn't used to going to the pub after work as some of my new colleagues did – it was not then 'the done thing' in Belfast and, as a Pioneer, I struggled with the entire concept.

Being a northerner in Dublin, I was seen as being different anyway. The 1970s was a time when northerners – especially ones who wore a Pioneer Pin and played Gaelic football – were viewed with scepticism in many segments of Dublin society. Predictably, many southerners' reactions to the North and northerners had changed significantly in the period following the onset of 'The Troubles'. Putting it bluntly, anyone identified as holding nationalist views, which included those of us who were associated with the GAA, ran the risk of being viewed with a suspicion, which bordered on an assumption that we were all probable 'closet Provos'. That was unfortunate and unfair.

But even worse was the elitism in certain segments of Dublin society in those days, especially in some of the wealthier parts. That was new to me. In the North, communal divisions influenced how one was perceived, but my experiences in Dublin society was unlike anything I'd previously experienced.

Twenty years later I discovered that, in some respects, nothing much had changed in some parts of Dublin society. Its media in particular continued, and still continue, to emphasise such differences. They do it very subtly – possibly so subtly that they do not realise that they are doing it; but they also do it very effectively. We are seen as different. Having a rural background, being a northerner, a non-drinker who wears a Pioneer Pin, a member of the GAA, or speaking Irish, are all factors which still create few friends in Dublin's media circles or in other parts of Dublin society, too. Carrying all those identities makes one very different.

Since most of our children have now accommodated very well to life there, something may have changed in the interim but, from my experiences, Dublin was a somewhat cold house for northern nationalists in the early and mid-1970s. Within six months of moving there, I was offered a fresh start in Manchester and happily accepted the post – a decision I've never regretted.

By then I had met the woman who was to become my wife. Though, for a time, I was in Manchester and she was in New York, we eventually married and raised a family – three of whom live in Dublin and support Dublin's hurlers and footballers with a passion.

14

Manchester

I had hardly been a proverbial wet week in Dublin before I was given the opportunity to join the Doctoral Programme at Manchester Business School (MBS), to work and also to study towards a PhD: The Dublin office had decided that they needed a person over in the UK who would keep them informed and updated on whatever new developments were occurring in the whole area of management education in Britain – a sort of monitoring role.

I was new to the place and therefore dispensable. I was still single, had a reasonably good academic record and was young enough to have no problem adjusting to change. So, I was selected to go and meet the Director of the Doctoral Programme in MBS to see if I would be acceptable. He was happy to take me on the programme, provided I sat the Princeton Test and scored highly enough to exceed the School's criterion, which I did easily enough.

I secured accommodation in Hale Barns, a rather affluent part of south Manchester, where I found myself sharing accommodation with one Gordon Ibbottson, who was already half-way through his doctorate in finance, and with whom I was to work for many years afterwards.

Prior to the first meeting of the doctoral students, I was concerned that I might be much older than the others but, to my surprise, I was wrong; in fact, I was about the median age. Many of the others had worked in either industry or academia before being accepted on the programme. MBS had a policy of preferring those with some experience of the world of work for all its post-graduate programmes, giving its students an older age-profile than was normal for academic institutions.

My time in Manchester got off to an embarrassing start. The day before I began, we'd been playing a home League game against Kinawley. We were winning fairly easily, when I dived to block an opponent's kick. Those were the days when players kicked the ball, before we developed this version of basketball which masquerades as Gaelic football. If I had any skills as a player, they were that I was fast, accurate and could block a kick by diving on an opponent's boot; otherwise, I was pretty useless. Over and over again, I had practised blocking kicks, until I was reasonably good at it. But against Kinawley, clearly I failed to put my practise into operation correctly. In any sport, but especially in a sport involving physical contact (which was then part of Gaelic football, though it appears not to be now) there is a price to be paid for getting things wrong.

When I dived on my opponent's foot, either the ball or his boot connected with my face – it was probably the ball, because there was relatively little blood – and, within minutes, I had as fine a 'shiner' as anyone ever saw. About twenty hours later, I was seated in Manchester, attempting to understand my first seminar on epistemology (the science or theory of knowledge), with classmates of ten different nationalities; and the only one with a 'black eye' was the Irishman. If ever anyone reinforced the stereotype of the 'fighting Irish', in the higher echelons of British academic life, I did it on that occasion. The most worrying aspect was that no one asked me how it had happened, they simply pretended not to notice something which could not be overlooked. I got the impression that they were afraid to ask, in case I caused some sort of ruction.

Several of my new classmates were asking questions and having exchanges with the lecturer about existentialism and empiricism, about rationalism, positivism and rational-positivism, about the philosophies of Descartes, Weber and Wittgenstein, about Kant, Neitzsche and Plato, about scientific induction and deduction, and about the theories of the Vienna Circle. I had never even heard of most of these guys and I knew absolutely nothing about the concepts they espoused or promoted.

I was very conscious of the black eye and more than slightly embarrassed. It would not have felt nearly as big if I had been in Ireland, but in the airport, on the flight, in the taxi and, now, among these strangers, it felt huge – easily the most prominent item in the room, as far as my perception ranged.

In the midst of that self-consciousness, I was completely lost in all this talk about philosophy and logic and reasoning, and long before the day ended, I was asking myself, *What the hell am I doing here?* I genuinely believed that I was out of my depth. Everyone else seemed to understand these esoteric concepts, even to have strong opinions about them. Apart from my limited knowledge of financial theory, all I knew anything about was milking cows, or making hay, or harvesting turf.

But oddly enough, before the year had passed, epistemology became a subject which I really enjoyed. I became particularly interested in the writings of the late Karl Popper and his 'empirical falsification' theories. He was, and still is, my favourite writer in this field of study though I no longer devote any of my reading time to such subjects.

By the end of that year, my paper on this subject, submitted as part of the doctoral programme requirements, was rated the best of the lot and I was urged, by a member of staff, to make a few modifications and improvements to it and have it published in one of the academic journals. I rejected the offer. I didn't want to be seen as an expert on any branch of philosophy because I knew I wasn't. But I did find some aspects of the broader subject quite interesting, if not always particularly practical. Such esoteric matters would certainly not have interested my father, with his down-to-earth approach to life and its problems.

It's hard to believe that within a few weeks of that poor, black-eyed start, I had settled very well into life in Manchester and into life as a student again. The change was probably made easier by the fact that I was flying back to Ireland every Friday evening, either to teach at Queen's on the Saturday morning, where I delivered a three-hour input on finance and related topics, or to play for Teemore on the Sunday afternoon, before flying back to Manchester later that evening. In effect, I was almost a commuter, especially since the teaching at Queen's continued into the closed season for football.

I had finished my Master's thesis shortly before I left for Manchester and the external examiner informed my supervisor that, if I spent another four to six months developing certain aspects of it, he'd have no problem awarding me a doctorate. If I'd been more sensible, I'd have opted for that easier route to getting my PhD, but by that stage I'd already decided to go to England and study for it there and I was determined to continue on that path.

In any event, I was thoroughly enjoying being a student again. It was better than lecturing to post-graduates and much, much better than teaching on an undergraduate programme. I was also very happy in Manchester. Despite all the negative comments from cricket commentators and others, and all their jokes about the high rainfall there, I loved the place, especially after I found a club which accepted me and allowed me to play with them for almost two years. Of course, they didn't realise that I was an illegal player.

To say that I enjoyed my time as a student in Manchester would be a huge understatement. It was incomparably more satisfying than my undergraduate years in Belfast. I enjoyed life and studying at the Business School where I was exposed to new ideas and areas of knowledge of which I had either barely been aware, or totally unaware. I enjoyed the colleagues I had there and found the staff to be entirely supportive of the doctoral students as the two groups coalesced into a small intimate group, with similar interests.

But best of all, I was very privileged to have had Professor Sir Douglas Hague as my economics tutor for a year. He gave me a completely new insight into economic theory and its practical application. Though not a particularly good public speaker – and his lectures suffered as a result – he was an outstanding tutor with a most unusual way of imparting knowledge. Later he was to become economic advisor to Margaret Thatcher, but I have long since forgiven him for that!

When I joined the GAA club in that city, I thoroughly enjoyed my involvement with the Irish community in Lancashire. They came from every walk of life, and from every county in Ireland, but they were united in their Irishness, at a time when being Irish in Britain carried certain risks. Some of them had been in England for up to two or three decades before I met them, had married and settled with their families in Manchester, but still saw Ireland as their real home.

What impressed me most about them was that, unlike what I had occasionally met in my own country, there was no sense of elitism, no snobbery, and no sense of either inferiority or superiority. It was like being back in the South Fermanagh of my teenage years and schooldays. Quite clearly, there was no special treatment for university graduates: if I missed a ball, which I should have won, I heard about it in no uncertain terms. They were very genuine people and I made many long-term friends there.

The friends I made in Manchester included several who were neither Irish nor British, but were no less genuine in their friendship for that. That two-year period has been one of the outstanding highlights of my life and career and, unexpectedly, it opened access to opportunities which I would never have uncovered otherwise. It led to a broadening of my experience and my expertise which has benefitted me greatly ever since.

Sometime about half-way through my first year, Bill Davies, then Director of the School's Management Development Programme, approached some of the doctoral students and explained that he had a number of very senior executives on one of his programmes who were complaining that they did not have a sufficient background in finance and accounting to get full benefit from the strategy sessions or some other parts of the programme, which he managed. He asked if any of us would be prepared to spend a couple of hours teaching basic finance and accounting to these executives, many of whom had a technical background and for whom this was a new language. Over time, I learned just how important it was for many of them, and I also began to understand their unwillingness to admit that they were lost in the financial jungle – though not nearly as lost as accountants and bankers tend to be in technical and production jungles.

I wasn't keen on volunteering but someone mentioned my teaching background. I could see Bill's scepticism about my ability to deliver what he needed. Still, no one else seemed to have had any experience of teaching finance so he offered me two seventy-five minute sessions. Two and a half hours was a bit short, but I knew I could give them what they needed, and I accepted.

The sessions went well – so well that there was a demand from virtually the entirety of the group (forty plus, in total) for some more and that was duly arranged. Course after course, the participants demanded more from 'the Irishman' and, over time, my input to those programmes increased significantly. I have no idea why they particularly liked my stuff, but it consistently secured very good evaluations from the participants; it might just have been the accent – 'the way I tell them', to quote Frank Carson – or the flippant humour, or the willingness to accept interruptions and deviate from the main subject, but it enhanced my reputation within the School.

Unfortunately for my academic progress, I had been assigned Bryan Elliott (of Clarkson and Elliott fame, which grew as a result of their then ground-breaking and very successful book 'Managing Money and Finance', published in 1969) as my tutor. Bryan was a tremendously focussed individual who had no time to waste, but was still likeable and generous with his time, provided he thought it was being used productively.

One had to have the subject matter of one's research agreed by the end of the first year, as well as showing the necessary competence in a variety of business-related activities. But Bryan became seriously ill in the second half of my first year and was unable to assist me in defining the scope of my research. Then sadly, early in my second year, he died. He was a great guy. No one else was appointed to replace him as my supervisor so I struggled for a while to make progress in my chosen area of study: defining the methodology appropriate to valuing private companies. My biggest problem was that I had no way of getting the necessary information from private businesses – an issue which would not have arisen had Bryan been in good health, because he had a huge network of contacts, at all levels in British industry.

About that same time, Manchester Business School established its International Banking Centre. Douglas Hague was its first Chairman and, indeed, the originator and inspiration behind the Centre which aimed to train bankers from all over the world, but especially in the British Isles and the former British dominions in Africa. Later, it expanded its operations to most parts of the developed and developing world. Its Managing Director was a Dublin man, Jim Byrne, who was then completing his doctorate. Two other significant contributors to its development and growth were Gordon Ibbottson and the late Doug Wood, each of whom had developed very good models for teaching practical finance. Better than that, they were great people to have as colleagues.

Between the four of them, they built the Centre into a major business within two or three years. I had developed some practical analytical tools and other material on a number of areas of corporate finance, including on credit appraisal within banks and, as a result, I was asked to contribute to the banking programmes. That was the first, major spin-off benefit from my involvement in the Management Development Programmes for Bill Davies. I was recruited on to the team to deliver part of the corporate finance content and continued to be part of that team until I found a different role for myself, more than a decade later.

Later, while I was involved in running a business, I developed a further range of practically based case studies. As a result of my experiences in that business, I have long taken a particular interest in the problems of small businesses and the threats to their survival, and since most of the customers of the commercial banks were SMEs, I developed a reasonably high level of competence in that area, and used that to my advantage in working with both British and overseas banks.

Subsequently during the 1980s, after I had sold my share of that business, I spent several years travelling throughout most of the world, speaking at various banking seminars, on aspects of business, which most people assume to be financially-based, but which are essentially about management generally, with the financial outcomes simply being the result of good or bad management, as the case might be.

Back then, one of my biggest problems used to be persuading bankers and accountants that problems, such as those which arise from poor profitability or over-trading or cost variances etc., did not have their primary roots in finance. Instead, they are the result of poor strategy or poor management, and reflect a whole range of management issues, including control issues, which would not normally be associated with financial management, at least not in the text books which I have seen.

As a result of those years of experience, I became convinced that bankers and the vast majority of professional accountants – by that, I mean those who remain in practice, as opposed to those who go into business – including some, with big reputations as administrators and receivers, are about the least competent people in the world to advise on business. Nothing which I've seen since has caused me to change my mind on that; on the contrary, I've seen plenty of confirmatory evidence. Bankers and accountants both tend to be good bookkeepers and strong on corporate governance, but the majority of them are total disasters when it comes to decision-making, taking risks, helping businesses to grow and develop or to diversify. There is more to running a business than governance. In fact, governance holds a very low priority for those who decide to devote their lives and their energies to creating and running a business, or to creating jobs and contributing to national wealth.

Annoyingly, the fees many of these people charge, and get, for delivering what is effectively a bureaucratic governance service, are absolutely staggering for such a low level of ability and complexity, and such obvious irrelevance to the real needs of the economy.

Despite dealing with that kind of incompetence, I enjoyed the combination of teaching, case work and consultancy on specific business problems, in which I was engaged for those years. In that role, I discovered that innovative solutions invariably met with suspicion, even hostility, from senior banking and accounting staff. Virtually without exception, they much preferred to play safe and avoid the implementation of recommendations which would involve risk. Their world is the antithesis of entrepreneurship.

By comparison, real business-people welcomed a bit of imagination and the challenge of implementing such recommendations and making a real difference to their community, their country and the world. Unfortunately, their voice is rarely heard.

Although I was spending too much time on teaching instead of learning, my assignments continued to secure some of the highest grades awarded by faculty members. But I was not there to teach, or to do assignments; I was there to do research and get a doctorate and by the middle of my second year, I was already beginning to fall behind some of my colleagues in that respect.

Still, my experiences in those two years were to stand me in good stead in later life and, subsequently, they provided the basis for most of my career. Even though I rarely l go to Manchester any more, MBS still holds very fond memories for me. I owe it a lot.

15

Back in Ireland

We were only a few months married when Mary announced that she was pregnant. In that case, we wanted to leave Manchester and get back to Ireland before the child was born. We were already looking forward to moving into the new house in Dublin, which we had bought shortly after she had returned from working in New York. Structurally, good progress had been made, but little progress was occurring inside the building. We had requested a few modifications, which were going to be costly and would stretch our budget to its limit, but we felt that they were necessary, and they were not what was holding up progress.

My research had not been going well. Access to data was still proving problematic and the School had not yet assigned a new tutor to replace Bryan. I had discussed some of the issues with other senior staff but they were all fully occupied with their own work and, in some cases, their own research students, and the School was diversifying its activities, so everyone was busy. The net result was that I got very little help. I'd done well in the preliminary phase and there may have been an expectation that I needed little help, but that was not my view, nor was it the reality.

Before Easter, the decision was taken that I should return to Ireland at the end of the academic year. I was told that I would be given time to complete my research on a part-time basis. We left on 30th June, with some regrets and plenty of memories. We'd been receiving telephone threats, which indicated that someone had been watching our comings and goings. Later we discovered that the threats had emanated from elements within the security forces, who apparently had difficulty reconciling our lifestyle with my being a student and feared that we might have had ulterior motives for being there. Effectively, they were concerned that we might be 'sleepers' for the Republican movement, but they were grossly mistaken.

At that time, there was a particularly high level of sensitivity to Irish people who were neither obviously employed, nor in receipt of unemployment benefit. Clearly, the people behind those calls were not aware that I was on a fully-paid secondment. I have since come to understand their concerns, but I cannot forgive them for frightening my wife, by threatening her when I was away.

Our first son was born in the Erne Hospital, Enniskillen, less than a fortnight after our return to Fermanagh. In those days, fathers were not welcome during the delivery process so I left Mary into the hospital, early in the morning, and went off to Cavan on business. When I arrived home, my mother told me that the midwife had phoned to say that Mary had given birth, but that she had to tell the father first, according to the hospital's protocols. So I rang, to be told that it was a boy, that both mother and baby were well and that I could to visit them as soon as I could get myself to Enniskillen. It didn't take me very long to travel the seventeen miles.

The pleasure of seeing one's newborn son, with his mother looking radiant despite the pain of childbirth, was euphoric: no other feeling can match it. That was, without a shadow of doubt, the happiest day of my life – certainly until then.

We had been living with my mother for the fortnight since we left Manchester. Because our new home wasn't ready, we decided to rent a house in Dundrum for a year and, just over a two weeks after mother and son arrived home, we moved to Dublin.

*****

We had been beaten in the Championship semi-final that year with virtually no contribution from me. Our trainer came to me after training one night and said, with his customary directness: "Peter, your legs are gone."

I was only thirty, but I'd already been playing senior football for sixteen years and the two years without serious training in Manchester were beginning to show. I couldn't argue with him because I knew he was right, however much I might have wished otherwise.

"We need a goalie," he continued. "I hear you played in goals as a young lad."

"I did, a bit," I replied, somewhat sheepishly.

"James is packing it in, and we need someone with a bit of experience. Would you do goals for a year or two?" he asked.

I knew that he was right about 'the legs' and that I was unlikely to retain my place in the forward line for much longer – free-taker or not. I also knew that I had done reasonably well in goals in the past and that this offer was better than being discarded entirely. However, I had some concerns that my kick-outs might not be long enough for senior football (which later proved to be the case), because taking frees in the forward line demands accuracy, rather than length. Nevertheless, without much hesitation, I agreed.

Two nights later, he came back to me. "You know," he said, "they're going to play the senior games before the junior games, next year."

"That's right," I answered, without knowing where this was leading.

"Well," he continued, "I was just thinking, if you played goals for the seniors, you could play full-forward for the juniors after it. You wouldn't have to kill yourself and you could help the young lads and maybe use your experience to bring them on a bit. What do you think?"

Anything for a quiet life and, even though I knew that I would have to do a bit more training about Bushy Park or Cuala, I agreed. And that was how I finished my career, winning my last two Championship medals and another League medal as the team's goalkeeper.

*****

Within months of my return to my employer, I was getting restless. Job satisfaction from teaching non-financial managers how to read a balance sheet tends to wane quickly, and I was never very good at disguising my restlessness. I had already lost most of a year struggling firstly with a methodology for my thesis and, when that was largely solved, struggling for access to the necessary data. More importantly, I was becoming disillusioned with academic research and was already thinking of 'doing my own thing', though I was not at all sure what that might be. But, for the first time since I decided against farming, I was becoming more and more attracted to owning my own business.

Again events produced change. I was working in my office one afternoon when my immediate superior – a friend and colleague – arrived back from a lunch meeting. Though he'd clearly enjoyed a considerable intake of wine with his lunch he wasn't in good humour, a fact that was underlined by his kicking over a rubber plant in the foyer on his way back to his office.

About fifteen minutes after he had returned to his office, he arrived at my door and asked to speak to me in his own office.

"I'm half-pissed and I'm also pissed off," he started, though I needed no confirmation of the former.

Then he continued, "I've just offered a job to a guy, but he has already been offered a post as European Chief Executive of a major American company based in Paris and on a salary which I could not match. So, he said no, and I can't blame him, but it leaves me stuck."

I can't remember how I responded, but probably with surprise since I would not normally have been privy to such information.

"I suppose you're wondering why I'm telling you this," he continued. "Well, I need someone with a financial background and I was wondering if you'd take it."

I was speechless, though not at all surprised when he added, "Now there'd be no increase in salary for you, at the start anyway."

"Ah, come on," I countered, "I have no experience of business, I'm just an academic. I'd go into a business for you some day and would have no idea what was wrong, and where would that leave both you and me?"

"It'll never happen, Quinn," he said with some conviction, which I felt might have been driven by the wine, or worse still, by an unhealthy combination of wine and 'rose-tinted spectacles'. "And, even if it did, the rest of us would be there to steer you in the right direction."

I wasn't convinced by his argument. Nevertheless, I saw a glimmer of an opportunity to become involved at the coal face of business, with the potential to achieve my ultimate ambition of going into business on my own account.

My assertion that the opportunity was coming too soon for me was immediately contradicted. I should have been more mindful of my father's view that 'you'll never learn younger – now'.

"I've been watching you for the past while and I think you could do it. You can make financial figures talk," he said.

I was intrigued by his answer. He had a waspish sense of humour, but I could see that he was genuine in both his request and his comment. At the same time, I could see that I was second choice, at best, but it was still a major vote of confidence in my potential, because I had not delivered much for them until then.

"How long have I got to make up my mind?" I asked, knowing that he would not give me very long – that was his style.

"You can tell me tomorrow morning," came the reply, with absolutely no hint of either sarcasm or annoyance.

After thinking about it overnight – Mary left the decision entirely to me – I decided to take the chance on offer. Two choices of career were definitely better than one and, in my experience, very few academics ever stray into the world of real, roll-up-the-sleeves business. A year or two in consultancy would help my career, or so I thought anyway.

I have never regretted that decision. I think it was one of the best I made in my entire career. My boss was a wonderful mentor and his initial assessment was entirely accurate – I never went into a business where I could not discern what was wrong pretty quickly, though I did not necessarily identify the solution quite so quickly. That short stint in 'academic consultancy' was the best learning experience of my entire life, though, as I look back, I still had a lot of learning to do later when I started the move from theory into practice.

The work was interesting – much more interesting than lecturing. I began to understand the problems involved in running a business, the risks attached to every major decision and the pressures on those in leadership positions. I also learned that what the owner, or owners, of the business believed to be the problem was often a million miles from the real issue. When that happened, I had to persuade them that they were tackling their problems from the wrong perspective and that was not always a welcome message. The fact that it frequently carried implied criticism of those who had offered us the assignment was even less welcome. Worse still, such a raw message was often complicated by the fact it was being delivered by a whipper-snapper, still wet behind the ears in business terms. I was frequently reminded of my lack of experience but, in the end, I won most of the arguments – and all of the crucial ones.

Ultimately, I actually relished the challenges we faced in helping businesses to cope with the trials confronting them. In the process, I learned that business-people occasionally make wrong judgements and that they can be very intolerant of different assessments. I remember speaking to a number of senior executives and recommending 'de-leveraging' (reducing their borrowings) early during the 1970s oil crisis, only to be told, in a very aggressively arrogant manner by the Chief Executive of a quoted Irish Plc, that I was talking nonsense and that any business which could borrow money, should do so to the maximum extent possible. His own company's results two years later proved that I had been right and his company has not been an Irish quoted Plc for several decades.

For all that – or probably as a result of interactions like that, because it was not an isolated event – my period in that role provided me with an outstanding learning experience and I was happy enough there, though I had already come to the conclusion that my longer-term future was unlikely to be in such an organisation. I had decided that I was destined for the business world, preferably on my own account. In any event, being a teetotaller and a Gaelic footballer was not an advantage in the segment of Dublin society to which the majority of my colleagues were linked: we were just 'culchies' on a lower rung of some imaginary ladder.

In my case it was worse than that – I was a northern culchie. Consequently, I had little in common with their view of the world and I hadn't integrated particularly well into the social culture of the organisation. I was becoming disillusioned with the place and leaving it would cause me no pain, though I was very happy with the work, which was not particularly taxing, but which provided great opportunities for learning and self-development. I also liked most – but not all – of my colleagues and found them easy to work with.

But again events intervened. I was less than a year in my new role, when I was approached by a member of its Council to undertake an assignment for the Institute of Chartered Accountants in Ireland (ICAI), reviewing its then examination systems and structures, and the educational support which it was providing for its students.

I was informed at the outset that the assignment arose because the Institute's then President had indicated, during a visit to Canada, that the standards being applied in Ireland were inadequate for the developing international profession and were considerably inferior to those in Canada. Why he would have said that was difficult to fathom because the comment was almost entirely unjustified. It was not the standards of those who passed which was the problem. The real problem was that the Institute was providing no reasonable educational support for its students as they struggled to achieve the standards needed to pass the examinations. The self-appointed genius who had made the comment had failed to distinguish between the standards of those who qualified and the standard of the educational support systems available to student accountants. It was a stupid mistake and a particularly stupid mistake for the President of the Institute to make.

Theoretically, I was being asked to take on this task on a secondment.

I was happy enough with that but, as the weeks passed, I began to realise that I would never be going back to my real employer. I had begun to realise that I had other fish to fry and that my future was not going to be with that organisation, though I had not yet decided precisely where it would be.

With my academic background, I had some interest in the education of accountants but I had absolutely no knowledge of the hoops through which prospective accountants in other countries had to jump in order to qualify. So, I had to do a vast amount of research – comparing, contrasting, assessing and thinking through the implications of potential changes and the related implementation processes; those latter were the really difficult aspects.

With more experience, it would have been an easy enough assignment, but I was a novice in the 'change game' and I struggled with the organisational aspects. Textbooks are of bugger-all use when it comes to the *realpolitik* of professional bodies, and commercial sense is equally useless in that context, but I didn't know that when I started the assignment.

I was reporting to a very high-powered committee and found the old saw about the camel being a horse designed by a committee to be entirely apt. In my entire career, this has been the only position I have ever held which I did not enjoy. To be fair, my new colleagues were wonderful people and I was lucky that I received very staunch support from both the full-time staff of the Institute and a minority of the committee members. Later, I was asked to sit as one of the three persons selected to oversee the implementation of my proposals, but I never succeeded in getting the support of the man who had created the problem in the first place.

One afternoon, while I was working in the ICAI office, I received a call from my ex-boss, telling me that the members of my former unit (since I was officially on secondment, it was still technically my current unit) were writing to the chairman to express their disagreement with the strategy being proposed for the future of that organisation. He asked if I would add my signature to the letter and, though I had no intention of going back there, I agreed to do so.

On the following Friday evening, I was at home having my tea when a taxi arrived. I went to the door and was presented with a sealed envelope. To say the least, I was surprised to read that I had been dismissed from my position with my former employer even though I was no longer working there; fortunately, that decision had no implications for what I had been doing and continued to do for the Institute. Apparently, our biggest mistake was to write to the chairman, whoever he was, because I had no idea who held that position. Looking back, that was a peculiar form of dispute resolution, grievance procedure or human resources policy.

Some months later, I received my share – the smallest share, for obvious reasons – of the money paid in lieu of our dismissal. In today's terms it would seem very small but it was then a very valuable bonus for me, because it helped to fund my share of the equity in the new business which I was buying in partnership with my brother. As they say, 'it's an ill wind...'

By that stage, Seán's business had grown to the point where he needed to expand geographically and wanted someone to help him. It was a good opportunity, although it would mean moving from Dublin. Mary and I now had two more children, both born in Dublin, and we were well settled into our new home. I negotiated the end of my assignment for the Institute and freed myself up for the start of the new project. After examining a number of diversification options for the business, Seán and I eventually settled on one and made an offer.

Within a couple of weeks, I had started to run a manufacturing company. The rest of my life was to be devoted to a variety of different business roles, in both manufacturing and service businesses. But manufacturing is what I really enjoy most.

16

In Business

Like most accountants, I thought I knew a bit about running a business when I took over the new plant. And, like most accountants, I was wrong. I have no idea what it is in our training which makes us so convinced that we know how to run a business, once we get the label after our names. But I do know that it is arrogant and ill-founded of us, as a profession, to believe that, on qualification, we know about business or management.

At that time, my view was that I had worked in audit for a couple of years, I had been awarded an MBA, I had taught finance, accounting, economics and even a small bit of mathematics, at third level, I had been involved in management consultancy and I had even done well on the doctoral programme in MBS. I appeared to be, and thought I was, better prepared than most – after all, I had spent years learning about business, and I was familiar with every page in the book.

But the real thing was a different experience altogether. It was a new learning experience with totally new problems, a different risk profile and hugely greater pressures, none of which were explained in the text books. I learned that my accountancy and academic backgrounds had not prepared me for *real* business. It would be an understatement to say that I struggled in the early months.

Firstly, what I was doing involved a massive capital investment programme, many millions of Euros in today's money, and it all had to be spent within a few months. I had to manage that capital expenditure programme while also running the operational side of the business.

Secondly, I was starting almost from zero base – trying to expand rapidly with employees, most of whom had no experience of the business, and with equipment which was being operated as soon as it was installed, sometimes before it had been properly commissioned.

Thirdly, having virtually no technical background, I was relying on someone else to install and operate the new plant.

Fourthly, I was selling into a market which was very competitive – we had three major competitors and a host of smaller ones within a twenty-mile radius – and in an environment where I was a stranger.

Finally, and most importantly, I was a novice in the business with no background in production or in producing real profits. Boy! Was that different from managing a Balance Sheet? You bet it was.

There was no time for slacking, much less for feeling sorry for oneself. I worked 70 to 80 hours per week, grabbing only a quick bite, which Mary prepared and delivered as she collected the children from school. Frequently, I went back out after nine or ten o'clock at night to collect money from debtors, some of whom were slow to pay but many of whom just could not afford to pay. It was hard work but, for the most part, I enjoyed it. There was a buzz about doing what should have been impossible. And there was a feeling of satisfaction, for someone with an economics background, from contributing to one's country's national product and one's community's economic prospects.

Notwithstanding the problems of a 'new start', and against all the odds, we were succeeding. Despite the disruption caused by the capital investment programme, we made a small profit in the first year and monthly sales had grown to about ten times what they were a year earlier. The second year started off reasonably well, too; we were breaking-even in the off-season and meeting our commitments to the banks without having to look for extensions to our loans. However, at one point we hit a problem over which we had no control and our borrowings rocketed – I faced several months of hardship, but we survived it.

Twenty-five months after I started, I'd taken the business to an annualised turnover of just over Stg£1million, 25 times what it was when I started. That had been one of my personal targets from the outset and I was quietly satisfied that things were going in the right direction.

But, eventually, I decided that I'd had enough, that I was being unfair to Mary and the children and that I should change direction again. I knew that I had the opportunity of a new career which was available to me. So, I sold my half of the business and walked away from it.

I was to spend the subsequent dozen or so years in a completely new role which involved travelling over most of the world: much of Africa, parts of the Far East, much of the Middle East, India, the main Caribbean Islands, North America, a couple of places in Europe and most of the main population centres in Britain. Some of those places seemed, and were, exotic at the start but, when the novelty wore off, they became progressively less attractive, until eventually they were just other places in which to work – fly in, do what had to be done and fly out again. Primarily because of the travelling, much of the work was physically challenging but some of it was mentally challenging, too – there was no place for mistakes.

Flying all over the world, at an average of about 120,000-150,000 miles per annum, is bad enough, but waiting for hours at airports, up to forty-odd weeks of the year, is no great thrill either. The work was attractive but the associated travel wasn't, though at least I have no fear of flying. I can look back and say truthfully that I enjoyed that decade and a half from the late '70s to the early '90s, but they were hard on me and even harder on Mary and the children. From a family perspective, the biggest problem in those years was that Mary had to rear the children, almost entirely on her own.

By the time we decided to return to Fermanagh, which we eventually did on the eve of the 1984 All-Ireland Hurling Final in Thurles, the GAA's Centenary Final, our eldest son was ten and facing a new school system, with the spectre of the 11-plus only two months away. Our youngest was only six months old and her sister was just starting school.

We were all facing new challenges. But certain aspects of my own life were already heading in new and very different directions.

17

Ulster Calling

I had spent a decade on the Ulster Council by the time nominations for the new officers became due, in 1980. Although I had already represented the Council at national level on two different committees, I was not the senior delegate from Fermanagh.

That was the late John Vesey, a Mayoman by birth who had played for that county before playing in Fermanagh. He had represented our county long before I became involved in county administration. John would not be pushed around easily but he was always reasonable and committed to the best interests of the Association, as he saw them. A man of strong convictions, who stuck to them without becoming doctrinaire or 'in-your-face', he was intelligent, capable, empathetic and very honourable; but most of all he was respected for his integrity and for his very sound judgement.

For me, John Vesey was a great and fearless friend, who had no hesitation in telling one that he was wrong, and we all need people who will tell us when we are 'out of order'. Real friends do not have to agree on everything and John and I saw many things differently, but we never fell out over them; we simply argued our respective cases and went home, only to meet again another day. I have worked with very few like him in my life. Without becoming annoyed, I would have taken comments and criticisms from John Vesey that I would have resented had they come from most other people.

Consequently in 1980, I had made the assumption that, if anyone from Fermanagh was to get a nomination for office on the Council, it would be John – and it would have been well deserved. I had also assumed that a nomination for any Fermanagh man was unlikely, given that Malachy Mahon, who had been the first Fermanagh man to be selected as Uachtarán, Comhairle Uladh, had completed his term in that office only three years earlier. A second senior officer within less than four years was, in my view, very unlikely for Ulster's 'Cinderella' county, the last of the nine to provide the Council with a President.

Therefore, I was surprised to discover that my name was being mentioned. I remain convinced, though I have no proof, that Vesey had suggested that I might eventually have something to offer at a higher level, and that he would stand aside to allow my name to go forward. It was a tribute to his own status that he was later appointed to all three of the main elected officerships on the Council, during the 1990s.

While I was surprised at being nominated, given that I was not living in either the county or the province at that time, I was even more surprised to learn that five or six of the nine counties had nominated me for the post of Council Treasurer, which normally led to subsequent promotions to Vice-President and then to President, though that could never be taken for granted.

The incoming President was an old friend and colleague of mine from Queen's days and afterwards through business, Peter Harte, from Tyrone. His brother, Mickey, is now nationally known and another brother, Martin, had played with me in Manchester – also illegally. The Vice-President was Phil Smith from Cavan, who was therefore destined to hold the position of Ulster President in the GAA's Centenary Year – a unique honour, which he fulfilled admirably.

Within a couple of months, Peter Harte was to show his courage and his integrity in a most unusual way. We had received a referee's report, which indicated that a player from Peter's own county had been sidelined for rough play in an inter-county Championship game. When the report was presented to the meeting, Peter refused to accept it, saying that he had been at the game and that it was not rough play but that it had involved a more serious offence. Pointing out that it 'mattered not a whit' what county was involved, he was not prepared to accept that sort of behaviour on a GAA pitch and he suggested that the report be returned to the referee for his further observations. When the report came back with no amendment Peter announced that, if no Council member wished to propose the longer sentence, he would rule on it and apply the appropriate sentence for the offence he had witnessed. Not many others would have shown that level of integrity and he got a proposer.

Between the three newly appointed officers, we had accumulated more than forty years' experience on the Council. In normal circumstances, our roles should have been largely administrative and prosaic, apart from Peter's, since he would become the public face of the Association in the province for the subsequent three years.

But the early 1980s were not normal times, in our province. We were in post only a few months when the North of Ireland was faced with the political and communal tsunami of the 'Hunger Strikes'. No organisation in that part of the country was immune to the consequences of those historic, traumatic and potentially disastrous events and, by virtue of its position within the nationalist community, the GAA was directly in the 'firing line'.

For more than a decade, we had been subjected to the burning of our dressing rooms, club houses and community centres, and damage to our other properties; our teams and players had been subjected to harassment and abuse and a number of our members had been murdered, for no reason other than their membership of their local club.

Some suffered more than others. The experiences of Ardoyne Kickhams and St Enda's in North Belfast, Crossmaglen Rangers in South Armagh, most of the clubs in West Belfast and the hurling clubs in the Ards Peninsula are generally well known, having received considerable publicity at the time. But rural clubs in both North and South Derry, throughout Antrim, the clubs around Lurgan and Portadown, other clubs in South Armagh, virtually every club in both East and West Tyrone and throughout Down, also suffered at some point over a period of three decades. Fermanagh suffered, too, losing both players and property, but the latter could be replaced.

The isolation of the Association in Ulster was compounded by the refusal of the audio-visual media in the North to recognise the GAA for what it was, or to cover its games. Indirectly, that implied that the local radio and television stations either perceived the Association as having a political dimension, or were biased against it for some other reason. A well-researched report produced some time earlier by the Down Communications Committee, under the guidance of Fergal McCormack, had raised the issue of the coverage of GAA activities by all the northern media but especially by the two television stations. In 1984, the GAA's Centenary Year, we decided to put some pressure on them and arranged to meet both stations, separately, on their own premises, to discuss our concerns.

Our first meeting was with the BBC. Our then President, Phil Smith, and our Secretary, Micheál Ó Finneadha, presented our case. It was not making much of an impression – they just did not want to know. Micheál emphasised the support for Gaelic Games in the province, quoted the attendance figures and their growth, and explained how our games were being disadvantaged by the policies of the BBC.

"And where is all this support, you say you have?" asked the senior of the station's two representatives.

"Well, we have very strong support in South Down, Monaghan, Cavan, the border areas of Fermanagh, South Armagh, the Glens of Antrim, West Belfast, South Derry, Donegal and most of Tyrone," Ó Finneadha replied.

"I thought so," was the reply. "Sure no one in any of those areas pays their licence fee. Why should we spend licence payers' money covering games, which none of our licence payers watch?" continued the non-neutral response.

There may have been some slight validity to the comment, but it was far from being completely true. However, that was the attitude of the then establishment in the North. It was a somewhat more refined, but equally one-sided, version of the loyalist slogans which adorned the walls of many streets in Belfast at that time. But this was a publicly funded company which was supposed to cater for all sections of the community on a fair and equal basis – at least we thought so, though clearly not everyone agreed.

A couple of weeks later, we had a similar experience with UTV. This time, the case advanced by our spokespersons was followed by an even more offensive question.

"Can you guarantee that there will be two Ulster teams in the Ulster final, every year?" we were asked, after we had made our 'pitch'.

Ó Finneadha nearly choked in his haste to respond.

"Where the f*** do you think they will come from? Do you think we'll have a team from Cork in the Ulster final?" he asked.

"Well, who was in it last year?" was the not unreasonable follow-up.

"Donegal and Cavan," he answered.

"There y'are now. No Ulster team in last year's Ulster final," replied the professor of geography, who was representing UTV on that occasion.

As the late Gene Larkin, who was part of our delegation at both meetings, said afterwards, it was time to drink as much whiskey as was being offered, because it was all we were going to get. Unfortunately for that option, three of the four of us were wearing Pioneer pins.

One of the consequences of the combined effects of the absence of coverage of our games, as a result of the combination of media bias and political disruption, was that Ulster teams became uncompetitive in the All-Ireland series. It would have taken a miracle to produce success, under those circumstances. After winning three All-Irelands in the 1960s, the Ulster Championship winners had to wait twenty-three years for another win with only two appearances in the final in the interim – Armagh in 1977 and Tyrone in 1986. Those were tough times for the Association in Ulster.

While the majority of the people of Cavan, Donegal and Monaghan were conscious of what was happening and gave us great support throughout that entire period, those from outside the northern province were largely unaware of the realities of those decades. Many had warped ideas of what was happening, others fed off propaganda and media perversions of the truth, some interpreted events through their own ignorance and got the wrong analysis, and others simply did not care – it was far enough away from them for indifference to take root and grow.

Unfortunately, there were also those from outside the province who thought that they knew what was happening at ground level and were prone to pontificating on the issues involved, using information from the so-called liberal press and other media to support their views. But the reality was – a realty which was, and is, well understood within the northern counties – that those who lived more than thirty miles from the border had no real idea of what was happening in the North. They were not aware of the consistent low-key harassment and abuse or of the provocation, the threats, the set-ups and the attempts to 'create' evidence. There was no way of learning about those from the media.

One did not have to be involved in any form of political activity, never mind paramilitary activity, to be a target. Most of our members who were murdered in those years had no involvement in any kind of illegal activity; just being a member of the GAA was enough to have them killed.

That is not to condone what was happening on the other side – it could not be condoned either, in any society. Murder is murder and must be condemned, whoever commits it or whatever the motivation. But the GAA was not murdering people. Nevertheless, its members were being murdered, simply for being members.

The Hunger Strikes brought all of this to a new level – more widespread, more vicious, more dangerous and with much, much more potential to do major damage to the GAA. While I was not living in the county, I had been playing for Teemore until 1977 and had been managing the club's senior team since 1979. That meant multiple trips per week to my native county over the second half of that decade and into the new decade. In the process I had been seeing, at first hand, what was happening and it was not a pretty sight. The cataclysmic events of 1981 were becoming inevitable, long before they actually occurred.

Within months of our appointment, we were beginning to realise the direction in which things were moving politically and we knew what the potential implications were likely to be for the Association. I had long admired Peter Harte's vision and his courage – especially his courage on the playing field – but I was also aware of his commitment to what he saw as 'right' and ethical. I can look back and say with absolute certainty that, without his leadership, his courage and his sense of what was achievable, the GAA would not have survived without some form of major split in the North in 1981. He had the courage to lead from the front and to lead successfully.

Throughout the worst parts of that period, the officers of the Council met in Monaghan on most Sunday mornings, sometimes with the officers of all nine Ulster counties (it was not just a Six-County issue) in an attempt to chart a strategy for the organisation, so as to minimise the damage to the Association. We were on our own and we knew it because, at central level, nobody seemed to want to know and nothing was being done, not because of indifference but because they did not know what to do and did not understand the reality of what was happening. The strategy had to be flexible, because we often had to react to changes or events which we'd never anticipated.

One such unexpected incident involved an invasion of the Clones pitch, at half time in an Ulster final, by a group proclaiming their support for the Hunger Strikers and demanding a stronger line in support for the dying men, from the GAA. Any move to evict them would almost certainly have led to violence. We were caught unaware, so we took a decision not to intervene. While there had been rumours of some sort of protest, we had not anticipated that it would occur on the pitch. By the time we realised what form the protest was taking, it was just too late to intervene. The result was that we took a lot of media-orchestrated criticism for not intervening, but we would probably have taken even more stick from our own members, if we had intervened, and the same media would have criticised us for that too. For us, it was a lose/lose situation.

Though it was embarrassing for us and we received much criticism for it, in the end we probably won, even if the victory was almost by default. We avoided violence and the protestors did not disrupt the day's programme.

Each of the six northern counties lost clubs during that episode and some lost several. They all lost members who felt that we were not being sufficiently proactive in support of the Hunger Strikers. Most of our members had great sympathy for those who were on strike and that support increased as people started to die.

In Dublin, it was seen as a political issue but, for us, it was much more acute and more direct than that. Some of our members were dying and many of our members were upset, annoyed, angry and, in a small minority of cases, hoping for revenge. The communities from which we were drawing support were being ravaged by division and members were voting with their feet. We needed wise leadership and we got it.

Peter Harte was determined to ensure that the Association in the North and the wider province would be protected. He himself came from a staunchly nationalist background. He knew some of those who were dying and, in common with most other nationalists, he probably empathised with some aspects of their cause. But he was willing to fight to protect the GAA, whatever the price might be for him personally. In the end, the majority of the clubs which had left returned. But some of our members stayed away for years and even decades. Most importantly the split, which at one point seemed inevitable, was avoided and Peter Harte was the man who led us through that trauma.

He has never received the credit he deserved for his courage, commitment and energy, or for the leadership he gave in that period. In my opinion, that is unfortunate. Others, who contributed much less, have claimed and received far greater credit. He sought none and, unfortunately, he has received far too little. But, without a shadow of doubt – and I was very close to what was happening in that period – he was the man who saved the Association in Ulster during the Hunger Strikes of 1981. Phil Smith, then Vice-President, gave him total support, as did Micheál Ó Finneadha, then Provincial Secretary. But Peter Harte led and he led courageously from the front.

By the end of that year, we knew with certainty that whatever issues might face us in the rest of our three-year period in office, we would be capable of managing them. Every one of us had been tempered in the red-hot heat of conflict and gained extra strength in the process. Losing members was undesirable and unhelpful, but dealing with a major split would have been a disaster and that was avoided, thanks to Peter Harte.

Progression followed the normal pattern. Phil Smith replaced Peter in 1983 and I became Phil's replacement as Vice-President, which was a particular honour in Centenary Year. That year marked a complete break with the trauma of three years earlier and we were finally in a position to close that chapter in the history of the Council. My greatest hope for the GAA is that it will never again have to face an issue comparable with the 1981 Hunger Strikes; but if we do, I hope we are being led by another Peter Harte when it happens.

As Vice-President of the Council, I had responsibility for the progress of hurling in the province. That was largely new to me. I'd never played the game and had never even seen it being played, until I attended my first Railway Cup final in my late teens. I was in Croke Park on that occasion, primarily to see PT Treacy win a Railway Cup medal, though I was delighted to see a host of hurlers, whose names were familiar to me from Michael O'Hehir's commentaries, with Christy Ring as *primus inter pares*.

Despite some dire warnings before I took on that role, I found it a pleasure to work with the likes of Seamus McGrattan, the late Neilly Patterson, the late Seán Hollywood, 'Gilly' McElhatton, Eddie Donnelly (and his brothers and cousins too), Willie Johnston, Jim Carlisle, Kevin Moen and the many others who were then promoting our national game in Ulster. For the first time, I really appreciated how much effort they invested in the game they loved – and 'loved' is not too strong a word for their commitment – and the obstacles they faced.

As a Fermanagh man and, more particularly, as a Teemore man, I was already very familiar with the problems of small population, low playing numbers, the effects of emigration, lack of volunteers and all the problems associated with the weak counties. But in my new role, I really began to understand that the efforts to promote hurling in the Ards Peninsula, North Antrim and Belfast have never been fully appreciated within our Association. It is even worse in the other seven counties and, in my opinion, the huge efforts being made in Armagh and Derry, in particular, deserve more recognition and better support from national level – even at a time when resources are stretched to breaking point.

The hurling fraternity in Ulster have a passion for their game, which matches that of their equivalents in the strong hurling counties of Leinster or Munster, or in Galway, but they do it with little hope of major rewards. Thankfully, they would never accept that they have no hope of winning something big. It isn't easy to promote hurling in any county, but it's definitely much more difficult in the so-called weaker counties, which may be weak in terms of results, but should never be described as 'weak' in terms of commitment.

It was a privilege to work with those people for three years and I, too, felt the heartache of several good performances in the inter-provincial series for forty or fifty minutes, only to finish with a scoreline which suggested that there was an even bigger gulf than was actually the case.

But there were interesting days, too. I remember a trial game which was organised by Seamus McGrattan for the purpose of selecting the Ulster panel for that year's Railway Cup. It was held in Corrigan Park, Belfast. Seamus knew every reasonably good player in the province but he still wanted to give everyone a chance.

He asked me to check the players' names and their clubs as they came through the entrance to the dressing rooms. They were trickling in slowly, in twos and threes, with an occasional lone player. I had been standing at the door for about ten minutes, with my little book, when two players arrived and announced that they were both McNaughtons from Cushendall. Five minutes later another two arrived and claimed that they, too, were McNaughtons from Cushendall and, eventually, a third pair arrived, apparently another two McNaughtons from Cushendall.

By now, I was becoming very suspicious, thinking that someone was 'taking the mickey', or that I had been set-up by McGrattan, who I knew was well capable of such a trick, so I asked them for their Christian names. One of them told me bluntly to get out of the bloody way, that they were there to play hurling and that he had no time for officialdom or notebooks. I saw that he was a very determined individual so I let him in, closed the door and went in search of McGrattan, to see who was responsible for making me look even more stupid than normal.

"McNaughtons? Ah, they'd be OK," he said; "Sure there's a slua of them ones up there, and they all play. There'll be some of them on the team."

That was my first encounter with Terence 'Sambo' McNaughton whom I now consider to be a friend and who was, in my opinion, jointly with Eddie Donnelly (Big Eddie), the best player I ever saw playing the game in Ulster. As it happened, Sambo was not selected in the first fifteen for that year's game against Munster, because Neilly Patterson said he was, "...too young yet, but he's going to be a good one."

How right he was – at least in his second comment. Sambo became an inspirational player for both club and county, as well as for Ulster, and deserved more than the one All Star award he received – in my view he probably deserved three. He has since contributed greatly to the county team as manager.

That trial provided me with a second memory. Antrim played the rest of Ulster, who had a big, strong, raw, ginger-haired lad at midfield. Every player who ever played football or hurling has had a game where everything went right, and another game where everything went wrong. On this occasion, everything went wrong for this big lad. When he went forward for the puck-out, the ball went long; when he went back for the long one, it went short. He looked completely lost – the proverbial 'fish out of water'. By half time, I was feeling sorry for him. I went over to McGrattan, who was refereeing the game and commented on this lad.

"You might not believe it, Peter," he said, "but that lad's a great hurler, one of the best hurlers in Ulster. Now, he's not a midfielder, he's a centre-half, that's where he plays for the club and for the county, but he's a very good hurler."

"You could have fooled me," I answered sceptically.

McGrattan picked up on the scepticism. "No," he said, "he's genuinely a good hurler, but he's out of position."

I wasn't convinced. What would I know anyway – I was only the chairman of the selection committee!

When we went in to select the team, later that evening, the big lad was not considered, not even for the subs.

Almost a year later, I went over to Ballyshannon to see a McKenna Cup game between Derry and Donegal. Derry had a fine, strapping, big lad wearing number eleven. He was new to the team – a good fielder, strong in the tackle and very powerful. I watched him carefully. He was raw, could have done with a bit of coaching, but I was impressed – very impressed. Everyone else seemed to be talking about a light young lad who was playing wing half-forward for Donegal and he was certainly good, too. I discovered later that his sister was married to Des Cahill of RTÉ, one of the best GAA presenters in the country – if not the best.

It was almost half time before I realised that the big centre half-forward was the same guy I'd seen playing in the previous year's hurling trial. I checked the name in the programme and, though it meant nothing to me, I was sure it was the same player.

Ten minutes from the end, the selectors replaced him. I was flabbergasted. To me, he was the best new prospect I'd seen in a long while. But who can read the mind of a selector? I had been there myself and I knew that selectors make mistakes too. I had done it in a county final when I'd taken off my own brother and it had probably cost us the match and the Championship.

Three or four months later, I was in the office from which we conducted the on-the-day administration of the Ulster final. Like every other final, the place was in a state of absolute chaos and uproar, when Kevin Heffernan entered. Kevin had been appointed manager of the Irish team to play Australia, in Australia, later that year. He went straight over to talk to Michael Feeney, then Secretary of the Ulster Council.

Michael called me over and introduced me to Kevin. I knew who he was – one of the greatest players and one of the greatest managers in the history of our Association. Not surprisingly, he had no idea who I was though I'd been a member of the Games Administration Committee which had dealt with the events of the 1983 All-Ireland final. He asked if I had seen the preliminary list, which he had announced for the trials. I had been working abroad for the previous fortnight and had not seen who was on it so he showed it to me.

"Kevin wants to know if there is anyone from Ulster, or anywhere else, not on that list, who you think should be given a chance," Feeney said.

I read the list and thought about it for a few seconds. It was fairly comprehensive, as I would have expected from Heffernan.

"There was a big lad who played for Derry in the McKenna Cup, at centre half-forward," I said. "I think he would be worth having a look at. He's raw, but he's brave and he's strong, and I think he'd suit that game."

"What's his name?" Heffernan asked.

"I don't know," I said, probably somewhat sheepishly, because it was an implausible scenario – my recommending someone, whose name I did not know.

"Now, he was taken off before the end," I added, "but I liked him. Contact any of the three selectors and they will give you his name. I would recommend you have a look at him."

I could see that Kevin was sceptical, particularly after I mentioned that the lad, whom I was recommending so strongly, had been withdrawn before the end of the game. Having said it, I was beginning to feel a bit stupid myself and was thinking that I should probably have kept my mouth shut. But I was still confident that, with a bit of coaching, this big lad would turn out to be a great prospect. But what if my judgement was totally wrong? I had long admired Heffernan's acumen and his understanding of how to win in Gaelic football, even with limited resources, and I had no desire to make a complete fool of myself in his presence.

Four or five months later, a big red-headed lad from Dungiven, in Derry, came back from Australia, carrying the trophy for 'player of the series'. He had played mainly at full-back in that series in which Ireland was successful and Heffernan's managerial prowess was confirmed – as if it needed confirmation. The play-anywhere, dual player was called Brian McGilligan. He'd been a surprise selection for the panel, because he was not well known at the time, but it turned out to be a successful one. He would later win an All Star award for his performances at midfield in helping Derry to win the 1993 All-Ireland, and was unlucky not to win more than one.

I have long been a great admirer of this big-hearted man as a hurler, as a person and as a footballer, for which he is, of course, best known. His tackle on Dublin's Jack Sheedy (another great midfielder) in the closing stages of the 1993 All-Ireland semi-final, was one of the hardest, fair tackles I ever saw. I am very pleased that Kevin Heffernan, notwithstanding his understandable scepticism about my recommendation, followed up on my suggestion and that it paid off.

Brian McGilligan would still claim that hurling is his first love. He has managed Derry hurlers and given that role the same sort of commitment as he gave to the Derry football team when he partnered another great midfielder, Anthony Tohill, over a period of five or six years. They complemented one another perfectly and made an outstanding pairing – one of the best I have seen.

Having started my career at midfield, I've always taken a particular interest in that aspect of the game. Of course, it has changed immensely over the past decade and, in my opinion, not for the better. Nevertheless, I tended and still tend, to be fascinated by what happens in that part of the pitch. In terms of partnerships, the Mick O'Connell–Seamus Murphy one was exceptional; they seemed to have a telepathic understanding, which was extremely difficult to disrupt. Jack O'Shea and Seán Walsh was another great partnership, until Seán was moved to full-back. McGilligan and Tohill, I have already mentioned, while Liam Hayes and Gerry McEntee were also very good, each with very different strengths – Hayes was a wonderful fielder, who was very mobile, while McEntee was immensely strong and very effective. Finally, Paul McGrane and John Toal were developing into another wonderful and greatly under-appreciated partnership, until John's unfortunate injury.

But apart from the great partnerships, there have also been great individual mid-fielders, in my era. I have taken great pleasure from watching the high fielding of Willie Bryans of Offaly, Brian Mullins of Dublin, Ray Carolan of Cavan, Mick Carley of Westmeath, Kevin Walsh of Galway, Willie Joe Padden of Mayo, John Galvin of Limerick (how and why did he retire without an All Star award?), Darragh Ó Sé of Kerry and many more. Good midfielders are the most complete footballers on the field in Gaelic football, in my view.

Unfortunately, that aspect of the game has been virtually eliminated by the more recent tactics being employed in Gaelic football, as have some of the other great characteristics and skills of a fantastic sport. Modern innovations have reduced our game to something much more akin to professional soccer than to the game I first knew and enjoyed. Effort has replaced skill, running has displaced tackling, mouthing has supplanted camaraderie, and high fielding has virtually disappeared. I fail to see the benefits, in terms of sporting enjoyment, from any of those changes.

The Association has a tendency to blame team managers for those changes, but that is wrong. It is not the managers who have destroyed football; it is those who have changed the rules for the worse, especially those who have changed refereeing to the point where Gaelic football, as we knew it, no longer exists. I am unhappy with what has replaced it and even less happy with what I see as an inevitable trend in the game

– the massed defence. Thank God for hurling. It gives us reason to live in hope of enjoying our native sports, as football becomes more and more of a non-contact sport and both player and spectator satisfaction decreases.

Looking back, three years is a very short time. My period as Vice-President of the Ulster Council seems to have passed in a flash. In February 1986, I succeeded Phil Smith as President, with Gene Larkin of Armagh as Vice-President.

My most vivid memory of that period is still my first meeting of Central Council, in May or June 1986. Both the late Micheál O'Connor, from Killarney (a man for whom I had outstanding respect and who would have made a great President of the Association) and I, were attending our first meeting, and we sat at the back of the room. After half an hour, we were looking at one another, in absolute bewilderment, as the proceedings drifted slowly along, punctuated by irrelevant comment after irrelevant comment, with no sense that it was dealing with business of any importance and, in reality, it wasn't. Neither of us could believe what we were seeing and hearing. It was a sobering lesson in the *realpolitik* of GAA administration – quite deflationary, in fact.

Within a few months of my acceding to the position, Tyrone had qualified for the All-Ireland final after a semi-final performance which is best forgotten. It was the first Ulster team in the final for nine years and expectations were high, although everyone knew that the great Kerry team would be hard to dethrone as they went in search of another three-in-a-row, having just failed in the attempt to achieve an historic five-in-a-row a few years earlier. Most of the Kerry panel were household names and the team contained some of the greatest players in the history of the sport, or of any sport on this island. One could go through the entire fifteen and find some reason to believe that Tyrone had only a slim chance, if even that. They had never been in the final before. It was a daunting task.

That Kerry team was an exceptional outfit. They had an outstanding manager in Mick O'Dwyer and they gave supreme pleasure to all who appreciated good football. In fact, no football team has ever given more enjoyment to so many people and no one could begrudge them any of their eight victories, including their last one, however much northerners would have wished for an Ulster win.

Tyrone's performance was one of the factors, which persuaded me to state, at my address to the Ulster Convention in 1988, that notwithstanding the effects of 'The Troubles', the main thing which Ulster teams needed was increased confidence and that, if one Ulster team could win the All-Ireland, it could and should act as the forerunner to a period of sustained success for Ulster teams at national level. That was to occur sooner than even I could have expected.

Later that year I was appointed to a sub-committee, which was established by Management Committee, and given the task of examining the personnel structures at central level. We recommended that staffing of central office should be reduced by five – from twenty-three to eighteen. But we also spent two full meetings and part of another, examining whether we should recommend much more drastic reorganisation. Eventually, on the Chairman's (the late Noel Drumgoole's) casting vote we decided not to make any more trenchant recommendations. We realised that pushing for more radical changes might be counter-productive, though we all knew that more radical change was desirable, if not essential.

When the report came before Coiste Bainistí, it became clear that some senior members of the management team were distinctly unhappy with our findings. On reaching Central Council for decision, the first few speakers spoke out very trenchantly against any redundancies, arguing for the maintenance of the status quo.

After about half an hour, I could see all of what we had decided going down some river without a paddle. I was not prepared to accept that without a fight. So, I stood and spoke as forcefully as I ever have in my life, arguing that we had recommended minimal change, by comparison with what some of the committee considered to be necessary. I countered the arguments from the floor, one by one, and proposed that the report be accepted as it was presented. Within a few minutes, it had been passed by an overwhelming majority.

Had we been even more radical, we would almost certainly have failed in getting any of it implemented. Some of the senior staff had taken great exception to our proposals and I had been identified as the prime mover. That was unfair to my colleagues: we were all agreed on the problem and differed only on what changes we thought would be accepted by the decision makers.

*****

I had absolutely no intention of running for the Presidency of the Association in the run-up to the election of a President-Elect at the 1987 Congress. John Vesey had indicated to me, a couple of years earlier, that I should run in order to have 'my hat in the ring' for the 1990 election, but I didn't accept his advice and was happy enough to lead the Association in Ulster. I felt that a sitting Provincial President should not run for higher office, as it could be construed as an insult to the office of Provincial President and, in any event, I was not really interested in the position. But, not for the first time in my life, I had reckoned without the impact of 'events'.

In early December, when the late John Dowling had already been installed as the overwhelming favourite for the position and had secured commitments from the majority of Ulster counties to support him, I received a telephone call, quite late on a Saturday night from the Secretary of Donegal County Board, Bart Whelan. He had an issue on which he wanted my opinion. It was not a complex question and I wondered why my view was being sought. When I gave him my opinion he responded, with no great excitement, "That's what I thought, all right." We chatted for a while longer, about things in general. Bart was great company and a chat with him was always a pleasant experience, so I was in no hurry to end the conversation.

Then he fired his Exocet: "Peter, that's not the real reason I was phoning you. What are you doing about the Presidency?"

I was slightly taken aback. "Nothing," I replied. "I haven't given it a thought."

"Well, we think you should be thinking about it and we intend to help your thought processes, because we intend to nominate you at our Convention tomorrow," he responded.

There is not much one can say in such circumstances. I was almost dumb-struck. I cannot remember if I replied, or what I said. It wasn't as if it hadn't been mentioned previously, but there is a big difference between a conversation about some hypothetical prospect and the certainty of a nomination within twenty-four hours.

By the Sunday afternoon, I was a candidate for the Presidency of the GAA. I am no different from most other people – if I was going to run, I wanted to win. But I had no confidence that I could overtake John Dowling.

On the evening before the Congress, I met the late John Doyle some place in the Burlington Hotel and we stopped for a chat.

"Well, Quinn," he said; "How is this election going for you?"

"Ah, sure you know yourself, John, you've been through elections often enough. If I get all the votes I have been promised I could win it but you and I know only too well, I'll not get all I have been promised," I replied.

"By Christ, you can swear that, Quinn. My advice to you is take the number of votes you were promised, divide it by two and subtract seven, and you'll be about right," he said, with a glint in his eye. And he was not too far off.

There were seven candidates. The final vote was between John Dowling and me. He won easily. In our hotel room, earlier that morning, I had drafted a few words to say, when I lost – Mary wanted to know why I had prepared nothing to say in the event that I would win. I was realistic enough to know that a 'good showing' was the best I could expect.

My loser's speech seemed to go down well with the delegates. I compared my contribution to the Association with John Dowling's and really there was no comparison. He had refereed All-Ireland finals in both football and hurling; his county had won All-Irelands in both codes during his period in office; he had contributed at both national and provincial level over several decades; and he fully deserved any honour which was accorded to him. Against that background, I assured the delegates that they had made the right decision and, while it was the politically correct thing to say, I was also sincere about it.

I would, however, be a liar if I did not admit that I was slightly disappointed. People came up to me and told me that I would win next time but that was like telling the losing team in a county final that they would win the next year's final. I had been there three times and I knew that such platitudes were nonsense; next year's final is a different competition entirely. So, it was back to the Ulster Council and total focus on its interests for the following two years. I was determined to enjoy them and, for the most part, I did.

Before my final days in the post, the selection of my successor became an issue. I'd encouraged the late Gene Larkin to run for the position of Treasurer six years earlier and for the Vice-Presidency three years earlier, but I had warned him that the Council conducted most of its business, including all meetings of the full Council, through Irish. I had advised him to take classes so that, even if he was not fluent, he would be capable of conducting the meetings through Irish.Gene Larkin was a great GAA man. He had played for his club, his county and his province, in a very successful career. His club's fight against the British army for the rights of the Crossmaglen club and its members, which he had led, was a supreme example of sustained commitment to a cause. He was articulate and committed, and fought the Rangers' case courageously, intelligently and unceasingly. I had great admiration for both the man and the cause.

As the Convention approached, Gene's Irish had not improved one iota. That was placing the Council in an invidious position. Eventually, the late Fr. Dan Gallogly decided to stand for the Presidency of the Council. Apart from being an historian, Fr. Dan had taught Irish and was totally committed to the Council's policy. He and I were very friendly – he was one of the finest men, I have known – and, when he won fairly easily, I was accused of organising a coup. There is no way one can change such perceptions and I had to take the abuse on the chin, but the reality was that I was not responsible and Gene was not really the issue. The Council's policy on Irish was the only issue. And while I was also totally committed to that policy, I had no interest in embarrassing or undermining Gene Larkin – then or since. He was far too good a GAA man for that.

But he believed that I had orchestrated a coup against him. There was no way that I could persuade him otherwise and I have had to live with that accusation.

But that aside, I was very happy that Fr. Dan would be do a good job. In the event, he did an even better job than I could have anticipated and I was very glad of his support over the subsequent few years, when I was in a different position.

18

Second Time Round

By the end of my term as Ulster President, I was still in my mid-forties, with an expanding portfolio of overseas commitments. Overseas business is hard won and there is little or no profit in the early assignments, as one spends time building contacts and relationships and refining presentations to prospective customers. Therefore, I needed to take advantage of the opportunities and networks, which I had developed in earlier years, and build on them. So, I went back to my business activities with considerable relish.

It had not been easy balancing commitments to the Ulster Council with the demands of clients who had never heard of the GAA and would not have been impressed by someone who said he had commitments to a sporting body, which might impact on the service being provided to them.

By mid-1989, I was devoting all my energies to the business, much to the relief of some of my colleagues who had been left a bit short-handed over the preceding three years; the business was expanding satisfactorily and my input was still needed. I had developed an expertise in one or two areas, which were perceived as being 'best in class' and I was frequently being asked to write a book on the subject.

But I had neither the time nor the inclination to do so.

Although I knew that I would be favourite for the election, which was due in the following April, by July or August I had decided not to run again. I told no one apart from Mary, who half agreed with me but advised me to think carefully about it because I might regret it in the future.

I was happy with my decision, having finally taken it and buried the uncertainty. So, I began devoting myself entirely to work. Deep down I knew that I had, at best, only another six or seven years in that sort of business, because the amount of travel was such that, by the time I reached fifty, I would have to start the process of disengagement, with a run-down of three or four years at most. In the meantime, there was a wide spectrum of opportunities and I needed to avail of as many as I could, while I still could.

As the seanchaí used to say, 'things rested so'. I had almost forgotten about the possibility of becoming President, until I got a call from Seán one day, in late summer or early autumn.

"What are you doing about this Presidency thing?" he asked.

"Nothing," I said, "I'm not running."

"You're what?" was the sharp response.

"I'm not running," I said.

The silence on the other end of the line was prolonged and deafening. Then it was broken by a decorated outburst, which I had never, in my wildest dreams, expected and which was certainly not normal from Seán. He lambasted me.

"You've wasted most of your bloody life on the GAA, when you could have been making yourself a wealthy man." He finished with, "Go out and fight for it and win the bloody thing," or words to that effect!

I recall that I laughed nervously because Seán rarely produced outbursts like that. We discussed the issue for more than half an hour, an unusually long time for a telephone conversation between us.

I argued that I didn't have time to run a campaign and that I was not prepared to canvass for the position. He responded that he would make a few calls on my behalf, that he had a good network of contacts and that there would be no need for me to canvass. He told me to talk it over with Mary and "go for it".

Later that evening, I relayed the conversation to Mary and, surprisingly, she backed Seán's view, repeating her argument that I might regret not running for it over the rest of my life. I had no such concerns. I knew that I had always been able to put the past behind me, without even the slightest backward glance.

Inevitably, having been the previous runner-up, I got a considerable number of nominations, but there was a big field. I did no canvassing other than contacting two people who sent messages asking that I should call them. I'd always had a concern that canvassing could lead to ill-judged commitments which might not be in the Association's best interests. That said, I was not standing to come second again, but neither was I going to be pressurised into making commitments.

April Fools' Day might be an appropriate day on which to elect a new President for the GAA and I won on that date. It was not exactly a shoo-in but I was ahead throughout the entire election count. I then had a year sitting on Coiste Bainistí under John Dowling, although I had left that committee only a year earlier, so I had a fair idea of what the current issues were.

The burning issue of that year was whether to rebuild Croke Park, and, if so, whether it should be done as a single phase, with major games being played elsewhere for a couple of years, or whether we should go for a completely new site. I favoured the latter option, with the then Phoenix Park Racecourse being my favoured location. However, the tradition associated with Hill 16 and Bloody Sunday, the vision shown in the early years of the Association, when the Jones' Road site was first acquired, and the overall history and heritage associated with the place, were all advanced as strong arguments for staying where we were. I empathised with those arguments but felt that the greater convenience and commercial advantage lay with a new site. In the end, I was happy enough with the decision. In fact, it was almost certainly the right decision.

During that year, Frank Fahy, then Minister for Sport, called the three main, Irish field-sports bodies to a meeting at which he indicated a willingness on the part of the Government to fund most of a new national stadium. His estimated cost of an all-seated stadium was IR£120 million, and he asked the three sports to provide IR£20 million each, with the Government funding the other half and any excesses. By any standards, it was a good offer.

John asked Liam Mulvihill and me to accompany him to the meetings. Although we had virtually no money at that time, we agreed to produce the required IR£20 million. The IRFU seemed reluctant, but said they could contribute IR£10 million, though they would struggle with anything beyond that; however, they were not opposed in principle. The FAI claimed that they had no money and effectively that, in the aftermath of their massive success at 'Italia 90', the country owed them a stadium. We were not impressed by that argument.

Fahy continued his efforts to broker a deal which would be acceptable to all parties, including the Government, over a period of about six months. It was not his fault that no deal was agreed; he invested a huge amount of energy in the project and appeared frustrated by the failure of the three sports to make the necessary commitments. Eventually, he and we accepted that the idea was 'going nowhere' and we felt that we had no choice but to tell the others that we would go ahead on our own if a deal was not agreed quickly. It wasn't and we did.

At that point, it had become clear that the GAA needed a new stadium. Despite the expenditure on Hill 16 in the late 1980s, Croke Park was in poor shape overall, with the regulatory authorities reducing its capacity on an almost annual basis. It was already down to less than 65,000 and we could see that, within less than a decade or so, it was likely to be not much more than 50,000, at best, as the required safety standards for such facilities were raised.

As far as I can ascertain, issues with the stadium had first been raised by Michael Horgan in a memorandum to Coiste Bainistí, in 1979, when he advised of the need to improve entry and egress facilities at the Cusack Stand and Canal End of the ground. But it was not until July, 1980, that Coiste Bainistí accepted the improvement of entrance and exit facilities as a 'long-term' ambition. Then in 1983, during Paddy Buggy's presidency, they decided to erect a covered stand over the existing Canal End terrace and convert that area into seated capacity, but Michael Horgan, then Managing Partner of Horgan Lynch and Partners, pointed out that it would not be possible to develop new seating because of the lack of exit and entry capacity for larger numbers.

In late 1983, following problems including a 'pitch invasion' near the end of that year's All-Ireland football final, Dublin Corporation contacted the Association about the need to improve aspects of the stadium. That led to a decision, in February 1984, to appoint Michael Horgan to draw up the Long-Term Development Plan for Croke Park. In his written acceptance of the assignment, Michael commented that, "...I have no doubt that the attainment of total formal capacities of 60,000 to 70,000 will definitely involve you in land and property acquisition."

In May of that year, Michael again wrote to the Association in a sort of interim report, indicating that, "We are dealing with a stadium which has presently a safe holding capacity of approx. 65,000, but with only a safe exit capacity of approx. 50,000." He ended his letter by stating, "Finally, the single key factor (apart from finance) is the element of acquisition mainly of the substantial strip of land from Belvedere."

The collapse of a screen wall in the toilets on the upper deck of the Hogan Stand, during the half-time interval on All-Ireland hurling final day, in 1985, increased the pressure for investment in the stadium. The reality was that it had passed its sell-by date. The fact that the Association was deemed liable for 20 per cent of the costs of that event helped to concentrate the minds of its administrators on the need to do something significant about the problem.

Later, the Taylor Report into the Hillsborough Disaster, in January 1990, and the subsequent report issued by the Government Safety Committee a month after that, proved conclusively that we had to do something substantial, or our capacity would be reduced to a level which would not be acceptable to our membership.

In so far as I am aware, and according to a January 1991 report to Coiste Bainistí from the Ard Stiúrthóir and the Uachtarán, the first formal approach to Belvedere College and the religious order which owned and ran it, was in May 1985 and it was on the basis of the GAA's acquiring a few strips of land, which would not impinge on the College's pitch. The College responded that it had no wish to move from its facilities. In response to a follow-up enquiry of November 1985, asking if they would consider selling the entire property, the College again responded in the negative.

Continued pressure from Dublin Corporation in 1987, confirmed to the Association that further reductions in the stadium's capacity, specifically in its entry and exit capacity, were inevitable. As a result, the Association negotiated a 'temporary licence agreement' allowing emergency exits onto the Belvedere pitch; those 'temporary' arrangements were later used on the occasion of the 1988 All-Ireland hurling final. Subsequently, the GAA approached the Clonliffe authorities about the possibility of providing Belvedere College with an alternative site for their pitch, but again, the response was negative.

In the meantime, the Association decided to re-build Hill 16, made an application for planning permission at the beginning of 1988 and, despite objections, received that permission within a few months.

Just after I ceased to be a member of Coite Bainistí, in April 1989, the HOK Lobb Partnership was appointed to produce a 'Master Plan' for the stadium, and shortly afterwards, the authorities in Belvedere were approached with a higher cash offer than the Association's previous offer, which had been determined more by the Association's financial position than by any imperative to acquire the property. Not surprisingly, that offer, too, was rejected.

Over the months, particularly in the second half of 1989, the Belvedere position appeared to soften and, by November 1989, the GAA had finally received a letter from a representative of the College, setting out a number of requirements if the College was to consider any sale of the site. Those demands were ambitious, but not unrealistic. By the early months of 1990, there was agreement in principle to sell. The GAA had increased its offer, but the offer was deemed inadequate by the negotiating team appointed to represent the College, which therefore said 'no' again.

In January 1991, I was added to the negotiating team, though John Dowling was still the team leader. Liam Mulvihill met with a senior representative of the College's authorities on his own and, it seemed to me, that his meeting moved things closer to a conclusion. The path to a final agreement – purchase of the entire property by the GAA – was becoming much clearer. It was now about money.

John Dowling led the final negotiations on the acquisition of the Belvedere College ground, which were finalised before I took office. We agreed to pay all fees, legal costs and stamp duty, as well as to do some infrastructural work to the grounds and compensate the College for a number of associated issues. In January 1990, before the agreement was concluded, journalist Martin Breheny disclosed that the final cost to the GAA was going to be IR£3 million, and he wasn't a mile away.

Largely as a result of the Belvedere deal, we had virtually no money by the time I became President. However, we were still in a good position to move forward with the project, on all other dimensions. The design consultants, HOK Lobb Partnership, together with architects Gilroy McMahon, led by former Tyrone player, Des McMahon, had produced an outline design using the then Joe Robbie Stadium in Miami as a prototype.

Subsequently, a local design team including architects, quantity surveyors, structural engineers, mechanical and electrical consultants, planning advisors and most of the other necessary specialists, had also been appointed and preliminary designs had already been produced by the time I came on board. That latter work had highlighted considerable problems with the site, which was too small for the sort of stadium being considered.

While I was involved in some of the later stages of the negotiation, it was fitting that they should have been completed during John

Dowling's period in office, since he and Liam Mulvihill had carried most of the load in bringing the matter to that stage. John had been centrally involved from early 1988 until the final agreement less than a month before he left office, and the Association owes him more than most members appreciate.

Even the acquisition of that property did not solve the space problems entirely. The old stadium had been built on a very confined site – though that might not have been obvious to those who had the courage to develop it in the first place. It was clear to the design team that using a conventional H-frame structure would result in one 'leg' of the H being outside the GAA's property, on the other side of the canal at one end, and very close, if not too close, to the boundary in other places, too.

Any solution to those issues was going to demand a high level of imagination and ingenuity, because acquiring more property would have been impossible, even if we could have afforded it.

Fortunately, the team which had been assembled by then, contained people with just such ingenuity. Gilroy McMahon, led by Des McMahon, and structural engineers, Horgan Lynch, led by Michael Horgan and Frank Murray, combined to develop a unique Y-frame structure – the first of its kind for such a project, anywhere in the world. It reduced many of the space problems, especially the access and egress issues raised by Michael Horgan as a limiting factor in his first assessment of the site. More importantly, it provided the structural strength and stability necessary in such a facility, though an immense battery of tests had to be undertaken before we could be absolutely certain of that.

The Y-frame was a massive breakthrough and a tremendous tribute to both the ingenuity and the design talents of an Irish team. It allowed us to develop a stadium with capacity originally set at over 84,000 spectators. Ultimately, that capacity was reduced by almost 2,000 in order to meet a variety of other design and operational requirements.

After I took over, the first source of frustration was the planning process. It proved to be immensely complex and bureaucratic, and it held us back for at least a year longer than we had anticipated, ultimately proving to be one of our biggest obstacles.

Our second problem was always going to be money, but, while we were still in the planning phase, I encountered other problems.

19

Becoming a Target

On the night before I was due to take over as President of the GAA, I did an interview with RTÉ for broadcast on the following day's News at One radio programme. Predictably in that interview, the issue of the then ban on the security forces in the North was raised. I knew only too well – as did most other members of the Association, including those in the North – that such a ban could not remain forever, but I was also sure that its removal at that time was just not an option – it would split the Association. Having been through the Hunger Strikes a decade earlier, I was not prepared to risk that again.

It was obvious to everyone who was close to the situation that, unless there was some movement on the political front and major changes in the structure and membership of the RUC, our members in the North, and a significant proportion of those in the South, just would not vote for the removal of the ban. Some of them would probably have seceded, thereby precipitating an even bigger split than that which had almost resulted from the Hunger Strikes.

Those of us who were dealing with these issues, generally on a daily basis, also knew that there was a 'liberal' faction with a political agenda for the GAA, mainly concentrated in sections of the Dublin-based media and the public sector, who did not understand that and did not want to understand it. I was more aware of the issues involved than most because, in those years, I was actually the nominated point of contact on behalf of the Association in Ulster for the collation of factual data on issues of the abuse of individual GAA members, on damage to club property, on security force interference with, and disruption to, the Association's activities, in most of the border areas. Belfast, Derry and Crossmaglen had their own reporting systems and did not fall within my remit. Clearly, I had to be reasonably impartial if I was to retain credibility in that role, which involved reporting such matters to a representative of the Republic's Department of Foreign Affairs.

At that time, those so-called liberal attitudes, and the people who espoused them, were far removed from the grass roots of northern society, including especially the nationalist community there. The reality was that such people and their views were much closer to being a problem than to having any realistic input to a solution. In such matters, timing is crucial and, just like an ill-timed tackle in football or hurling, any mistiming of responses to such issues tends to have serious and negative repercussions.

It was clear that either those people were not aware of that, or they did not accept it – they were entirely convinced that they knew what was right for Ireland, for northern nationalists and for the GAA. That took some arrogance from people who hardly ever crossed the border. They clearly felt that they knew more than those of us who were dealing with these problems on a daily or a weekly basis. Such people were actually an impediment to real reconciliation, even if they were too naïve to appreciate that.

The cheerleader for that view in the sports media was the late Raymond Smith, a journalist with the Independent Group, but he had plenty of acolytes, though some of those who supported his view did so fairly and without converting their views into personalised attacks.

Raymond Smith had a great knowledge of the statistics associated with our games but very little understanding of either the games themselves or of the views of the vast majority of members, including virtually all our members in the North. He was primarily a political journalist rather than a sports journalist; that was his background and he was happy to use the GAA to promote his personal political agenda. Given his experiences in the then Congo, he should have known better.

The last thing the GAA needed, at that point, was political interference or interpretation of its activities in a political context. We were doing our utmost to avoid any form of political involvement and, with considerable and growing pressure from many sides, that was becoming progressively more difficult. Comments from pseudo-liberals, living sixty-odd miles from the border – and even farther from where the real pressures were – were unlikely to be helpful.

Against that background, it would have been entirely stupid of me, whatever my personal views, to indicate any form of unilateral concession to those whose own position needed to change and change dramatically – as it eventually did, or was forced to do, and within a decade, too. I used a quotation from Chris Ryder, in his book 'The RUC – Force Under Fire', where he described the North's police force as being viewed by nationalists as "… the armed wing of Unionism". I also quoted the reference for the comment so it should have been clear that I was not expressing a uniquely personal opinion, but that I was reflecting a view which was widely held and recognised by even the most ardent supporters of that force, even if most of them would not have accepted its validity.

Nevertheless, my comment provoked a negative reaction in some quarters, though that was not clear until later. Obviously, it confirmed a stereotype of me, which had been developed, by someone, or some group, with a political bias. In the immediate aftermath of that broadcast, I received only a single letter of criticism (which I still have), and that criticism was both personal and ignorant. It came from an Antrim man who was working and living in Fermanagh and who was a member of a professedly pro-unionist party.

A few weeks later, on an afternoon programme on RTÉ Radio, to which I happened to be listening while in the car, Raymond Smith launched a bitter personal attack on me on the basis that I had not indicated that part of my Presidency would be devoted to easing tensions between the two communities in the North. I was and still am indebted to Micheál Ó Muircheartaigh, who was in the studio on the same programme, for pointing out that I was "hardly a wet week in office", though that did not stop the verbal onslaught.

That was the first salvo in a personal campaign against me, by sections of the national media. I was being branded as a northerner, first and foremost, but, worse than that, as a republican who was militantly anti-unionist and who was operating to a political agenda. The reality was, and still is, that in my entire life, I have been a member of only one political party and it was, and is, totally committed to democratic and constitutional means of creating change in the North and everywhere else either. But the northern badge was enough to raise the hackles of the liberal media in Dublin. Even the hint of a republican opinion was enough to make me persona non grata with those bigots.

I have never denied that I am a nationalist. Equally, I cannot deny that I was born and reared in the North, nor would I ever want to – in fact I am proud of it. And I will not deny that I saw change in the structure, membership and performance of the security forces in the North as an essential element of any progress towards real reconciliation. I am not ashamed of any of those facts or views. As I proved later, when the opportunity to contribute to the easing of tensions and to promoting reconciliation was open to me, I did my bit and more, and I think that those who worked with me in those years would accept that I did it well.

The thing that has really 'bugged' me about that ever since, is my conviction that, had some of my detractors been in the position of having to negotiate under pressure in an Orange Hall in Portadown or North Antrim, or with some of the leading and, allegedly, most volatile and violent loyalists, when they were armed, in a number of the most dangerous areas of the North (East Belfast, Portadown or North Antrim) or in an RUC barracks, as I had to do with absolutely no security, they would have spent most of their time in the toilets.

I am proud to say that I was always prepared to fight my corner in a realistic, non-dogmatic way, on the ground and face-to-face, rather than in words or print from a distance. It is easy to be brave, fighting from a distance of a hundred miles, with a pen. It is considerably more daunting to argue face-to-face with someone to whom your life means absolutely nothing when both he and you know that. It's all the more so when you know, with 100 per cent certainty, that he has already been responsible for several murders, most of which he committed himself. I was taught by my father that cowardice was one of the greatest faults from which any man could suffer and I now know that he was right. I hate all cowards but I consider cowards who use pen, print and paper, or electronic media, to be the worst of the lot.

I became more aware of the problems which I was about to face in 1991, although I did not fully realise what was in store for me. I was invited to speak at an awards ceremony sponsored and organised by a national newspaper within the Independent Group, some weeks after that year's All-Ireland football final. I sat at the top table beside the editor and we seemed to get along quite well. He was the first speaker and he made some comment about the differences between sports coverage in the USA and that in Ireland; it was an entirely inoffensive comment and I had no reason to take exception to it, nor did I.

I had no prepared speech. In the course of my comments, I made a throwaway remark about American sports not having to deal with an Irish media. It was meant to be flippant, in response to the comment from the previous speaker and, though it could hardly have been described as witty, I would not have considered it to be provocative.

But, as I frequently discovered later, flippant comments can land one in bother. In fact, most of the times when I have had problems arising from something I said, they arose out of some flippant, caustic or witty remark which was never meant to be insulting or controversial, but which was so interpreted by someone in the audience.

When an executive from the Group addressed the event, he launched into a prolonged and vituperative tirade about my comment and then proceeded to castigate and insult me in several ways. His attack lasted for more than five minutes; that allows for a lot of words and considerable negativity, when they are directed at oneself. I considered walking out, but stayed.

When the formal proceedings ended, I spent a few minutes talking to various people and then decided to leave. It had not been a particularly enjoyable event for me but I was aware of the 'sticks and stones' syndrome and, even though I was slightly annoyed, I did not see it as all that important. On my way out, I was intercepted by someone who was close to the newspaper itself. He was clearly quite agitated – more than I had ever seen him previously or subsequently – and was obviously wary of being seen talking to me. He told me to 'watch my back' and warned me that life was going to be made as difficult and as uncomfortable as possible for me. He was careful to minimise the time he spent with me. In fact, he did not even allow me time to ask him any questions before he walked away as I attempted to query him.

I could see that he was visibly upset on my behalf and, while I appreciated his candour and his courage in alerting me, I was absolutely stunned by his statement. In fact, when I gave it further thought on my way home, I was not disposed to believe him especially since he had refused to elaborate on it. Nevertheless, I was not happy about the comment, though I never expected that it would cost me any loss of sleep.

I was, however, surprised that the only one of the senior people from the sponsors, the late Jackie Gilroy, a great St Vincent's man, bothered to speak to me as I was leaving. I met Jackie only once after that but I have never forgotten his gesture on that evening and, over time, it became even more symbolic. To the best of my memory, that was also the only event I attended in all those years, where the organiser did not make a point of thanking me as I left. That fact has caused me no great concern since then. I consider it more of a reflection on their behaviour, than on me.

To this day, I find it impossible to determine what was 'cause' and what was 'effect'. But what is certain is that it was not long before the *Independent* and the other southern media got their chance and, boy, did they take it!

In September 1991, Down won the All-Ireland senior football final with Pete McGrath as manager. They had been very lucky to survive in an earlier game in the Ulster Championship, when a point from a sixty-yard free by Ross Carr, in the very last seconds of the game, secured them a replay which they won. Down have a great ability to improve as they progress in the Championship but, in 1991, no one gave them much chance of winning an All-Ireland, based on their performances in Ulster. In fact, very few gave them much chance of winning Ulster, but they did.

The 1991 football Championship had been dominated by the four-game saga between Dublin and Meath, when Dublin dominated about three-quarters of each of the four games, but Meath, thanks to Kevin Foley's late goal and David Beggy's even later point, eventually prevailed due to a massive level of resilience, confidence and determination. Both teams deserved All-Ireland medals for their efforts and for the pleasure they gave GAA fans across the country over those four epic games.

It was, therefore, a major surprise when Down won the final, though by winning again three years later, that Down team proved that it was no flash in the pan. Liam Hayes was the Meath captain on the day and he almost turned the game in their favour, with an outstanding goal from twenty-plus yards as the game entered the final quarter. As one of the highest-fielding and most mobile mid-fielders of his era, he deserved to captain a winning All-Ireland team, but it was not to be. All of Ulster rejoiced at Down's breakthrough, after so many years without a northern win, but many of us felt sorry for Meath too, given what they had to do to reach that final.

As I had predicted three years earlier, that Down win heralded a succession of wins for Ulster teams – four in succession, with first Donegal and then Derry, following in Down's footsteps, before Down returned to win another and give Ulster its first-ever four-in-a-row. It could have been five because, in 1995, Tyrone were unlucky against a very good Dublin squad – though, given their number of 'near misses' in previous years, no one could begrudge Dublin that victory, apart from Tyrone and most of the rest of Ulster. Three different Ulster counties winning the All-Ireland in my three years in office, was to become one of the hallmarks of my presidency though I cannot take any credit for it.

In that same period, Tipperary won the 1991 hurling title and Kilkenny won two-in-a-row, in 1992 and 1993.

About two months after the 1991 finals, I read an article in one of the Sunday papers about a proposed game between the All-Ireland champions Down and the Dublin team, which had made Meath battle until the last second, in Leinster. The game was to be played in the RDS on a joint bill with a soccer game involving Shamrock Rovers. I was somewhat surprised that it appeared not to have been raised with the Association, at least not to my knowledge, but I was not particularly exercised about the protocol or lack of it. I gave the matter very little heed.

On the following Tuesday morning, I was at home, doing some preparatory work for an up-coming overseas project, when I had a call from an officer of the Clann na Gael Fontenoy club, who told me that he wanted to inform me about a proposed game, which the club hoped to organise in the RDS jointly with Shamrock Rovers and with a soccer game on the same bill; he wanted me to support the proposal. When I let him know that I had already learned about it from the previous Sunday's paper he said he had hoped to contact me before I learned about it from any other source. Clearly, he'd failed in that regard but I gave him no indication as to whether I was in favour of it, or not.

We had a Coiste Bainistí meeting on the following Friday. The minutes of that meeting, under the heading, 'Items for Noting', record a minute indicating that "Coiste Riaracháin na gCluichí had refused permission to Clann na Gael Fontenoys for a game involving Dublin v Down". No details were provided and the matter was simply noted, with no discussion, as Coiste Bainistí did not have to take a decision on it. Assuming the minutes provide an accurate record of the meeting, no one asked for any details and none were provided.

The minutes of the subsequent Coiste Bainistí meeting of November 29, 1991 (page 11) record the hearing of an appeal by Clann na Gael

Fontenoys against the decision of Coiste Riaracháin na gCluichí. The club was represented by John Egan and Michael Fitzgerald and GAC was represented by S Mac Thaídhg (Cathaoirleach) and S Ó Laoire (Runaí).

The club argued that they needed to have the game played in Dublin 4 and that the RDS ground was the only venue, in that area, capable of hosting such a game, but it was not available on any Sunday, other than the date of a soccer game. According to the minutes, the GAC representatives, "...outlined the various reasons for concern felt by them when the application had been received and stated that a lot of information had been given to An Coiste Bainistí about the proposed fixture which had not been available to them initially".

Under the heading 'Decision of An Coiste Bainistí', the minute of that meeting of Coiste Bainistí read as follows:

"It was decided that the appeal failed as Coiste Riaracháin na gCluichí had not broken any rule in dealing with the matter. However, it was decided to invite the club to make a new request pointing out the various matters which had been stated at the meeting and that Coiste Riaracháin na gCluichí would set down the conditions under which the game could be played."

Clearly, Coiste Bainistí did not set any specific conditions – that was left to Coiste Riaracháin na gCluichí to decide.

That minute was subsequently accepted, at the following meeting, as an accurate record of the decision which was taken. In effect, it was passing the issue back to Coiste Riaracháin na gCluichí to negotiate a resolution to any issues associated with the proposal.

The reality was that the Coiste Bainistí decision was entirely in accordance with the Association's rules and the supplementary comment provided the club with an opportunity to make another application to Coiste Riaracháin na gCluichí. Such a 'rider' was going well beyond normal protocol in the case of a failed appeal and suggested that the Association, through its Coiste Bainistí, was not entirely opposed to the game, but wished to have certain issues resolved in advance of the granting of any such permission.

I left on the following evening, a Sunday, to undertake an assignment, which had been awarded to me some time earlier, by a company which was aware of my role in the GAA. The contract had been awarded on the *express condition* that I would not be contactable during the period of the assignment (Sunday evening until mid-afternoon on the following Friday), because of its nature. Clearly, that company was very sensitive about anything which might have a disruptive effect on the outcome, or the delivery, of the assignment which I was being paid to undertake – those who pay earn such rights.

Consequently, I was not in contact with (nor under my contract was I allowed to have contact with) Croke Park at any time during that week and was entirely unaware of what had been happening there. With hindsight, my being away when a major issue was developing was a most unfortunate coincidence but it did not seem to be a potentially major issue on the following Saturday.

I arrived back in Dublin on the Friday evening and went straight to Croke Park to meet Liam Mulvihill, the Director General.

I had difficulty believing what I was being told. Some of the events which had occurred in my absence were, in my opinion and subsequently in the opinion of the other members of Coiste Bainistí and Árd Comhairle, too, directly contrary to both the Association's rules and to what had been determined by Coiste Bainistí and Coiste Riaracháin na gCluichí a week earlier. I drove back to Fermanagh, more than slightly annoyed with one or two members of staff.

As was normal at that time, prior to every Central Council meeting, we had a special meeting of Coiste Bainistí scheduled for the following morning, with the meeting of Central Council in the afternoon. Before the commencement of the following morning's meeting, both the officers of Coiste Riaracháin na gCluichí and I were informed, by Down County Committee, that An Dún had decided to withdraw from the game as the spokesmen for both the GAA club and Shamrock Rovers had stated that it was going to be a joint promotion which was contrary to what had been stated to Coiste Bainistí at its previous meeting. I had had no contact with Down County Committee at any time during that period so I was surprised by this turn of events.

As a result of that morning's communication, I advised the members of Coiste Bainistí at the start of the meeting that the game was unlikely to be played because, as I had been told, tickets for the game were being sold contrary to the specifications set down by Coiste Riaracháin na gCluichí and agreed with Down County Committee.

In my business career, I had always had a policy of not intervening in the affairs of any subordinate entity which reported to me, unless something was going seriously wrong, and I still abide by that convention. Since this fixture was entirely a matter for Coiste Riaracháin na gCluichí, there was no obvious need for me to become involved unless, or until, there was a clear challenge to the Association's rules. Consequently, I did not get involved at that point.

Shortly before the scheduled end of the meeting of Coiste Bainistí, we received a hand-written note from a senior officer of Dublin County Board containing a request for a meeting to discuss the issue. We agreed to adjourn the Coiste Bainistí meeting in order to facilitate a meeting between the representatives of Dublin, Down and GAC. I was present at and chaired that meeting. The representatives of both Coiste an Dhúin and Coiste Riaracháin na gCluichí indicated their unhappiness with the proposed arrangements and their reluctance to proceed with the game on the basis being suggested. Dublin County Board argued that it should be allowed to proceed.

When that short meeting ended, I reconvened Coiste Bainistí and advised the members that neither Down nor Coiste Riaracháin na gCluichí was happy that the conditions set out were being applied, that Down had withdrawn from the fixture and that the game would not be going ahead. I explained that Dublin had expressed a different view and a Dublin delegate argued his county's position fairly and fearlessly. I also indicated that Central Council would be asked to rule on whether the fixture, as it was being advertised, was in breach of the Association's (then) Rule 5 and that the matter would be raised under AOB on the Central Council agenda.

All these facts are detailed in the minutes of the meeting of Coiste

Bainistí of December 7, 1991 (pages 14 and 17) and Central Council approved the decisions taken by Coiste Bainistí at its meeting later that afternoon by a considerable majority, and that, too, is recorded in the minutes. Whatever sympathy there was for the club, and there was considerable sympathy for it, was not sufficient to persuade the Association's main decision-making bodies that what was being proposed conformed to what was needed. But the reality was and is that neither Coiste Bainistí nor Árd Comhairle was ever asked to make a decision on the merits or otherwise of the proposal. The crucial decisions were taken by Coiste Riaracháin na gCluichí and Coiste an Dhúin; Coiste Bainistí simply recorded the results. But obviously certain interests, including some members of the media with their own agenda, expected that I should overrule both of those; that reflects little understanding of how organisations operate and how governance works.

Later that evening, I was due to present the All-Ireland medals to the victorious Down team. As I was driving to Down, listening to the radio in the car, I heard comments about the decision, from the late Mick Dunne, whose report was factually accurate and whose comments were entirely fair. But from other reports, it was already becoming clear that others in the media were unhappy with the decision. The media was taking the lead on this matter.

Over the next week, the issue grew legs and coverage became progressively more critical of the GAA, with much of the criticism being directed at me as its President. There were some who criticised the decision (as was their right), but not the President personally. I had no problem with their views, although even they were operating from limited awareness of the facts. I had taken a decision not to do or say anything, which would be seen as an attempt to transfer the blame to anyone else, or to any other committee and, while I was unhappy at having to take the blame myself, I felt that it was the 'least worst' option.

Predictably in the light of what I had been told a couple of months earlier, the *Independent* was particularly negative in its comments about the decision and in its personal criticism of the President. Raymond Smith was especially critical, but he was not alone – in fact only one person in that media group supported me, though that was not entirely surprising. Unfortunately, some of the staff of *The Irish Times* were no better and RTÉ was just as bad as the *Independent*. In RTÉ's case the main criticism came from people who were not from the sports department – in fact, those in the sports department were generally very reasonable in their comments. Why those others led on this issue was, for me, somewhat of a conundrum, until I realised that RTÉ also contained individuals with an anti-northern nationalist agenda and I was fair game for them on that front.

I was getting fed-up with the tone of some of the comment. As I saw it, journalists were supposed to deal in facts, not in perversions of the truth disseminated from a source, which had a vested interest in deflecting the blame. I would have had no problem accepting my fair share of any blame if I had been directly involved in the decision, but the real decisions had not been taken by me, nor was I responsible for the clear ignoring of decisions of Riarachán na gCluichí or of those of Coiste Bainistí.

On the following Sunday, the newspapers and the audio-visual media were full of comment and 'facts' about the issue, including the sequence of events, how decisions had been reached and who had made the decisions.

Much of the content was absolute rubbish without any foundation and some of it had clearly been 'leaked' from a source which had a vested interest in the issue. I realised who the likely source was, and why, but that didn't excuse the outrageously inaccurate reporting by some of the journalists. The anti-northern agenda was being pushed to its limits and my totally justifiable comments on the RUC were being used to diminish me as a person, as much as to abuse me as President of the Country's best-supported sports organisation. To this day, I view some of those journalists involved back then with utter disdain and contempt and more recent events have reinforced that view and confirmed the existence of an anti-northern agenda among major sections of the Dublin and Cork based media.

For me, the worst aspect was the effect on Mary and the children. As usual, Mary was completely supportive. The children were mostly old enough to read the papers and understand what was happening. They pretended that everything was all right and that they were not upset but it was obvious that it was just a pretence; they were suffering gravely. Those journalists who engage in this kind of agenda-driven reporting and personal attacks have no interest in the target's family, they don't care. What a despicable shower!

The fact that I had been away when the real problems had occurred was ignored entirely. I knew that I could not use that as an excuse and that I had to accept the public element of any criticism since, in times of difficulty, the President represents the Association, wherever he is, or whatever his level of direct involvement. It was becoming more and more obvious that certain people, including some within the senior echelons of the GAA, were running scared and diverting the blame towards me. Until now, I have never given my side of the story.

I decided that, given the level of personal antipathy, there was no point in raising the issue of my absence when the mistakes, if any, were made. It would have made no difference to the opinions of my detractors anyway. But I was particularly annoyed that I was receiving very little direct support from within sections of the Association structures.

A number of the articles were clearly defamatory. I talked the matter over with members of the family and we decided to take legal action over several ill-informed articles in newspapers owned by the Independent Group and a radio interview. We decided not to sue anyone from a GAA background.

My solicitor recommended a Senior Counsel of considerable repute – he has since progressed to even greater heights, and, on the basis of my experience with him, deservedly so. Within the family, we later decided to add another well-known Senior Counsel to the team, someone who could bring a totally different dimension to the proceedings. I had very little knowledge of the legal profession prior to that – thankfully, I'd never had any need for such support – but, like most other people, I had a somewhat cynical impression to the professionals who provided expert legal advice on complex cases. That episode changed my whole attitude to the legal profession; good lawyers are worth their weight in gold and more, but, as I have learned since, there are some not very nice people at a senior level in that profession, too.

Legal people are, by their nature and instinct, not prone to overstating the strength of one's claim. I talked to the first Counsel, who asked me to prepare a dossier of factual information covering both the sequence of events and the articles to which I had taken exception. When I met him later that same week (in his own home, on a Saturday night!), he was clinical in his evaluation of the content and quite bullish about the outcome of any legal action, whilst warning me of the vagaries of the judicial system and of judicial processes generally.

Afterwards, when we had decided to add the second Senior to the case, my solicitor cleared the way for a two-barrister representation team.

We scheduled a meeting in the Four Courts, for 3.30pm. I arrived on time and both my solicitor and the first Senior Counsel were already present, but there was no sign of the second man. He arrived, a couple of hours late, with his hands in his pockets, in his full legal robes and with not a semblance of a note with him. He moved straight to the case, with barely an apology.

I was annoyed, because I thought that he had done nothing with the documentation which had been forwarded to him; I even suspected that he might not have read it. Consequently, I was gobsmacked when he told me that he could not give me a realistic opinion on the strength of my case because there were ten items of information, which he needed, before he could make a judgment. Then, from memory, he listed the entire ten without hesitation. I was seriously impressed and made a mental note not to underestimate this guy again. We agreed to get the additional information to him within forty-eight hours and to re-convene, at the same time, a week later.

Again he was late, though not by nearly as much. This time, he had no notes either. I wanted to know whether he thought I had a good case.

"I read your file on Friday night and again last night," he started.

"Well," I said, "have I a case?"

"You have a good case – a strong case," he said, "you were clearly defamed."

My relief probably showed. That was, until he continued.

"But that's not the issue," he said.

"Of course that's the issue – the only issue," I retorted. His comment irked me, but by then I knew that he was also very sharp, so I had better remain civil with him.

"No, Peter," he said. "You think it's the issue, but it's not the real issue. I have no doubt that a court would find that you have been defamed but there are two other issues, which you are not taking into account and they are just as important."

"And what are they?" I asked.

"Well, firstly, you could win the case and get derisory damages. You could get £100, or £20 or even £1, which would mean that, technically, you had won, but in the public perception, you would have lost. If you got a South Dublin jury they might find for you and give you very little. You need to take that into account."

There was clearly considerable sense in what he had just said, though it had never occurred to me. But I wanted everything on the table, so I responded: "OK, that's probably a fair assessment. But you said there was a second factor - what was it?"

"That's the real issue," he said, "in a way, it doesn't matter whether you win or not."

"Of course, it bloody matters. How can you say that it doesn't matter? It's the only thing that matters," I retorted, quite sharply. I was exasperated by his comment. By now, my frustration was getting out of hand, but he was in total control.

"You think it's the only thing that matters," he explained, "but it's only incidental to the real issue. It's my assessment that you have been let down by certain people and you must know that."

Obviously, I did, but I had never said so to anyone and I would not have admitted it in public either. I did not reply. I wanted to see where he was going with these comments.

"In my opinion," he continued, "if you go ahead with this case, whether you win it, or lose it, you will have to address the issue of who let you down. Now, if you do that, you'll be running the risk of splitting the Association. Is that a risk you are prepared to take?"

I hesitated. Mentally, I was working out the implications. If he was right – and I was beginning to realise that he probably was – how would I handle this new situation? I needed to think this through carefully. I needed time. But I was not going to get much of it.

"What are you going to do?" he asked. "Are you going to risk a split in the Association, or do you wish to go ahead regardless? It's up to you. I can't make that decision for you."

"I don't know," I answered. "I'd need time to think about it."

I turned to the other Senior Counsel and asked him for his opinion. I was 'playing for time'.

"I never thought of it like that," he said; "But now that [his colleague] has said it, I would have to agree with him. I think he's right. It's certainly a consideration which you cannot afford to ignore."

With hindsight, the proceedings had a sense of unreality. The two Senior Counsels, who were very familiar with each other, were addressing one another as 'Mister', while I was addressing both by their Christian names. It was only later that I realised how incongruous the whole situation was. I have never met either man since, but I was highly impressed by their capacity to absorb information and to get to the kernel of the issue and I am still thankful to both of them. If professionalism means anything, they had it in spades.

The first speaker came back again: "Peter, I'll make you an offer that might help to concentrate your thinking. If you decide to withdraw from this case, in the next fifteen minutes, I'll waive my fees to date. If you decide to proceed, the clock starts now."

I thought about what needed to be done if the Croke Park project was to be accepted within the Association and proceed to a conclusion

– it was already getting very close to a start. I thought about how a prolonged legal battle would affect my credibility in leading the re-building project. I thought about the implications of a split and how close we had been ten years earlier because of a different issue. I thought about the worry associated with a prolonged legal battle and I had no doubt that sections of the media would string the issue out, for as long as possible.

I knew that the same entities would do their damnedest to destroy my reputation – what little of it was still going to be intact after this episode – even if they ceased their animosity towards me, which I was pretty confident they would not. Twenty years later, I discovered that there would have been no such cessation – that particular media stance back then was not driven by fairness or integrity, and nothing much has changed since then. Cowards are like that. Ultimately, I realised only too well that my period in office and my reputation had both already been damaged, either way.

In reality, I could not think clearly. I was angry, confused, feeling besieged and under pressure. Eventually, I decided that I should wave goodbye to any vindication and go ahead to do what I could do best. I said that I would withdraw and both the other Senior Counsel and my solicitor matched the first Counsel's offer. I had to pay the Junior Counsel.

Nearly two decades later, I still have mixed feelings about certain aspects of my decision. I am still not sure that I would not have served the Association better by addressing the staff issue and by suing the media involved; in fact, I'm reasonably sure that I should have taken on both issues.

But it would have made getting support for the Croke Park development much more difficult and might even have temporarily scuppered that project, though, on balance, I think not. Overall, I often think that I probably called it wrong that day. But it no longer matters.

What I learned from the whole episode is that, like the Mounties, the media always get their man. There is no story if there is no scapegoat, and I became the scapegoat – I would not be the last Quinn to fill that role. I also learned that, despite their desire to portray themselves as liberal, fair and anti-establishment, ultimately, journalists will always support the establishment. The establishment will survive any individual and where access to information is crucial, and access to All-Ireland tickets is critical, staying on-side with the establishment makes for an easier life for a journalist. Thirdly, I learned that when one media organ targets an individual, the 'herd instinct' takes over; the target becomes fair game for them all. And finally, I discovered that 'outsiders', including northerners, are especially fair game for the Dublin scribes –just ask John Hume about how he was treated by some of the self-serving organs of right and liberalism, when he dared to consider getting involved in quasi-political affairs in the South!

In my case, the Independent Group got its pound of flesh – big time. They had made their judgement about my political leanings and they did not like what they had concluded, though they had no basis, or evidence, for their judgement. A northern nationalist has no right to his or her opinion if it does not coincide with the 'liberal unionist' view which pervades much of the Independent Group but which, in reality, was and still is far from liberal – in fact, it is extremely 'right wing' and illiberal. We northerners are entitled to any opinion so long as we bow to the superiority of Dublin 4's intelligentsia, even when those smart asses know very little about what they are pontificating on. Clearly the media is always right – what a joke!

In that respect, nothing has changed. Ever since I ceased to be a public figure, I have received only unfavourable press from that source, even when I was working for causes which they claimed to support. That did not cause me any loss of sleep because, if I was receiving praise from that quarter, I would have had to question the validity of what I was doing. Neither has anyone else connected to me, whether directly or indirectly, ever received support or even fairness from that section of our media.

For a long time, I felt that I had been targeted simply because I had annoyed someone in a high place with my interview on RTÉ. But, over time, I began to realise that the real issue was that I was from the

North. I concluded that antipathy to what had been happening there over the previous two decades was reflecting on me personally, despite the fact that I had spent more than three-quarters of that time outside the North.

It was a realisation which was hard to accept. I had been born and reared less than a mile from the border. My neighbours in Ballyconnell, in the rest of West Cavan and most of the rest of County Cavan; those whom I knew in Leitrim and Monaghan, the two counties which were next nearest to where I lived; and those in Donegal, understood what nationalists in the North had been suffering and demonstrated great empathy with our position.

As nationalists, we had always seen our true affinity as being with the Republic rather than with Britain, but we had murdered or injured nobody in support of that aspiration, nor had we driven anyone from his, or her, home. Neither had we fallen out with any of our neighbours of any political persuasion. By far the majority of the Unionist community supported us in business, as they still do, and we continued to maintain strong cross-community economic and social relationships. Our neighbours have always been very important to us and they still are, and those feelings are reciprocated.

It was, therefore, a culture shock (to put it mildly) to realise that we were not wanted in the South – especially in parts of Dublin and in the Dublin media, but in other pockets and population centres of the country, too. A few months after the RDS issue, I experienced the same view at a meeting in north Cork, where I had spent a day visiting local schools and was invited to attend a meeting of the local Board, on a snowy night, when the roads were dangerous. However, by then I had developed an immunity to such attitudes, I still believe that, in most instances, apart from the media, they are minority views.

Some time ago, in his weekly column in *The Irish Times* (Thursday, October 20, 2011) David Adams, who would not have shared many of my aspirations – either cultural or political – though we might share many social and economic views, wrote, a very perceptive piece on the 2011 Presidential election campaign in the Republic.

Under the headline, 'Reality is us northerners are not liked down here', he wrote: "It has become crystal clear during this campaign that people 'down here' don't like us northerners very much ... To the southern mind, we're too abrasive, overly aggressive and, when it suits us, pigheadedly literal (the grating accent doesn't help much, either). And that's not the half of it. Ultimately, we're seen as outsiders – if not quite foreigners – poking our noses into a polity that's none of our business."

Referring to the circumstances which had allowed Mary McAleese to get elected as President of Ireland, he surmised that another northerner would not be acceptable – ever. That is how much things have changed in 14 years – a time, when we had the best President in the history of the State (and I say that as someone who has long been a great admirer of the late Paddy Hillery, also a great President). Adams finished his column by stating, somewhat 'tongue in cheek', that he suspected that Martin McGuinness was probably, "thinking the previously unimaginable – 'Good God, these people make even the unionists seem friendly ...'" and that the Presidential election, "has, in its own fashion, even helped with mutual understanding in Northern Ireland."

I have no doubt that there are many in the South, and a clear majority in the North, who would empathise entirely with the sentiments expressed by David Adams. It obviously applies in major segments of the 'political classes' and of the media, but it goes much wider than that. Equally, I have no doubt that he is right and that such attitudes are neither new, nor unique to a Presidential election. As a nationalist, I find that regrettable, but I have long known that it is a very accurate view of reality. And it applies to a very wide range of areas, including the business world, where attitudes to those from the North and the border counties are entirely different to attitudes towards those who happen to live within 'The Pale'.

Even governmental decisions are influenced by such attitudes, which are particularly prevalent in certain sections of the public service. But at least we northerners are now beginning to understand where we stand in the minds and hearts of many in the Republic, and in a majority of those within 'The Pale'. Unfortunately for me, and for other members of the family, we were too late in coming to a full realisation of that situation, though I had been partly aware of it for some time – not least from my time in Dublin.

But what disappointed me most was the number of GAA journalists who gave the establishment's side of the story without checking the facts. I understand, but do not like, their rationale: I would be gone as President in three years and, therefore, I was dispensable. It would have been easy to be angry, but that would have got me nowhere. Nevertheless, while I tried not to allow it to affect my presidency or my relations with staff during the remainder of those three years (and I think I succeeded to a reasonable extent), I would have to admit to being quite annoyed – then and still – with some of the people involved and by some of the comments made and some of the 'stories' leaked. I will forever be grateful to those, including that minority in the media, who gave me their support during that period.

I received a number of letters – including a death threat which I ignored and mentioned to no one, including Mary – from various sources who knew nothing about the facts, but believed what was written in the papers. I still have those letters. They are among the very few items which I have retained from my time as President and I have no idea why I still keep them. They included one from a former prominent Armagh footballer and another from an equally prominent former Cavan player. To say the least, they were less than supportive and less than well-informed, but full of arrogance, self-righteousness and aggression. Thankfully, I have never met either of those individuals since then and I have no desire to do so; they are not very nice people.

Overall, I was then, and continue to be, annoyed by continuous snide references to me as 'controversial' based on that incident, though I am not surprised by such comments. My view was, and still is, that if others had done what they were mandated and paid to do, there would have been no controversy. I would have expected better from some of the journalists who, prior to that, had represented themselves as friendly towards me. I would certainly have expected better from a paper which had the doyen of Gaelic sports journalists on its staff for so long, in the late, great Paddy Downey. Paddy was one of the best and most respected commentators on the GAA ever, and the best and fairest I have ever read – a man whom I visited a couple of times in the early stages of his illness. And I would have expected better from a minority in RTÉ, at that time, too – though I never lost respect for Seán Óg Ó Ceallachain, who was one of the best GAA men I ever met.

Since then, I have not read anything written by a number of so-called GAA reporters and I have not bought the *Irish Independent* or any of its sister papers in over twenty years. At this point, I would not even welcome a favourable comment from any of them – not that I have a pup's chance of getting one anyway. In my mind, it would simply be worthless.

Nevertheless, I have huge respect for many people in the media. In a way, I have no choice since I have been chairman of six different media businesses at different times, over the past two decades – and lost money on most of them. I believe that the media can, and should, play a very beneficial role in national life. But it should aim to be primarily positive and upbeat, instead of being continuously negative and critical – always whingeing, criticising and complaining. From a variety of perspectives, the media has now become the main determinant of national opinion, attitudes and morale, and its employees clearly relish that role. Given that context, Ireland deserves better from its media.

At the end of my term in office, the BBC commissioned a programme which concentrated on my alleged republican views and how they influenced 'my' decisions on the RDS issue. (For the record, I have never been a member of any party with paramilitary links.) Much of that programme's content was factually inaccurate. They even got a person from England to front it who knew virtually nothing about the GAA and absolutely nothing about how nationalists felt on certain issues. Fortunately, the programme didn't damage my reputation any further. Most people with whom I was in contact at that time, identified that programme as "rubbish" and I would not dissent from that view. Unfortunately, the view applied to much of the other coverage, too.

20

Back to Building

With the RDS saga consigned to the rear-view mirror – at least as far as I was concerned – and my reputation well and truly tarnished, it was time to turn to more real issues. The project to redevelop Croke Park was reaching the 'go/no go' point. The battles with the planners were coming to an end and the design team was well advanced with the finalisation of its proposals and keen to get things moving. It was time for decisions and action.

In reality, there was no option but to proceed with the development. The collapse of Frank Fahy's National Stadium proposal, combined with the rapidly deteriorating condition of Croke Park, dictated that we had to go ahead with the project, provided we could fund it. But could we? Many of our members – possibly a majority – thought not. With Belvedere College having been paid, it was time to turn our minds to matters of money.

Excluding the acquisition, the overall project was structured into four phases, which would be built over fourteen or fifteen years and financed over twenty-plus.

Our first job was to select a contractor and there was no shortage of interested parties. I had to do an assessment of the financial strength of each company which expressed an interest, before we produced our short-list. At least, I knew with certainty that I could get that bit right. We finished up interviewing six companies. All of them had the ability to do the job but in the end we selected Sisk as the main contractor; their submission was both good and competitive, and it turned out to be a good decision. By normal construction standards, they proved easy to work with, though I was not the main contact point (that was Jim Dent, who was appointed as Project Manager), so I never saw the real working relationship, but I was happy enough with progress.

I was also very happy working with the design team. We had weekly meetings to monitor progress at which we sometimes had what might be termed 'robust discussions', but our working relationships survived them. When someone lost his temper it was normally yours truly, but such events were quite rare. On the whole, we worked well together and became good friends but always within the limits that we expected them to deliver according to the demands of the plans and the construction schedule.

None of the GAA staff had any background in either corporate finance or construction, so there was no help available from that quarter. As a result, I was forced to rely heavily on Des McMahon, our outstanding architect, Jim Dent the Project Manager, and Frank Murray our structural engineer, who had a wonderful ability to crystallise what was feasible and what was not. By and large, they made my life easy. My previous experience in construction, and the mistakes which I had made then, helped enormously, too; mistakes are a costly, but very effective, way of learning.

Unfortunately, we hit a few hurdles with some of the more complicated concrete pours in the construction of the roof and, for a time, it looked as if we would miss the construction programme by a considerable margin, but ultimately the project progressed broadly on schedule. Such projects rarely operate entirely to schedule, in my experience.

But the money issue was always the ghost in the background – the shadow overhanging our optimism. For the first phase, we set a budget of IR£37.75 million, to include property acquisitions and fees, as well as building costs. We had just 7.5 per cent of that when we started and needed almost IR£35 million more to be safe. In 1991, when we thought we were in a recession, that was a lot of money and we were going to need high borrowing and major fund-raising.

The first problem was always going to be convincing our members that the project was necessary – the easy part – and then that we could fund it – the difficult part. Clearly, we were going to have to raise a substantial proportion from within the Association. That reality worried many within our membership. Clubs were struggling financially; many, if not most, were losing players to emigration; the economy was performing badly; the people of Ireland were being told by their leaders to 'tighten their belts'. It was not a good time to be begging for money or support.

Those were years when Ireland was exporting 40,000 or 50,000 of its citizens per annum. It is easy to look back and understand why our members were worried but, at the time, we felt that the concerns were being overstated. With hindsight, we were probably far too bullish, or at least I was. It was a much bigger gamble than we realised at the time. But, they say that fortune favours the brave and we were fortunate.

I was particularly fortunate, in that I had an exceptional Management Committee. By its structure, Coiste Bainistí changes almost entirely within the three-year period of any President. A good Management Committee is invaluable to any leader whatever title he, or she, carries; the reality is that in GAA terms, it contributes massively to defining a Presidency. Without naming them, and they know who they are, I have to say that they gave me tremendous support. I was blessed to have such men supporting me as we tackled the biggest project ever undertaken by a sporting organisation in Ireland. Without exception, they were behind me when difficulties arose, as they did – and as they do in every three-year period. They deserve huge credit for what was achieved at that time.

Before we finished the first phase, Jack Boothman had been elected to succeed me, though he was not on Coiste Bainistí during much of that time. There is only one Jack Boothman! He is highly intelligent, direct, gregarious and very popular as well as witty and occasionally irreverent, but with a deceptively astute brain. When major issues are involved, when important decisions have to be taken and when things get serious, he becomes, contrary to his public image, the most serious of committee men. He has a very infectious personality and a great 'feel' for the so-called 'grass-roots' and he was never afraid to ask the difficult questions, which others preferred to avoid. I found him a great help in the latter stages of the first phase of the new stadium.

The pre-sale of tickets for the All-Ireland finals had been used before and a much larger scheme, to be operated on a similar basis, was adopted to start the fund-raising ball rolling. It would be complemented by the pre-sale of the proposed corporate seats, in the new stadium. We offered four tickets to every club, for both the hurling and the football All-Ireland finals for ten years, at a discount of about 30 per cent. We hoped that that would ease some of the concerns.

But before we could test that assumption, we needed to get the support of the county boards and the broad membership of the Association for the redevelopment. Cynics might have argued that the offer of the 'term' tickets to the clubs was designed to swing some of the doubters as we canvassed for that support, and they may well have been right.

It was Des McMahon who first suggested that we should get someone to build a model of what the final stadium would look like and use it in our marketing campaign. If the clubs and the counties could see what the new stadium would look like when it was finished, they might be more receptive to what we were trying to do. It was a brilliant suggestion and achieved precisely what Des had indicated it would. The model seemed expensive at the time but it produced the best value for money of any of our marketing expenditures.

Our first problem was Central Council. I knew very well that there was a strong view among some of the members that this was a high-risk project and that funding it might reduce the availability of funds for physical development within the counties. The latter would be an issue for all the members. Talk of a total cost of between IR£105 million and IR£110 million was seen by many of them as involving a project which was completely beyond anything we could fund. There was also a concern that, if we included corporate facilities, the business and banking sectors would then have control of the stadium and, by implication, of the Association and its value system, too. I had difficulty with that latter leap of logic, but I had to deal with it. The fact that the funding for over 28 per cent of the cost of the first phase would, if our plan worked, be provided through the sale of less than 11 per cent of the seats did not cut much ice with some people.

Once I saw it, I knew that the model would have a positive impact on the members of Ard Comhairle and it did – they were the first to see it, apart from those directly involved in the project. Nevertheless, I needed to make sure that the opposition view did not get early traction, during the debate. At that time, by far the most influential members of Central Council were Seán McCague, Ger McKenna from Kerry and the late Art Nolan from Dublin. Since Dublin was entirely supportive of the project from the outset, the latter was going to be no problem and, as he was then a member of Coiste Bainistí, neither was Seán. So before the meeting started, I made a point of speaking to McKenna.

"Ger," I said, "I need your support for the stadium project, when it comes up for decision on today's agenda."

In his best Kerry accent he replied, "Sure, you know I'm not in favour of it, Peter."

I was not sure whether he was pulling my leg or not, and I still don't know, so I played safe.

"I know you're not," I lied, "but I still need your support."

"I'll not let you down, Quinn," he said. I knew once he said it, that he wouldn't. And he didn't.

When the discussion started I was faced with a few negative comments but, though they were pretty weak, that did not mean that I could simply wish them away. It was clear that there were reservations. For a start, there was a concern that we simply could not afford it and that was a valid concern. But the biggest single issue was a perception that we were building a stadium for the 'big bucks' at the expense of the ordinary members. It was not easy to convince some of those present that we had no intention of reducing the number of tickets for ordinary members and that if we did nothing to improve our facilities, the statutory authorities would reduce access for ordinary members and extra-ordinary ones alike and we would have no say in their decisions.

Then McCague spoke and supported the project strongly and eloquently, and the mood started to change. But the 'clincher' was when McKenna spoke. He probably started with a couple of words in Latin but, whatever his starting point was, he supported the project and then proposed that Central Council should support the Uachtarán and the project, without ever hinting whether he himself had any reservations. With the strength of their support, the motion sailed through and we had entered the stadium redevelopment business for real. To this day, I am indebted to Ger McKenna for his support on that occasion and at other times, too. He is an exceptional man. For him, the Association always came first and he remains one of the best GAA men I ever met.

We then scheduled a series of meetings with our clubs, around the country. First was the launch in Dublin, in Croke Park, where representatives from Louth, Meath, Kildare and Wicklow were also invited. The model created a great impact, as it did subsequently at all the other meetings. I made the pitch and the response was generally, but not exclusively, positive. Nevertheless, it was better and easier than I had anticipated and I was becoming very upbeat about it all. I had finished taking questions and was about to wind up proceedings, when I was interrupted by a lady, whom I did not recognise, but who proceeded to criticise the proposed project and then to lambast me personally for the lack of consultation with local residents, the almost certain reduction in the value of local properties and the overall disruption to local people from the games there, with significantly increased attendances and higher noise levels.

Liam kept nudging me and telling me not to lose my temper. I was probably becoming annoyed and I have never been very good at hiding my annoyance. I was particularly upset at the fact that she claimed that the local residents had not been consulted or kept informed about the project. We'd made arrangements for such consultations, both during the planning process and subsequently. I had no idea whether much, or indeed if any, contact had been made since I was not personally involved, and I still have no idea. But obviously, it either hadn't happened or certainly had not been done to the satisfaction of the local residents. To quote a famous British lady, I was not amused!

We subsequently set up further arrangements for keeping local residents fully informed and also for employing local people. As we made greater efforts to meet their needs, relationships between the Association and the residents improved greatly. Although I was not involved in any of those meetings, I can say with certainty that the residents were generally agreeable people. It was clear that they were genuinely worried about what the project was going to mean for them and that such uncertainty was our fault. They were right and we should not have allowed such uncertainty to fester.

After that, we set off around the country, armed with our model and a new-found conviction that we would get a very positive hearing. Our first meeting was in Mullingar, for the Midland counties. To use a Fermanagh phrase, we were in for a 'gunk'. Some of the reception was less than positive: there was no need for such a project; we could never fund it; we should refurbish what we had; it would take money from the clubs and the counties; the 'big bucks' would control it; I had lost the run of myself and was biting off more than the Association could chew.

Nobody actually told me that I was mad, but it was clearly implied.

The RDS saga had clearly damaged my reputation and the ordinary members' confidence in me as their leader, and I was not going to be allowed to forget it.

I'd just returned from an overseas assignment in the Far East a day earlier and was both tired and tetchy, at least partly from jet lag. On that night, it showed. I did not quite lose my temper but I was not as diplomatic as I could and should have been, especially with one particular member who was fully entitled to her opinion, but who received short shrift from me. I handled that meeting particularly badly and came away not knowing whether those present would support the project or not, though, on balance, I felt that a majority was opposed. In the event, when we subsequently started to sell the term tickets, that was one of only two areas of the country where support, as reflected in ticket purchases, was particularly poor. Almost certainly, my performance on the night contributed to that outcome. Instead of acting as a motivator, I had de-motivated them.

After that we moved to Ulster. The support in both Enniskillen and Armagh was tremendous – more than 95 per cent in both places – and I cannot remember any real opposition. People who had been dealing with other, more serious, problems for more than two decades were energised by the prospect of a new, state-of-the-art stadium, which would put down a marker for the GAA and, by implication, for nationalist Ireland. I left both those venues with absolutely no doubt in my mind that I had the almost unanimous support of my own province, at least. Adding the support from Dublin and the surrounding counties put a positive complexion on progress.

The meeting in the south-east of the country was the most interesting. By then I knew the issues and objections, the pros and the cons, and I could respond to most of them. My memory of that night is of something of the order of a 60-20-20 split. Almost two-thirds were fully supportive. Less than a quarter, led by a senior officer from one county, was adamantly opposed. The same arguments were advanced, but more forcefully.

But, by that point, I was beginning to realise that the objections were based on real concerns about, and fears for, the future of the Association. It was not 'opposition for opposition's sake'. These were ordinary members of the Association who were worried about the future of their Association and concerned that someone from a business background was leading it in a direction which was both risky and overly commercial. These were entirely genuine members and their opposition had to be viewed in that context.

Finally, and for the first time in this process, there were a few others who seemed not to care one way or the other – they gave the most powerful display of apathy I encountered during the entire process.

That sense of apathy was reinforced at a poorly attended meeting of the Connacht counties. There, I estimated the split as being more like 40-30-30. Members and former members of Coiste Bainistí were supportive and so, too, were the Leitrim representatives – possibly, the 'neighbour's child' syndrome was a contributory factor. But the overall attitude was one of 'sure, it doesn't matter to us' or 'it doesn't affect us'. Notwithstanding the successes of Galway hurlers a short few years earlier, and Mayo's performance against Cork in a recent All-Ireland football final, morale appeared to be low in that province.

As we headed off to Munster, we were ahead in that we were convinced that more of our members supported the plan than opposed it, but not by as much as I would have liked. I had never said so to any of my colleagues, but I was then at the point where I was beginning to feel that the Munster response was going to make or break the project. I would have been reluctant to proceed with less than 70 per cent support, however strong the imperative created by the deteriorating state of our existing facilities, and, unfortunately, I had no alternative proposal for solving our problem.

The Munster canvas – for the entire process was becoming very like a political campaign – consisted of two meetings on the same day; a Saturday morning in Cork, from which we were due to go directly to Limerick for a session on that same evening. Although I was now feeling a bit of pressure, I was very cool and calm during the Cork meeting. I realised that this was a crucial meeting – probably a make or break meeting.

The support in Cork that morning was up-lifting. Two clubs, some of whose representatives had both northern accents and obviously left-wing views, led the opposition, with the same arguments as we had met earlier in the campaign, but this time they were couched in more overtly political terms. Almost without exception, the others were supportive – in several cases very strongly in support. Frank Murphy, for whom I always had, and still have, great respect (even when I disagree with him, which occasionally I do) had clearly done his homework – but then Frank always does his homework. The debate was well argued and the meeting lasted until into the early afternoon, but it was well worth it. We finished with a very clear and very strong endorsement, from the best-attended meeting of them all. I set off for Limerick in a very positive frame of mind. In effect, Cork had clinched it for us.

That day's weather was awful with non-stop rain and wind. Roads were flooded, trees were down and diversions occurred every few miles. We arrived in Limerick much later than we had planned so it was literally out of the car, up the steps and straight on to the stage to start the meeting.

Micheál Maher, then Chairman of the Munster Council, met us at the top of the steps and welcomed us. He took me aside to let me know that, while he personally supported the project, which I already knew from his support at Coiste Bainistí, the mood in the hall was almost entirely opposed.

"It seems to me that there is not a single supporter of the scheme in that hall," he told me. I was going to be 'up against it', in a big way. At least I knew what was coming.

Because of the weather, it was a poorly attended meeting but, right from the outset, the overall view was both consistently and strongly opposed to the redevelopment – at least as it was being proposed. Prior warning, even at relatively short notice, is a great asset in such circumstances. I'd had just enough time to steel myself for defending our proposal. One man was particularly articulate and he was best prepared of those who opposed the development. His arguments were logical, well presented and had considerable merit but we had already evaluated most of the issues he raised before we had made our decision, and had concluded that the balance of advantage rested with going ahead with the project.

I set out our stall forcefully, but not too aggressively – Mullingar had demonstrated the undesirability of that latter element of my previous approach. I explained the alternatives, or, more precisely, the absence of alternatives. I argued the advantages of the proposed funding package and asked the members present to look at what we could have and to compare it with what we then had. I described how we proposed to undertake the development in four phases, over a period of about fifteen years, and how we would pay for it over twenty-five, or more, years. I assured them that we would not be proposing the entire scheme if we were not sure that it was in the best long-term interest of the Association.

Before we ended the meeting, I asked for the conventional 'show of hands' to indicate support or opposition. In light of what had been said earlier, it was a surprise – a very pleasant surprise – that, although not everyone indicated their support, not a single person indicated outright opposition. That was a real vote of confidence.

We had a mandate – not a unanimous mandate but an acceptable one. By my estimate we were being supported by well over my target of 70 per cent of the county and club officers. Though I had no idea what the generality of the membership was thinking, my expectation was that it would not be too different from the club and county figures.

And then, out of left field, as the Americans would say, I encountered another problem with further potential to make my period in office memorable for all the wrong reasons.

Our contract with RTÉ had expired and was due for renewal. I had only once been involved in negotiations relating to the media sector prior to that, when we negotiated a deal for the Ulster Championship with BBC Northern Ireland. We had wanted that deal primarily for promotional purposes so, in those negotiations, the value of the cash was less important than the value of the exposure. That did not apply to the RTÉ contract, since its value was already well established. Nevertheless, I had only a layman's idea of the value of the coverage to the national broadcaster.

At that point, my relationship with RTÉ's Head of Sport was not great. Negotiations are always easier when the chemistry between the two sides, and especially between the two team leaders, is good. Our negotiations reflected that. We finished in entrenched positions and neither of us was prepared to concede. Congress was fast approaching and we needed a result before then, but no agreement was forthcoming. I spent much of the week prior to Congress, steeling myself for the apparently inevitable announcement that our senior inter-county competition would not be covered on television for that year and the first game was only three or four weeks away. I needed such a problem like a hole in the head, but there seemed to be no prospect of a resolution.

On the Friday morning, with Congress due to start that evening, I received a call from the office of RTÉ's Director General, Joe Barry, asking if he could meet me before lunch. I had met Joe, a proud Corkman and a staunch supporter of Cork hurling, several times previously and we had developed a good, friendly relationship. I made the GAA's position clear and he explained the RTÉ position.

This time the chemistry was right. We both moved a bit, then a bit further and, within about three-quarters of an hour, we had a deal. I have no idea whether Joe was relieved but I certainly was and, to cap it all, I had the very pleasant task of presenting the Sam Maguire Cup to Anthony Molloy later that year, in front of the RTÉ cameras. It would have been some disaster if Donegal's victory had not been covered by television – I would have had to emigrate!

Because of all the time invested in getting the green light from the membership, and sorting out all the other issues, the whole issue of funding had been receiving less attention than it deserved. I eventually signed off on the contract and then set about finalising the funding arrangements. I accept that this was the wrong sequence, but that was how we did it.

The corporate boxes and the premium seats were going to be crucial to the overall funding of the stadium and I had already signed a contract, which included almost 2,500 corporate seats in the first phase – the Cusack Stand. Then we got a shock. The company which was charged with selling the corporate facilities told us that their research indicated that there was a market for only 500 premium seats, altogether – possibly 600-750, if the commission rate was increased. Why the hell had I signed off on a contract, based on a design involving

2,450 seats, in the first phase alone?

I was not happy. I was particularly unhappy that we had not been alerted to this until after the contract had been agreed. But I simply did not really believe the research. Even if I was disposed to believing it, I could not afford to accept that the reported numbers were an accurate reflection of the size of the market.

Having previously been in consultancy myself, I knew precisely what to do when a professional produces the 'wrong answer' – get another consultant to produce a different answer.

A new company came back with higher figures: 1,000-1200, but not more than 1,300-1,500. There were two more phases to come, with the same design, which would mean we'd have over 6,500 seats. Now we were being told that we there would only be demand for a maximum of 1,500 sales – a potential market for less than 25 per cent of the proposed capacity.

Liam and I had a meeting. I told him that I disagreed with the figures and had no faith in marketing but that I believed, totally, in salesmanship and selling. Now, where could we get someone who could sell? Liam suggested that I should approach Pat Molloy, then Chief Executive of Bank of Ireland (and now, its Chairman), to see if he would be in a position to offer us someone who could do the job – sell 2,450 immediately and 6,500 in total – not 500, or 1,500. Possibly, Liam suggested, he would give us Dermot Power, who was then administering the GAA All Stars.

"Call Pat," I said.

Liam made the call and put me on the line. I asked if I could meet him as soon as possible. We were in his office within half an hour, and I put my request to him.

"Have you anyone in mind?" he asked.

"We were thinking that Dermot Power might do it, if you would make him available," I answered, with no great confidence.

"Well, if you think he is the right man and that he could do it, we can work out some mutually agreeable arrangement," he responded. I was looking for some indication, from his demeanour or his body language, as to whether he thought Dermot could do the job, but Pat was too shrewd to let his personal views on a member of his staff be known to any outsider. We agreed to take Dermot.

Within a couple of weeks, arrangements had been agreed with both the bank and Dermot (Dee), though none of us had any idea as to whether he was a good choice, or not. Still, he was all we had.

In later years, I did not always agree with Dee. We've had different views on how the Association should be managed, but we never fell out. He became very close to Liam when I felt that he should have been 'his own man' to a much greater extent. But, ultimately, I have to say fair play to him! He sold the lot in about eleven months and got the money in. It was an outstanding performance; he gave it everything he had and he made it work. I have never forgotten his contribution to the 'new' Croke Park, nor will I – it was a massive achievement and I will always feel indebted to him. And so should our Association.

By the time the stadium was completed and we had finished selling the premium tickets, there was a growing waiting list for them. In later years, the Association has had to increase the prices significantly in order to reduce the demand because virtually everyone who had that sort of ticket renewed the agreement at the end of the ten years. Neither have I ever forgotten the market research: Ultimately, it was proven wrong but only after a lot of time, effort, our money and probably a small copse too was expended on it.

In the meantime, there were large numbers of volunteers, right across the country and beyond, trying to sell the term tickets to the clubs. We had discovered that some clubs were not interested in buying them, or could not afford to buy them, so we agreed to allow individual members of those clubs who could afford them to make the purchase, provided the club itself was satisfied with the bona fides of the alternative purchaser – i.e. that he or she was a club member and was buying the ticket(s) for his or her own use and not for selling at a profit on the big days.

In some parts of the country, the term ticket scheme was a resounding success, but there were areas where its success was limited. The North and the Greater Dublin area were, by far, the most enthusiastic supporters of that scheme, with demand far outstripping supply in both of those areas. We had allocated 4,000 tickets for it, but the final number was well above that.

My most vivid memory of that part of the campaign is of arriving in Croke Park one morning with over IR£121,000, in a combination of cash and personal cheques, for term tickets. Most of it had been collected for me by a business and personal friend who was a former inter-county player. He had decided to make his personal contribution to ensuring the success of the scheme and of the overall funding of the project. I was the most relieved man in Dublin when I handed over the bag containing the money to a member of staff; I had been worried that someone might find out that I was carrying a large amount of cash and would decide to take a share of the action. There is a lot of selling in £121,000+, at £800/£1,100 per ticket, around the shores of Lough Neagh and in Fermanagh. Well done to that man.

Equally good was the day I received a phone call from a financial institution, to ask if I could call to its head office to collect a cheque for a combination of premium tickets and corporate boxes. I had no idea of how much they had purchased, but I arrived back with a cheque which was just short of IR£1,000,000. While I was absolutely delighted with it, there was just a tinge of disappointment that the extra bit was missing – it would have been wonderful to bring back a cheque with a seven-figure amount on it. I'd never seen such a cheque at that point in my life.

In the meantime, we'd started meeting regularly at 8am on Tuesdays to move the construction side of the project forward. Like Topsy, attendances at the meetings seemed to grow and grow. While I could see the professional fees increasing by the minute, we managed to restrict the meetings to no more than two hours maximum. Any longer would have driven me to distraction, because I had to be on the road just after 5am for those meetings while others could leave at 7am.

My abiding memories of those meetings are mixed. There was a clear atmosphere of excitement, of doing something new and interesting, progressive, and at the same time somewhat risky. Overall, we felt we were doing something which would make a difference to the future of the GAA and that feeling of euphoria lasted until Phase 1 was completed.

But there were worries, too. There was an unspoken concern that something might go wrong and we would all be made to look like idiots – and I was very conscious of who would become the scapegoat, though I lost no sleep over it. There was an appreciation that only a small proportion of the people of Ireland were in any way interested in what we were doing and that was confirmed by the extremely high level of criticism when the then Taoiseach, Albert Reynolds, and his Minister for Finance, Bertie Aherne, approved a grant of IR£5 million for the first phase of the project. There were the usual inter-professional tensions associated with most projects of this kind, and a need for me, as President and chairman of those meetings, to keep such tensions from boiling over. There were lingering concerns about the Y-frame and its validity as a structure; we were convinced, and yet...? As with all such projects, there was a need for constant monitoring of progress against the construction schedule. And there were still massive concerns about the finances: whether there were going to be cost over-runs, or indeed, if some had already occurred; whether the funding could be raised within the time-frame agreed with the banks; and what effects such a project would have on the future allocations of funding for other essential projects.

But most of all, I remember the palpable sense of achievement as the project progressed. And then I remember Liam and his penchant for recording everything that was said, but saying very little in the exchanges – though, in fairness, he would always intervene to calm things, if issues ever became heated.

Liam was, and is, a very complex man. When he is relaxed, he is very good company, witty and entertaining, with a huge store of anecdotes which make any social conversation with him a most enjoyable experience. He also has a good brain, though his approach is often more academic than practical – at least, in my opinion. At times, he would come up with something totally unexpected and innovative, often containing the undeveloped germ of an idea, which might be well worth pursuing. On other occasions, he can be distant, acerbic, and annoyingly sarcastic. His is a very complex personality.

For the most part, he and I got along well and, on most issues, I found him entirely supportive. But our relationship never progressed to the sort of friendship which had applied to his relationship with Paddy McFlynn or, later, with Jack Boothman. But then Jack is a completely different character from me.

In my mind, Liam – a former teacher – was an administrator rather than a manager and I felt some of his greatest strengths were not utilised in running an organisation like the GAA.

In general, I believe that a background in the public sector is not ideal for managing multi-million Euro businesses. Such a background – and there are always exceptions to any such rule – can lead to a tendency towards bureaucracy and defensiveness, a tolerance of inefficiency and low productivity, and an inability to take criticism. Civil servants, especially teachers, throughout Ireland have made an outstanding contribution to the growth and development of the GAA. Without them, we would be nowhere near as strong as we are at present and some of our greatest Presidents have come from that background. In my view, teachers are especially well equipped for roles like the Presidential role. However, the role of President is very different from that of Ard Stiurthóir, or Chief Executive. It requires very different skills – skills which, I believe, are best honed in environments other than in the public sector.

I liked Liam as a person, and I still do, and his three children are fine young people – well-mannered, intelligent and friendly. Later, I had huge sympathy for him, his wife, his sons and Daráinne herself, when Daráinne suffered meningitis and lost the use of some of her limbs. From my own family's experiences with Miriam, I fully understood the pressures of such an event. Thankfully, Daráinne has shown tremendous courage, has recovered remarkably well and has made a successful career for herself. She is a lovely person and deserves all the success which comes her way.

As I suspect he was with all the other Presidents who served with him, Liam was always supportive of me in that role. What most people wouldn't have known, as I did, was that Liam was persistently being undermined in his role and that greatly complicated things. Nevertheless, there was a persistent ambivalence to our relationship which would have been better avoided. Whether it arose because of individual issues, or because of our very different personalities, I don't know and it is no longer relevant. But it existed and I would accept that part of it, possibly most of it, was attributable to me.

I developed reasonably good relationships with most of the other staff, too. Almost without exception, they were totally committed to the Association, so that their work coincided with their main interest, which is always a good starting point for any voluntary organisation.

I considered the female staff to be very efficient and to portray a good image for the Association, and I had particular sympathy for those members of the female staff who were regularly interacting with the public. I could not believe the abuse which the receptionists, as well as Joan Cooney and Siobhan Brady, all of whom were in regular contact with the public, had to take from irate and bad-mannered callers, most of whom were our own members. Occasionally, it was outrageous and contemptible, but they handled it well though they shouldn't have had to handle it at all.

In the preceding three years, I had worked closely with Pat Daly and found him to be an exceptionally productive employee. In my years since then, I have never changed my view on that issue. He has a vision for our games and he has the persistence to make things happen, even if he might ruffle a few feathers in the process – but who am I to complain about that! He is a huge asset to the Association.

*****

Virtually from the outset, the project moved ahead on schedule. Occasionally, Jim Dent would ring me asking me to approve some item of expenditure, which had not been budgeted. My response was always the same: "Jim, ring me back as soon as you can, to let me know where you will save that amount elsewhere in the project and then I will approve your additional item." He never failed to find a saving somewhere and our relationship was consistently positive. Jim's background was in rugby, but he was a professional and he treated the Cusack Stand part of the redevelopment programme as if it was his own. It was a pleasure to work with him.

Before we had reached the half way stage of the Cusack side, it became clear that we would not be in a position to undertake the redevelopment of the Hogan side unless we acquired more property. There was a factory beside the bridge on Jones' Road and it was certain to create major access and construction problems on that side. Indeed, it would have created problems for the development of the Canal End before then, since it would impede access for the lorry traffic. We needed to buy it.

An intermediary was mandated to talk to the owners about selling the property to us and relocating. As it happened, they were already considering a move out to a custom-built property which would involve significant relocation costs. The intermediary's first offer was rejected – it was far too low. I was annoyed by the offer as I felt that it had the potential to derail any real negotiations. So, I decided to take matters into my own hands.

I contacted the late Ciarán Ó Neill, then one of the most senior members of staff, and asked him if he could arrange a meeting between the owners and me – preferably for later that day. The business was owned by a father-son partnership, both of whom I discovered were very commercial, but also very friendly and reasonable.

The younger of the partners agreed to meet, early that afternoon. I wasted very little time on small talk and moved to the reason for my visit fairly promptly. He told me his asking price; it was higher than I had expected, but it was not outlandish. There was potential for a deal. I bid him a bit more than twice our initial offer but there was still a significant gap to be bridged. He reduced his demand slightly but enough to give me more hope of a reasonable deal. Eventually, he told me that he could not finalise a deal without consulting with his father. We agreed that I would return a week later, on a day when the older man would be available. When we reconvened, the gap was still significant but it was now clear to me that a deal could be done. We haggled for a bit and I made a 'final' offer. A cup of tea, some small talk, a little bit of movement on both sides and we had a deal. Although I have never met either of them since, I would have to say that they were two very honourable men.

I was delighted with myself as I walked back the fifty or so yards to the office. Ciarán was first to meet me and asked how I had fared. I told him that I had done a deal, asked him to get our solicitors to sort out the paperwork and told him to organise the money to pay for it. When I told him the price, he was not impressed – putting it mildly! He thought I had paid far too much – shades of the Belvedere negotiations of a few years earlier. I knew that I hadn't, so I just ignored the implied criticism. I was very well aware that I had got good value; if we had waited to buy it a few years later, it would probably have cost us multiples of what I had agreed. Essentially, it would then have been identified as a 'ransom strip' and it could, and almost certainly would, have cost us many millions more. I had been there before, in business deals, and learned the consequences of timidity in such circumstances. It was, in my opinion, one of the best deals I ever did and I had no problem in having it ratified at the subsequent meeting of Coiste Bainistí.

*****

In my three years, I visited every one of the thirty-two counties, most of them several times, and I attended functions in several parts of Britain and the United States. I visited either all, or most of, the schools in a number of counties and I attended innumerable dinner dances, presentations and other functions all over the country. By and large, I enjoyed them, though leaving a function at 1.30am or even an hour later than that – in one case, it was just after 4.30am – to drive a couple of hundred miles back to Fermanagh, on my own, was not exactly my idea of fun. As a consequence, I feel very strongly that, if a President is expected to do such things, he should have access to both a car and a driver. I was not supplied with a car, never mind a driver, though I understand that, now, the President gets a car, as well as a whole lot of other benefits, which were not available in my time.

I also represented the Association at a number of international conferences, speaking on issues such as 'The Role of Sport in a Divided Society'. That one, under a variety of different titles, was especially common and sometimes quite challenging. I spoke on that broad subject in a variety of places, and was once attacked by a Dutchman about the ban on the security forces at a conference in Belgium! I never discovered who prompted him, but he probably had a friend somewhere in the Independent Group. I also delivered talks on issues such as 'Minority/Indigenous Sports in Europe', 'The Role of Sport in Society' and other similar topics.

Many of the dinner dances and presentations were memorable for one reason or another. One such was the presentation of the All-Ireland Under-21 Hurling medals to a Waterford team, captained by Tony Browne, with players like Fergal Hartley, a young Paul Flynn (still a minor) and a number of others who went on to play for the county at senior level. The sheer joy of that event could never be replicated by any of the counties to whom success comes more regularly.

Another was a major celebration by the St John's Club in West Belfast at a time when celebrations in West Belfast were rare. On that night they proved that, Troubles or not, those from the Whiterock Road and their friends knew how to enjoy a good night out.

But probably the most memorable of all was the Centenary Dinner of Mullahoran Dreadnoughts in south Cavan. There was a most unusual backdrop to that one. One afternoon, a couple of weeks earlier, I was returning from a meeting of the design team in Croke Park. At that time, Aghalane Bridge near Belturbet, one of the boundaries of my own club area, had been blown up by loyalists supporters and we had to use the Wattlebridge road from Newtownbutler to Butlersbridge, as an alternative route to Dublin, with very substandard roads. There was an army checkpoint about half a mile on the northern side of the border. I arrived at the checkpoint and was asked for my driving licence by a member of the infamous parachute regiment, with his distinctive cap. I was well used to that and well used to being treated 'as an enemy' by the army; that had been going on even before I returned to live in Fermanagh.

I could see the flashes, where they were photocopying my licence. I'm not sure how many flashes I saw, but they finished with multiple copies of my licence but I was well used to that, too. About fifteen minutes later the soldier returned and apologised for the delay, claiming that they were trying to check my identity. I was sceptical about his claim.

Ten or fifteen minutes later he returned, apologised again and disappeared again. I was beginning to lose patience. By about the fourth time and after the best part of an hour, I was fuming. I searched my wallet, where I knew I had the business card of one of the senior security personnel in the Northern Ireland Office, whom I had sometimes used to try and ensure that the Ulster final would not he disrupted by unnecessary checkpoints in Newtownbutler or Lisnaskea, through which much of the Ulster final traffic from the North would pass.

When he eventually returned with my licence, he apologised again and it was obvious that he had been purposely trying my patience.

"It took a while to confirm your identity," he said, with a grin, which gave away his satisfaction at holding me for so long.

"It had nothing to do with checking my identity," I snarled back at him; "You just wanted to see if you could provoke me into doing something rash," I added.

"OK," he retorted. Pulling a notebook and pencil from his breast pocket, he grinned nastily again. "If you wish to make a complaint, I'll take the details," he said.

"If I decide to make a complaint, I'll make to there," I responded, flashing the business card.

He read it and the smart-assed smile vanished immediately. I moved off as quickly as I could – an angry soldier can be dangerous! I decided that for the next month or so I would go round by Ballyconnell, an extra twelve or thirteen miles, until that regiment had left the area.

On the afternoon of the Mullahoran dinner, I was working in Donegal and was a bit later leaving than I had anticipated. Normally, I would have travelled by the mountain road in order to avoid the army checkpoint outside Belleek, but it is a longer route and I opted for the direct route, taking my chances with the army. It was a bad call.

They held me for about twenty minutes which, when added to my delayed start, was putting me under time pressure. When I arrived home, Mary was already dressed, but I needed a shower. By the time we were ready to leave, it was getting close to the time we should have been arriving in South Cavan.

Again, we decided to go via Ballyconnell. When we arrived near the checkpoint, beyond where my mother was still living in our former home, there was a queue about 500 yards long and it was moving slowly. After half an hour, we felt like turning and going some other way, but that could lead to the soldiers shooting if they thought someone was trying to avoid being searched. We sat, and we sat, and then we sat some more.

Eventually, we got through and arrived in Ballyconnell some time after 11pm, having spent almost two hours in the queue. I decided that we should go back home, but Mary insisted that we should continue. They would be expecting us and it would be bad manners to disappoint them, even if all the speeches were over, she said.

It was almost midnight when we arrived. I was met at the door by the then Club Chairman, the late John Brady, of the famous 'Gunner' family, and uncle of Ireland's current outstanding handballer, who holds innumerable national and world titles. The 'Gunner' name became nationally known, through the late Phil, who was full-back on the very successful Cavan teams which won All-Irelands in 1947 in the famous Polo Grounds final, in 1948 against Mayo and in 1952 against Meath, as well as losing the 1949 final to Meath.

"Peter, I'm sorry about this," he said, as he welcomed me.

"It's not your fault," I responded; "I'm to blame. We were late leaving and then we got delayed by the army."

"No," he said, ignoring my apology, "Tynan is nearly finished an interview he is doing with John Dowling. After that, he wants to interview you, and then we'll be ready to start the meal."

What a relief! It was almost 1am by the time the meal started. The late Fr Dan Gallogly and John Wilson (former Tánaiste and a club member) gave brilliant speeches. It was one of the best functions I ever attended – almost worth the hassle from the army, to be there.

As a post-script, about three weeks later, I was again running behind schedule for a Croke Park project meeting in Dublin and decided that the regiment which included my friend from the prolonged hold-up would almost certainly have gone, so I could go back via Wattlebridge. I came round the corner before the checkpoint and immediately recognised the man on duty. This will take a while, I thought, and I'm already late.

As I was pulling up, with the window down, my friend clearly recognised me, too.

Removing the barrier, he smiled down at me and, in his most polite voice, said: "Good morning, Mr Quinn … go ahead." In this world, you never can tell what will happen next!

* * * * *

Phase 1 was virtually completed by the time my term of office ended. As usual in such projects, the finishing of the contract took much longer than anyone expected. By then, Jack Boothman had been elected to succeed me and he had sat on Coiste Bainistí throughout my final year.

In almost every way, Jack and I were, and are, different. We have very different personalities and backgrounds, which I would describe in the following terms though Jack might, or might not, agree. He is gregarious – I am relatively private and not always at ease with people I do not know; he is instinctive and intuitive – I am analytical and commercial; he is a people person – I am a numbers man; his background is Protestant, rugby school and pro-establishment – mine is Catholic, Gaelic, nationalist/republican and anti-establishment; Jack likes a drink with the lads – I am a teetotaller and rarely socialise in a pub; he comes from a background of relatively well-off farming – I come from a small farmer background. In so many ways, we are absolutely poles apart but, when it involves the GAA, our views are normally very similar.

Towards the end of my term, major changes were occurring in Irish political life. After a quarter of a century of sustained conflict in the North, there was the possibility of some form of resolution or, at least, a reduction in violence. Albert Reynolds, in his role as Taoiseach and leader of a coalition government, developed a promising relationship with the British Prime Minister, John Major which led to the Downing Street Declaration, of December 1993.

Reynolds continued to promote a Peace Process in the North and enlisted the support of John Hume and Gerry Adams. For all three of them this was a risky initiative. John Hume had to bury long-held ideals in the interest of his country; it is said that some of the senior members of the Reynolds cabinet did not support him or the initiative; and Gerry Adams did not have the support of many in the Republican community for his involvement.

That was the political context in which Jack Boothman acceded to the Presidency of the GAA. It would be entirely wrong to evaluate Jack's election to that position in either political or religious terms only. Quite simply, he was elected because he was the best man for the job at that time. He deserved to be elected on that basis and on that basis only, and any other assumption would be entirely unfair to him. He had given me a tough contest three years earlier and was very popular with the membership, as indeed he still is. Jack's ability to communicate with the ordinary member of the Association was unrivalled. His family was immersed in the games and the Association: his son was on the Wicklow senior football panel and he had been a very good Chairman of the Leinster Council. He had the necessary pedigree and I was delighted with his election.

Nevertheless, even if it was entirely coincidental, the fact is that, if ever there was a time when the election of a man with Jack Boothman's background was in the best interests of the GAA, it was then. His election reflected the dynamic of the changes which were occurring in the North and had immense symbolism for the GAA, nationally and internationally. I have always been appreciative of the symbolism of having Jack as our leader for those three years.

In the event, he was to lead the Association very well over his period in office. In his first year, he had the honour of presiding over the official opening of the 'new' Cusack Stand. When it opened, the borrowing negotiated at the outset had been almost entirely eliminated and the Association was in a position where it could, if it so wished, proceed to the next phase well ahead of the original schedule. The final outcome in cost terms was also very favourable: the original budget, inclusive of property purchases, was almost IR£38 million but the actual expenditure was more than IR£½ million below that figure. That gave me considerable satisfaction because I had gone to great lengths to control costs in such a way as to avoid breaching the budget. I was very conscious that the Association had a poor record in that respect on many of its other projects.

Before I completed my term, there was one final issue to resolve – how the new Croke Park would be managed. Despite some trenchant opposition from within the organisation at both staff and Central Council level, we decided that the new stadium and, by implication, the subsequent phases of the redevelopment programme would be managed by a new appointee, who would be called the Stadium Manager. He, or she, would have their own staff which would operate independently of the Ard Comhairle staff.

The main reporting structure would be to a Stadium Executive, which would be selected for its members' business expertise, but would include some representatives from within the Association's main structures. In GAA terms, these were two innovations about which there were serious reservations from a variety of interests. Both were without precedent and both have since proved very effective. Recent changes in the structure of the Association at central level have modified some of them, but the core of the system has continued.

I spent a couple of days doing the interviews and we eventually selected Peter McKenna, who had previously held a senior position in the Smurfit Group. Based on a harsh learning experience, which I had in the late 1970s when I did a similar job for a public utility, I have always conducted interviews for senior positions with a view to establishing how interviewees are likely to react under pressure – as only one of a number of variables. Consequently, those interviews were conducted on quite an aggressive basis. Peter later told me that, as he left the interview, he believed that I was 'a right bastard' – and he was probably right. But we worked very well together on later phases of the project and we continue to be good friends. He has proved to be an excellent appointment.

Equally importantly, the Stadium Executive proved to be a very effective board and has consistently fulfilled its remit to a very high standard and with a high level of initiative and imagination. I believe that we left the new facilities in very good order.

21

There's Nothing so Past as a Past President

For the last six months of my term as President, I had been thinking mainly about life after the Presidency and how I could make up for lost time, in career and business terms. In reality, the period between the All-Ireland finals in September and the change of President in April, following the election of the President-elect, is a fallow one, apart from the Congress which marks the official end of one's term. The outgoing man is winding down, psychologically at least – but motivation starts to decline, too, while the incoming man is beginning to attract all the attention. Had it not been for the stadium project, I would have seen that period as a complete waste of time and energy, but the building programme was still in full operation and there was an imperative to ensure that the project did not over-run the budget. I knew that it was not going to be too far off but I wanted to bring it in under budget.

Nevertheless, I was mentally disengaging from the role for several months before it ended. Several of my predecessors had told me that they had suffered something akin to 'withdrawal symptoms' when their terms had ended. I had no such problems. For me, it might be an exaggeration to say that it was a relief, but it was certainly about moving on to the next phase of my life with no looking back. I can honestly say that I never missed it for a second and I have not missed it since. Neither did the family – they were delighted.

The 1994 Congress was in the Slieve Russell Hotel near Ballyconnell. I would be a liar if I did not acknowledge that there was, for me, a huge emotional significance to that location. The land on which it is located had been bought for me over forty years earlier, sold over twenty years earlier and repurchased less than ten years previously. I had fed cattle there, mowed meadows, lapped and pitched hay, bottled sick animals with all sorts of remedies, operated both horse-drawn and mechanically-driven equipment at different times, and sweated salty perspiration in those fields as a youngster. Sometimes, I had been completely bored with it, other times energised by it, but at all times until we sold it, it was seen as part of me and of my future, if that was what I had decided to do.

I had played imaginary Ulster and All-Ireland finals, won county finals, scored brilliant goals, and turned certain defeat into unbelievable victory, as I worked there. Of course the majority of those dreams had never converted to reality, but all children are entitled to their dreams, even if they are highly unlikely to be realised – that's what being a child is all about. For the only time in my Presidency, I was moved to genuine emotion on that final afternoon. I recalled those dreams and simply wondered why things had not turned out according to plan. But in most ways, I was also relieved. I had done my stint and now it was over. It was time to move on.

While I missed a few meetings of Coiste Bainistí during my year as ex-President as the enthusiasm waned, I still made myself available to Jack whenever he needed me. He used my services on two projects – the negotiation of the GAA's first-ever sponsorship of its football Championship with Bank of Ireland, and acting as chairman of the committee he established to review the Association's rules on 'amateur status'. Both were interesting and both were challenging, but I was always conscious that the final say rested with Jack, not with me. Jack also allowed me to chair the final meetings of the stadium design group, which monitored the redevelopment project and I was very happy to do that.

The negotiations with Bank of Ireland were stimulating. While I had previously been involved in negotiations with broadcasters in the North, sponsorship of the Championship was a totally different issue. I had no real idea of the value of what we were offering and neither did anyone else on our negotiating team. As the negotiations progressed I began to understand that, while the bank had other sponsorships with which to compare our proposal, they were not sure of its value either. It was clear to us that the bank's Regional Directors saw a link with the GAA as being of immense value to their areas of business but it was also clear that those from head office were placing a lower value on such a relationship. Another example of the differences between bureaucratic pen-pushers and those at the sharp end of a business!

In those negotiations, we were at a significant disadvantage in that we were not just sellers, but we were sellers who were under pressure to get a sale. We needed the money for a variety of reasons, not least to support development nationally, as most of our central funds had already been earmarked for supporting the Croke Park development. This time, there were no other buyers at the fair and, in poker terms, we were holding no aces.

From very early in the process, the negotiating variables had been reduced, in that both sides had already agreed on a five-year contract and there were unwritten understandings about some of the details – the broad level of promotional support to be provided by the bank; the number and approximate distribution of advertising hoardings; our commitment to prevent, as far as we could, 'ambush marketing' by the bank's competitors etc. These would all be made explicit in the final contract, but we knew broadly what the bank would be seeking and we were prepared to give them most of what they wanted.

My operating style in such situations where I am not the team leader, has always been to let others make the initial running while I try to assess where everyone stands – though I sometimes get it wrong! – and work out what might be feasible. Rightly or wrongly, in our previous meetings, I had already identified the late Paul Hartnett, Regional Manager for Leinster, (he died only a few months after we finalised the deal but was someone for whom I had a very high regard) as our strongest advocate on the bank team and he had almost equally strong support from John McNamara in the west. At most of the meetings, those two were seated beside one another and almost directly across the table from me.

At what seemed likely to be the final meeting, I saw a note being passed surreptitiously from Paul to John and back again. I suspected that no one else on our team had seen it and I also thought that it was likely to contain some indication of how far the bank was willing to go. My judgement was that the passing of the note indicated that, at least as far as Paul and John were concerned, we were getting close to the bank's breaking point and that a reasonable compromise would seal the deal while an unreasonable demand would probably end negotiations.

No one on our side of the table had much doubt about that meeting's being a make or break event. If those negotiations failed, it was unlikely that there would be another meeting for some considerable time – a year or more most likely, so at least one year's income would be lost. Therefore I decided that it was time to step in with a compromise suggestion. I was familiar with such a scenario from cattle fairs, 30 years earlier. There I had seen men spit on their hands, split the difference and then slap hands in agreement. This time, there was no spitting, but there was agreement. From start to finish, the entire process was completed in about six weeks and without rancour because the 'chemistry' was good.

As we were breaking up to leave, I asked Paul to show me the number written on the piece of paper. In reality, it would make no difference – the deal had already been agreed – but I was curious. He smiled and showed it to me. I had hit on a figure, which was less than 3 per cent below the bank's top line.

By agreement with the bank, we never released the figure, and that resulted in considerable speculation in the press. The suggested figure ranged from less than one million to almost three million for the five-year deal. The late Peadar O'Brien, in his Sunday column, suggested that he had reason to believe that it was about a million and a half. About a year later, he contacted me about something else and, as we were about to finish, he said, almost accusingly:

"You never announced what you got from Bank of Ireland for the sponsorship, Peter."

"Sure, there was no need," I responded, "didn't you tell the nation what it was?"

He chuckled, in Peadar style.

"But was I right?" he asked.

"Well, if you give, or take, 100 per cent, you would have been close," I answered.

There was a silence from the other end of the phone. Clearly he was doing his sums.

"You never got three million," he said with the disbelief dripping from his tone.

"Peadar," I replied, "you can do the sums, yourself. There was more than 100 per cent of your figure in the difference." I still do not know whether he believed me, but I assume that he knew that I had no reason to lie.

Chairing the Amateur Status Committee was a different proposition altogether. We had a very tight agenda and a very tight timescale. The seven-member group included three future Presidents of the Association, Seán McCague, Nicky Brennan and Christy Cooney, as well as a Dublin player, Paddy Moran of Whitehall Colmcille, who won an All-Ireland in 1995.

Looking back from where we are now, the conclusions from that review, of almost two decades ago, might appear almost antediluvian. But it must be remembered that, until then, the Association had been purportedly entirely amateur, apart from paid administrative staff. However, even then, there were suggestions that managers of county teams, in particular, were being paid and it subsequently transpired that so too were some club managers. But I also discovered that some of the claims being made at that time were absolute rubbish. Indeed, right up to the present day the sums being quoted by some people are so far away from reality that they are ridiculous. No 'county' through any mechanism, whether overt or covert, could or does pay some of the amounts being quoted. Many managers are now being paid, but simply not as much as some reports would suggest.

I had always been, and still am, an unequivocal supporter of the amateur ethos of the GAA. In fact, when I became President, the holder of that post was entitled (on what basis, I'm not sure, but I assume it was precedent) to a mileage rate of 5p per mile more than was being paid to the members of Central Council, who were, at that time, getting 25p. I refused to take the extra 5p on the basis that, whatever the rate for Central Council was, it should be the rate for everyone.

Without rehearsing all the arguments or even the individual conclusions, that Amateur Status committee's proposals were influenced by the changed and changing society in Ireland and, in that context, its conclusions were both obvious and necessary.

Firstly, it explicitly identified 'pay for play' as a potentially serious threat to the future of the Association, but acknowledged that better treatment of players, short of payment for playing, was rapidly becoming more and more essential. We argued strongly against semi-professionalism, though I think we all realised that we had already entered the era of 'shamateurism' in relation to managers. We felt it would be impossible to turn that clock back but we could impede its progress. Within our conclusions there was an explicit acceptance that the GAA was as much a communal organisation as a sporting one.

Secondly, it concluded that the ban on players' undertaking product endorsements or other promotions was out-dated and should be removed. A number of factors demanded such action viz.: the Association's own acceptance of sponsorship some time earlier; the changing economic, social and sporting environment in Ireland; the increasing profile of GAA inter-county players and the value of those profiles in commercial terms; the Association's investments in improving its facilities and the potential to harness those assets in generating revenues; and the continuing growth in attendances and gate receipts.

There was a very strong lobby that any revenue from endorsements and promotions should be divided between the player involved and the rest of the team panel – and the report contained proposals to that effect. Personally, I considered any such division to be both unrealistic and ill advised, in that it would inevitably lead to violations of the rules and to further accusations of 'shamateurism'. However, the view from a small majority of the other members was so strong that their suggestion was included as a recommendation, but with no corresponding proposal on how it should be monitored or on penalties for any violation.

Thirdly and most importantly, it recommended significant improvements in the expenses paid to players and in their general treatment, both for training sessions and on match days, including the provision of better equipment and better facilities. That also involved better and quicker access to medical support and more prompt payment of expenses. Those improvements were introduced gradually over the following years. While they have resulted in increased costs of running county teams and consequent funding problems for some county boards, they were and are essential.

Implicitly, it concluded that evidence of payments to managers was impossible to uncover, since most such payments were being funded outside the normal Association structures and would be difficult to control. Our recommendations under that heading were no more than pious platitudes, which could never be enforced, and we knew that.

Given developments and changes in the interim, none of those conclusions was earth-shattering. Nevertheless, many of the specific proposals were strongly opposed at the special Congress which dealt with the report. That opposition applied particularly to the proposed increase in travel expenses for players and the increased investment in equipment and facilities, both of which had implications for the viability of county boards. In the end, most of our concrete proposals were accepted.

The second phase of the redevelopment – the building of the new

Canal End – did not commence until three years after the completion of Phase 1 and I was not involved in it.

Later, Seán McCague asked me to become involved in Phase 3 – the Hogan Stand side – as Chairman of the Project Committee. By that point, Peter McKenna was taking a very active role in the overall redevelopment project and he was a tremendous support. He maintained a sort of informal, parallel, cost record, just as I had done for Phase 1, and it was tremendously useful to me in monitoring cost. For the first six months of that phase, I was having major difficulty in reconciling the data being provided to the Project Committee. In certain fundamental ways, which might have seemed minor to some of the other attendees, but which I considered to be major, the reporting system was significantly different from that used in Phase 1. I was confused by the reporting and assessment of performance against budget and the treatment of 'extras'. I had been satisfied with the systems used in the previous phase, but not with the changes since then, though no one else seemed to notice despite the fact they had significant funding implications.

Of the three phases for which I had some responsibility, Phase 3 was, by far, the most difficult to manage, though it should have been the easiest since the main construction problems had all been addressed in the two prior phases. But much of management is about interpersonal relationships and the confidence which one person has in another. In this case my relationships with, and confidence in, some of the advisors were not as strong as they might have been. I found this phase of the project very trying and was immensely disappointed that the savings on budget, which should have been possible, were not going to be achieved.

Fortunately, Seán McCague negotiated additional financial support from the Government, which left our borrowing position in a much healthier state than we could reasonably have expected. It was a marvellous piece of negotiation by Seán and a huge credit to both the man's personal standing and his negotiating skills.

By that point, the new facilities were being very well received by the corporate sector and, with the additional government grant, our finances were in good shape, too. Consequently, as we approached the end of Phase 3, we concluded that we should proceed directly to Phase 4 – the redevelopment of the northern end, including the iconic Hill 16 which is so beloved by Dublin's staunch supporters. The Dubs create an atmosphere there, which is not reproduced in any stand, in any stadium, in any sport, in Europe; they are wonderful supporters.

Our recommendation was based primarily on the potential for cost savings, which we had assessed as being significant, by avoiding further preliminary expenditures. Despite that, there was opposition, with by far the strongest opposition emanating from within sections of the staff attached to Central Council. I have never understood the real basis for that opposition, but obviously there were those who wished to defer completion for probably several years.

Seán Kelly, by then the President, asked me to make a presentation to Coiste Bainistí on our proposal. Before we made that presentation, David Mackey (who was then Chairman of the Stadium Executive) and I were alerted to the fact that certain staff and some others were adamantly opposed to our proposal. However, the presentation seemed to be well accepted and Coiste Bainistí agreed to refer it to Central Council. Far more important than any immediate reaction, was the fact that it gave us a clear insight into the issues, which might be used against us at the following day's meeting of Ard Comhairle.

A day later, I again made the presentation. But overnight, I had changed it to address the opposing views which we had heard on the previous evening and, again, the reaction was positive. Seán Kelly made his support for our proposal quite clear – in fact, Seán was consistently supportive of our management of the project. We already had reasonably firm estimates of the cost but we were also evaluating the possibility of having the 'cast' components produced off-site, with the potential for further saving.

Ultimately, I had to promise Council members that total Association borrowing, when Phase 4 would be completed, would not exceed €52 million. I was in a position to make that commitment in the certain knowledge that only the most adverse of circumstances would involve breaching that limit or even getting close to it. In the event, we never came near that level of borrowing, because we saved at least €6 million by sub-contracting part of the work to a company based in Offaly – Banagher Concrete – which had very strong GAA connections and also provided the lowest-cost tender for that element of the work. The rest of that phase of the development was also completed below budget, though only marginally so.

From our point of view, getting the approval of Central Council was a confidence booster and it was hugely satisfying when the press release announcing the green light was written and released. Phase 4 caused far less problems than any of the other three. We had a new team of professionals, which included some of the former team, and it gelled superbly. A number of the new personnel had a strong background in the GAA which helped considerably in a number of ways and eased the pressures on the rest of us.

What none of us had factored into our assessment of the cost of the redevelopment of Croke Park was the fact that, being a phased development, Phase 1 would require further expenditure on up-grading before the overall project was finished. As expectations increased, and as some areas predictably deteriorated as a result of use, there were frequent demands for further investment in some of the 'older' parts of the 'new' stadium. We could afford to make those extra investments, given the savings generated in Phase 4.

Thankfully, Peter McKenna has proved very adept at generating income from these facilities and, after loans had been repaid, funds became available for investment in other aspects of the Association's national activities. Ultimately, that project has proved very successful for the Association, in a wide variety of ways – image, funding, pride and status and the availability of money for other projects being among the most important.

While the GAA was still in the process of completing the redevelopment project, Seán McCague asked me to chair a 'Strategic Review of the Association', which he was planning and which he hoped would chart a future for the Association well into the new millennium. The previous such review had occurred in the late 1960s and was not considered by Congress until 1970, at a special session of Congress, which Malachy Mahon asked me to attend and which was my first experience of Congress.

In 1969, I was a young university lecturer with absolutely no experience of administration within the Association beyond club level. For some reason, I was asked to make a submission to that previous group, which was chaired by the late Pádraig Mac Con Midhe. Pádraig had been President of the Association from 1938 to 1943, serving during the early part of World War 2 when travel was difficult, and he was the last President to have served more than three years in office. That report had been both innovative and controversial in its time.

Chairing the review had the potential to be an exciting and fulfilling venture and I accepted it gladly. McCague had selected a very broadly-based group; Martin Rafferty and Gerry Cloherty, two Galwaymen who had been on the previous commission, several of the group had a background in business, some would later become Association Presidents, and some had a political background. It was an eclectic group which included the four provincial secretaries in Danny Murphy (Ulster), John Prenty (Connacht), Michael Delaney (Leinster) and Donie Nealon (Munster).

It was a pleasure to work with that group which combined wonderful enthusiasm and outstanding commitment. Some of the discussions could be described as 'animated' and one could never have expected the diversity of opinion, which existed within that group. Totally contrary to the view of the Association as being 'of one mind' on all issues, these guys were 'of one mind' on almost no issues! And our deliberations were all the better for that.

The final report was published in early 2002, though its findings were too late for discussion and debate at that year's Annual Congress. I do not propose to describe its outcome in any detail and will restrict my comments to some of the implications.

In preparing the draft report, we decided to create sub-groups to deal with different issues and provide the overall committee with regular reports on progress and an opportunity to discuss any preliminary findings or conclusions. In addition, we had professional inputs from Brendan Watters and Enda Gunnell, as well as from a market research company and other professionals. And the Committee met a range of other interests who gave their insights into the core issues, without any restrictions on the issues they could address.

One consequence was that production of the final version involved very considerable editing in order to give it continuity and a common structure. The sub-groups had reported in a wide variety of formats and I wanted the report to read as a single document, not as a compendium of different inputs, and the level of diversity in presentational formats was amazing. I lost all of the Christmas 2001 and New Year 2002 period in that editing process, and most of the rest of January in proofreading the draft print versions (and the final version still contained errors, including the omission of John Prenty's name from the list of members – renewed apologies, John).

One of the sub-groups dealt with the situation in Dublin and the need to improve the Association's penetration of the Dublin market. That sub-group was chaired by Christy Cooney and central to its conclusions was the need for greater investment in coaching and games development in that city. It also concluded that the future of the Association would be better served by dividing the capital city into two separate units – North Dublin and South Dublin – for GAA purposes, because of the disproportionate scale of its population.

I could see some merit in their suggestion at underage level, but was not convinced of its appropriateness at adult level. In fairness to the sub-group, I think that most of its members saw it primarily as a comment (albeit a provocative comment) which would stimulate debate on how the Association could make greater and faster progress in Dublin, and possibly promote greater attention to, and investment in, the growth and development of our games in that city – which it did.

The overall review group was divided on its merits, largely because we could not get any reasonable 'read' on what Dublin wanted, or would accept, from its senior people. Ultimately, we decided to include the now infamous North and South Dublin proposal in our recommendations. When the report was finally published at the beginning of 2002, that was the recommendation which received virtually all the attention and all the media coverage. Though it wasn't central to the overall thrust of the report, it became central to both the media coverage and the subsequent debate on the report.

The most unfortunate consequence of that distraction was that it diverted attention away from many of the core proposals in the report. They related primarily to the need to strengthen the Association's role within its communities – hence the sub-title, 'Enhancing Community Identity'. It also sought to promote greater mobility within the management and control structures, especially at county level, but also at central and provincial level and at club level, too. That was to be facilitated by imposing limits on the terms of office of elected representatives and we always knew that this part of our proposals would create opposition.

Such opposition was not restricted to the longer serving members of the Association. In fact many of them, while disappointed to see a limit on their terms of office, accepted the desirability of regular infusions of new blood into the Association's administrative structures. Unfortunately, a minority of the staff in Croke Park (one of whom announced proudly that '… we saw off the staff review and we'll make sure that this one is buried too … ') felt threatened by the conclusions and recommendations and quietly canvassed support for opposition to our proposals. They used the limitation of terms of office as a major plank for generating support for their opposition.

While there were some implied criticisms (there were no direct criticisms) of the performances of certain sections of the Association's full-time staff, they were relatively mild and would not have justified the orchestration of serious opposition to the overall document. But even minor criticisms were treated as serious attacks or threats and that made the 'selling' of our proposals more difficult than it should have been.

At the Special Congress called to deal with the report, only slightly more than 40 per cent of our proposals were accepted. I was disappointed, but not surprised. However, since then, acceptance has risen to more than 90 per cent – or so I'm told, because I have not myself counted the number of our recommendations which have since been adopted.

My final contributions to the Association, at central level, occurred indirectly. Firstly, Seán McCague decided that the time had come to remove the ban on the security forces in the North. Seán had stood four-square behind that ban when its removal would not have been in the Association's best interest – living less than a linear mile from the border, he was very conscious of the implications of such a proposal and had opposed its adoption when he thought the time was not right. But with the changes to policing in the North and the hugely significant movements towards the possibility of a lasting peace there, he felt that the time for change was right. He was right about that.

Like McCague, I had opposed the removal of the ban when I felt that removing it would produce a massively negative reaction among our northern membership – probably leading to a split. I became very conscious that some of our fellow members in the Republic did not appreciate that and spoke in support of its removal when they were totally ignorant of the reality of life and politics in the North. When such a decision was taken, the time and the circumstances had to be right.

Like McCague, too, I had by then come to the conclusion that the GAA could not be seen, nor allow itself to be seen, as an impediment to the consummation of an acceptable peace process and an acceptable system of policing. Those were now realistic propositions, for the first time in half a century. The time was right and we needed to be in the vanguard of such change. It was time for pragmatism to take precedence over idealism. Our world was changing and we needed to change too.

He rang me to see if I agreed with his view. I agreed totally. He told me that he was establishing a sub-committee to deal with the issue and invited me to be a member, and I accepted. But I knew that there would be resistance and I understood why that resistance existed. Many, probably most, of our senior members in the North had suffered unjustifiably at the hands of the former security forces. Many of them felt that things had not yet progressed to the point where they felt that all the threats and the harassment could be ignored. The truth was that they weren't really being ignored, but they were being put to one side, in the broader national interest. Many members simply thought that it was too soon and some others may have had a political agenda, though they were probably in the minority.

Still, this was a courageous and potentially dangerous move by a President from Ulster. But Seán McCague was never short of courage. My role was to try to convince the northern county representatives that the time for change had come, but this was entirely Seán's initiative.

Many people are aware that I have long rated Seán McCague very highly, both as a man and as a President of the GAA. He was, in my opinion, one of the very best Presidents the Association ever had. His vision in identifying the convergence of the need and the opportunity to address the issue of the ban on the security forces, his courage in getting broad support for his initiative and his handling of that Special Congress, where he proposed the motion himself, confirmed my views. I realise that most northern delegates, including my own county – though by only a very narrow margin, at the County Board meeting – voted against it, but even they realised the necessity for what he was doing and he made no enemies in the process. Ten, or even five, years earlier that would have been impossible but 'cometh the hour, cometh the man'. I was delighted that Seán McCague was the person, who steered this change through the Association's decision-making system.

My final contribution was also indirect. At the Congress in Galway, I had chaired one of the sub-committees for which Peadar Murray of Armagh was acting as rapporteur to the body of Congress. A number of issues had been raised in relation to the state of the Association's finances and the need to get greater benefit from our new stadium when it was completed. In my contribution in support of Peadar Murray's report to that Congress, I reacted aggressively to a provocatively negative comment from the floor and, in the process, raised the issue of possible 'foreign' games in Croke Park. It was partly as a warning, given the financial position which the sub-committee had reviewed but, partly too, it was a positive option. Predictably, it received considerable coverage in the media.

Over the following few years, I was occasionally invited by RTÉ as a guest on their Questions and Answers programme, which was hosted by John Bowman for over twenty years. I had, and still have, great admiration for Bowman, as both a historian and a television presenter – unfortunately, RTÉ has not many like him. On a couple of occasions, questions about Croke Park and its possible use for rugby and soccer internationals were raised.

When it became obvious that the Landsdowne Road stadium was to be demolished and rebuilt and that our sporting competitors would have no venue in which to play their home games, I made my views very clear. I argued, as well as I could, that it was not in Ireland's economic, cultural or sporting interest that Irish international teams, in any code, should be forced to play their 'home' games in Britain. That possibility made no sense to me. As a national organisation, which had received public funding for the development of our new facilities, I felt that we had a responsibility to Ireland and to its people to change our rules on a temporary basis, and I said so. But I realised very well that my view was not held unanimously within the Association.

Don't get me wrong. Instinctively, I had no great desire to see other games – especially so-called foreign games – being played in Croke Park. I understood why people would be upset and why some would feel 'let down'. The original Gaelic games facility there had been built by our members; it was the scene of the Bloody Sunday Massacre; Hill 16 had tremendous national symbolism; it had been our home for decades; great men had played there and great games had been played there. But we were now being faced with more than just a sporting issue. The decision was about the best interests of Ireland Inc, about the benefit, or loss, to the economy of Dublin and Ireland and about our standing as a nation and the GAA's standing as an Association in the eyes of both foreign and domestic opponents, many of whom would have been only too happy to have another excuse to 'have a go' at us. I could not support any position which would make either Ireland or the GAA an international laughing stock.

Consequently, when Seán Kelly contacted me to see if I would support his efforts to change our rules, I agreed and I gave him as much assistance as I could. But this was Seán Kelly's initiative, not mine, and I would have no right to claim any part of the credit. The fact is that history suggests that the GAA did the right and honourable thing, however painful it was for some – and it was very painful for a minority and I fully understood their pain – but the 'greater good' demanded that we should do what we had to do, pain or no pain. That is what leadership is about.

By the end of all that, I concluded that it was time for me to opt out of active service within the Association. I was involved in other things which had no connection with the Association and I decided that I had done my stint. I still love the games and attend them regularly but, that apart, I am no longer involved at national level and I do not intend to hold any such role in the future. Truth to tell, I was becoming disillusioned with certain aspects of our activities.

Looking back, as an Ulsterman and proud of it, I am happy to have presented the Sam Maguire Cup to Paddy O'Rourke, Anthony Molloy and Henry Downey in my three years. Such an outcome would have been inconceivable, when I was elected in 1990. That and the redevelopment gave me most satisfaction in my three years, and they still do.

22

Where Are We Now?

I suspect that, in many ways, a past President is not best placed to comment on what has happened since he finished his term. There are those who believe that, like Alan Ladd, in that great cowboy epic, Shane, he should fade away into the sunset when his task has been completed. I accept that there is considerable validity in that view but it was never my way of dealing with issues about which I feel strongly. Therefore, since I am on record as expressing disappointment with some aspects of the recent management of the Association, it would be remiss of me not to comment on my view of where we are at this time.

My concerns relate mainly, but not exclusively, to two broad areas.

Firstly, I am very unhappy with the on-going process of 'bureaucratisation' of the Association – replacing real management with poor administration and reducing our effectiveness in the process.

Secondly, I am very unhappy with recent trends in our games – football especially.

I fully accept that the GAA needs to be both efficient and effective, that our central administrative structures must operate professionally and productively, and that the GAA must meet broadly similar governance requirements to those which exist in all well-managed, major organisations. But I also believe very strongly that it is, first and foremost, a membership and community-based organisation whose real strengths lie nearer its base than in its higher echelons. My recent experiences of the Association suggest that it has become administratively top-heavy with far too little support for the clubs especially, but for county boards, too.

As an example – and it is purely as an example – a couple of years ago, I was asked by one of our club officers to assist with the submission of a claim, under the players' injury scheme. Most of the claim (over 70 per cent of the total) related to one of our county's very few All Stars, who had received a completely accidental injury in a game which was attended by over 35,000 spectators and seen by hundreds of thousands on television. But, to give the full picture and be fair to the person involved, there were a number of other cases involved, too.

Our club secretary had resigned without warning early in the year and, for various reasons, a replacement was not appointed for some months. When he took over the role, the new appointee was not aware that the injury claims had neither been processed nor paid and another three months passed before he became aware of the situation. The total involved came to over Stg£22,000, which the club had paid, out of its own resources, pending recovery from the players' injury scheme.

Ours is a small rural club, with a growing population of just over 600 persons in approximately 150 houses. Unfortunately, about 20 per cent of locals would not support the GAA, for political reasons, though some of them would encourage us quietly. Realistically, that gives us a total population base of about 450 persons in total. In many counties we would not survive and we very nearly went out of existence in the 1950s.

When I contacted Croke Park, I was told bluntly that the claim was out of date and would not be considered. A similar one had been submitted from Armagh a couple of weeks earlier which had also been refused – Croke Park would make no exceptions. On asking why, I was told that a time limit had been introduced because the Association had discovered in the mid-2000s that there was a hidden liability of almost

€2 million and that it had decided to ensure that its scheme would never face having to pay such a sum.

But every insurance company in the world has an IBNR (Incurred But Not Reported) figure, which is normally a large proportion of its reserves and for which it provides annually, and survives. Over time, that figure stabilises at its appropriate level and having to pay such an amount in any year, or over a couple of years, is not a realistic concern. Why should we be different? If we are to be different, it should be because we are more lenient with our members rather than being more bureaucratic.

Fortunately, the Shamrocks were strong enough to sustain such a loss because they then had a good supporter, who would never have allowed us to become short of money. But that has changed in the recent past, and we could not afford such a cost now.

In the context of such bureaucracy, I have huge sympathy for the current Ard Stiurthóir, Páraic Duffy. No organisation can operate effectively with two bosses and there has been an increasing trend for the President to take an executive role. In my view, involvement by the President on a day-to-day basis undermines the Chief Executive and promotes a drift towards a full-time, paid President. Thankfully, Liam O'Neill appears to be less involved in that respect than some of his predecessors and he appears to be doing a good job in the process. But the two roles have not been defined adequately and there is now far too much overlap, which is not working to the Association's advantage.

For what it is worth, I see the President's role as being very similar to that of a voluntary chairman in organisations like charities or other not-for-profit organisations. Such a role is about providing leadership and defining a vision for the future, not about being involved in the on-going activities, which should properly be the role of the Chief Executive.

The President's role should be strategic, not operational. It is not a full-time role. In fact, it operates best when it is entirely divorced from the full-time, operational roles of a central administrative, or managerial, structure. It should be outward looking, identifying where we are in terms of our markets, and our competitors, whether we are exploiting our strengths, addressing our weaknesses, taking advantage of the available opportunities, anticipating potential threats and introducing actions to avoid or overcome those threats. It is a 'strategic role' and any good, feasible strategy takes full cognisance of what resources are available and what is realistically deliverable.

The Chief Executive's role is entirely different. It should be a managerial role, designed to ensure delivery of the strategy. If the strategy is unclear, ambiguous, replete with internal contradictions or so idealistic as to be undeliverable, then the Chief Executive's job becomes impossible and the Chief Executive cannot be held responsible in those circumstances. The blame then rests entirely with the Board – Ard Comhairle, in the GAA's case – and the Chairman – or the President in the case of the GAA.

Interference by a President who changes every three years leaves a Chief Executive faced with implementing a strategy which changes far too often in its emphasis. That can result in strategies being produced by outside consultants who might know very little about the GAA and its culture, or of running a business but who want to come up with something new.

I hope to live long enough to see a consultant's strategy report which says bluntly, "There is nothing wrong with the existing strategy; just carry on and implement it well – preferably better than at present."

The best strategies are invariably produced by the relevant Board, not by external people, which gathers the information from within the organisation anyway.

The 'culture' of an organisation is a critical determinant of its success – probably the single most crucial aspect of success or failure. The GAA has a particularly strong organisational and communal culture, built on the voluntary effort and ethos which sustains it. It is very difficult for outsiders to harness that culture or develop a strategy based on that culture – in fact, they invariably struggle to understand it because it is almost unique. But failure to recognise that culture and to develop a strategy, which suits that culture, is a recipe for an irrelevant and non-feasible strategy. In that event, the new strategy is reduced to a meaningless 'wish-list'.

That appears to be what has happened to the GAA over the past half decade, when 'outsiders' have been given the task of producing strategies, and the staff have been left to pick up the pieces. I do not envy them their job as it is an impossible role.

I believe that the modern GAA needs a more focussed strategy, which concentrates on strategic issues only. It should be vision-driven, with a clear focus on objectives and outputs at a macro level. Most of all, it should be consistent with the organisation's culture and it should identify who has responsibility for monitoring the achievement of the specified targets. It most certainly should not be driven by its structure, as most bureaucracies are, nor by the creation of roles for individuals.

What that means is that the President should preside, the Management Committee should monitor the control and governance aspects, and the Chief Executive should execute – and be left to execute without interference. For those who fail, the old business maxim 'back him, or sack him' should operate and that, too, has to be part of the President's role.

Given my view on how the GAA should be managed, it cannot be a surprise that I am absolutely and unequivocally opposed to a paid Presidency, or to a President who interferes in matters which are the prerogative of the executive staff. I am just as implacably opposed to an organisation which is bureaucratic, inefficient or ineffective. We could finish up in that position if we pursue a strategy which is designed to satisfy everyone. Satisfying everyone is just not possible.

I believe strongly the President should be provided with a car and a driver as the driving was easily the worst part of the role, in my experience. Beyond that, he –or she, and I look forward to a female President in the not too distant future – should be recompensed for vouched expenditures only and should get no 'allowances' for outgoings which may, or may not, be either necessary or expended.

Finally in this area, I do not support the trend towards greater centralisation. My professional experience suggests that a well-managed, decentralised structure is far more effective than a centralised one: it generates greater commitment and loyalty, it is easier to get change accepted within and through such a structure, contacts tend to be closer and there's far more potential for progress, when change is needed.

There are those who believe that the provincial councils are outdated and an impediment to progress but I disagree fundamentally. Given the culture and ethos of the GAA, local is better. Whatever chance we have of implementing change in the organisation, it will have to be done through the provincial councils. Even today, the reaction to 'dem wans up there' is invariably negative among the clubs and most of the activists at county level. Managed change and development will need the input and support of the provincial councils, otherwise it will not work.

The GAA needs managed development, not revolutionary change. It needs to remain amateur if it is to grow and fulfil its role as a major feature of the sporting, social and, especially, communal development of Ireland and of Irish communities outside Ireland. Paying those who should not be paid clearly threatens that ethos, damages others' perceptions of our role and constrains our potential for growth and development.

I also believe that in choosing a Chief Executive for the GAA, a background in the Association would be useful but it should be much less important than his understanding of and experience of managing an organisation. We are far too prone to look inwards for such persons, while looking outwards for those with broader experiences would, in my opinion, serve the Association better, by bringing new ideas, broader experiences and a wider vision to the role. That will be essential in a future of more rapid change and greater external threats – and we are already facing serious threats. Finally, I am convinced that no Chief Executive of any sporting organisation, which by its nature deals primarily with young people, should hold the position for more than about seven years – and I feel strongly about that, too.

If I am unhappy about how our organisational structures have developed, especially over the past decade, I am even more concerned about recent trends in our games. I never played hurling and, therefore, I have no right to comment on its playing rules. I am utterly convinced that only the occasional, very able individual, who has not experienced a game as a player, can understand it fully. Unfortunately, I do not have that sort of experience of hurling.

Nevertheless, I am absolutely convinced that hurling is the best field game in the world – it is certainly the best of those I have seen. If anyone had any doubts, they should have been erased by, firstly, the draw in the 2013 final, and then by the replay – what a contest!

When it is well refereed, it provides a brilliant experience for the spectator. The Kilkenny-Tipperary final of September 2011, was such a game – Brian Gavin gave a wonderful display of the art of refereeing. I shudder to think of what would have happened if some of the 'bookies' and 'yellow-card merchants' who now referee football had been in charge on that occasion. Hard tackles were taken and given, with no diving and no whingeing. It was a privilege to be there, watching real men play a real game under a referee who didn't want to be the centre of either attraction or controversy and who took his 'clip of the hurley' like a man.

That approach should be the example and the *modus operandi* for our football referees, too. I did a bit of refereeing for a couple years (although I was never really interested in being a referee) until I left Fermanagh to live elsewhere. So I fully recognise that refereeing is a thankless task and I have loads of sympathy for referees. Most of them are good men, who wish to make a contribution to the Association and to society. I would not consider myself a 'referee basher', but I have serious concerns about refereeing standards in football, and especially about referees who want to be the centre of attention.

I have been lucky enough to have seen many great referees of Gaelic Football, though I really took relatively little notice of the referee until the 1970s or later. For me, Paddy Collins and Pat McEneany were the two best I have seen and I would not choose between them. Tommy Sugrue was probably next best; his refereeing of that famous game in

Celtic Park in 1994, when the 1991 and 1994 All-Ireland champions defeated the 1993 champions, was outstanding in by far the greatest game of Gaelic football I have ever witnessed. And when a game is that good, the referee has to be given some of the credit, though Tommy's pedigree was well established long before that. Incidentally, the 2013 game between Dublin and Kerry was the second best, in my opinion, with Dublin and Kerry in 1977 being third.

In my early days, I played under and admired many of the leading Ulster referees of that era. And we had in Fermanagh six or seven referees who refereed at provincial and national level and playing under them was an entirely satisfying experience, although I might have let some of them know that I didn't entirely agree with their decisions from time to time. In every case, when we meet, we reminisce, we joke, sometimes we 'slag', but we always enjoy such meetings. I'm not sure that will apply to some of the current referees in their futures.

Given my lack of physique, I should have preferred referees who would not allow hard play, but I never wanted that. Getting in a good strong tackle was one of the most satisfying aspects of the game but if one enjoyed giving it, one had to be prepared to take it.

That is one of the problems with refereeing and referees today. Many cannot distinguish between hard play and dirty play, or between an accidental collision and a pre-meditated dirty tackle. And even if they could, they know only too well that someone is doing an assessment from the safety of the stand. That is the core of our current problems – referees now have one eye on the assessor in the stand and only one on the game on the pitch.

I was at an Ulster Championship game some time back. An 'away' player made one of the best tackles I have seen in a very long time. He hit an oncoming player with his shoulder as that player soloed along the sideline towards the rival goals. It was as hard a tackle as I have seen in many years, but it was fair and the timing was perfect – shoulder to shoulder although it was towards the front of each shoulder. I was sitting very close to it. The attacking player was knocked into the advertising hoardings, but he was not injured. That sort of tackle was common when I was playing and one simply got up and got on with the game after it. I would have gone home a very proud man, if I had made such a tackle, but unfortunately I was never strong enough for that.

The crowd bayed for a red card but he no more deserved a red card than I did and I was sitting quietly in the stand. In the end, the player was given a yellow card – fortunately his only of the day – which I could not agree with as the rules of Gaelic football do not ban hard tackles.

Someone up there is watching too much soccer. Gaelic football is meant to be a physical contact sport. That is what the supporters go to see, that is why players play it, if they wanted a non-contact sport they would not play Gaelic football. It is conning spectators out of their money to interpret such things as fouls, never mind to give yellow or red cards for them – even if a few biased supporters howl for retribution.

I understand that referees are now being told at training courses not to apply common sense when refereeing – just apply the rules. What a joke! Common sense is the main factor which distinguishes humans from other animals, and referees are being told not to use it! It is time someone wised up, before our game is ruined completely.

In one match, I witnessed a series of cards caused largely by the incompetence of the referee who lost control of the game in the first ten minutes by giving a series of decisions, which neither the players nor the spectators understood. That led to frustration, on and off the field. The linesmen did not help either.

Soon after, I watched another referee who let hard tackles go if they were fair, who did not want to be the centre of attention and who helped to produce one of the year's best games. Eddie Kinsella is not one of our best-known referees, but he gave a superb exhibition on that occasion. The other referee is better known but he was a disaster. One would have to ask 'why the difference?'

Over the past number of years, the inter-county referees' panel has included a few referees who are not good enough to be refereeing at that level – possibly at any level. One of them has refereed an All-Ireland final and did not cover himself with glory, but he still gets major games. I am sure the Referees Committee knows who they are but if they are in any doubt, all they have to do is ask any genuine and regular supporter, and they will get a short-list with which I am unlikely to disagree. Refereeing is now a favourite topic of conversation at most GAA gatherings around the country. That was not the case when I was playing and it should not be the case now either.

I have a particular objection to any referee walking away from the player to whom he wishes to speak and standing with the little book and pencil, pointing towards his toes and demanding that the player to be chastised should stand directly in front of him to get a dressing-down. A bad teacher would not do that to a bold six-year-old in this modern era. Referees should not do it either.

Such actions make a complete mockery of the Association's 'Respect' programme. Respect has to be earned before it is awarded. Yes, referees deserve respect and they should get respect. But when referees themselves show that sort of disrespect, they forfeit the right to respect and they certainly lose the respect of the supporters in the stand when they do things like that. The referees whom I respected as a player, and those whom I respect today as a supporter, always made/make sure they were/are not seen as being disrespectful to players. I compare referees who do otherwise to candidates for the driving test; they might pass the theory test, but they cannot drive. They do not deserve their licence.

It is easy to criticise, but not so easy to mend. Therefore, my suggestions for improving refereeing are as follows. Firstly, get rid of those stupid assessments and get rid of the assessors, too. Secondly, let the referees use their common sense; if they are good enough to be selected in the first place, they are good enough to be capable of applying their most valuable God-given asset. Thirdly, select a panel of about 20-25 referees for special development as inter-county referees and provide them with the coaching needed for the role, recognising that our game of football is a physical contact sport – and that latter is crucial. Then pay them to act as the Association's inter-county referees' panel for two-year periods – everyone else is getting paid anyway.

The criteria to be used in refereeing inter-county games and other high profile games should be developed jointly by a referees panel and selected, or all, senior inter-county team managers. At the end of every season, in the autumn, each senior inter-county team manager should be asked to rank (not score them – that would be too dangerous) every single member of the inter-county referees panel, so that those responsible for appointing referees would know who has the respect of the players and managers and who is performing well. Those rankings should then be used in determining who gets the major games in the following year. At the end of each two-year period, the panel should be re-assessed, based largely on the managers' evaluations. Those who have not been performing well should be dropped and replaced by new nominees.

But clearly, not all of the problems with Gaelic football and the refereeing of that game can be laid at the feet of the referees. Essentially, those problems derive primarily from the rules, and the current rules do not serve the game well. Our legislators have not covered themselves in glory in terms of the rules of Gaelic football. They have to be blamed for the current defensive formations being used by many teams, for the excessive use of low-grade basketball skills and for the slow movement of the ball. These innovations are diminishing the attractiveness of the game. If the rules are not changed, Gaelic football as we know it will die, as it ceases to be attractive to either players or supporters. That makes me fear for the future of the Association, though the current Dublin team and two or three others (Kerry, Meath and Mayo, in particular) appear to be trying to save Gaelic football.

As the rules now apply, there is a serious imbalance between the rights of forwards and those of defenders and that is giving rise to massed defences. Team managers are doing what the legislators have failed to do with regards to providing a proper balance between defence and attack. Unfortunately, the response by some team managers has destroyed the game as a spectacle and made it less attractive to play.

But referees add to the problem; when they see two players 'tussling' off the ball, they are happy to run fifty or sixty yards to award a free to the attacker. Someone should tell them that forwards foul too – I know I did from time to time and I would have been very happy to get a free for it.

Today, defenders in Gaelic football have no chance against intelligent forwards. Intelligent forwards do not kick the ball, they carry it almost directly into the tackle, then hand-pass it and defenders have no realistic chance of inhibiting their progress or depriving them of possession. That leads to frustration and loss of discipline and the players and managers take the blame – not the rule-makers.

In the old days, a defender could dive on a forward's foot and block his kick. It was one of the great skills of the game and one of the greatest sources of satisfaction when it succeeded. Today, only an idiot would dive on a forward's foot because hardly anyone kicks the ball any more. Certainly a forward, when faced by a defender, will not kick the ball – he will lay it off to a colleague, who cannot be tackled until he has possession – and rightly so.

The reality is that under the current rules, there is no realistic way – there are theoretical ways but they are absurd in practice – in which a forward can be dispossessed, unless he makes a mistake. The good ones don't. That imbalance needs to be addressed, otherwise why have open play? Just crowd the space completely out – and that is what is happening.

In my view, if Gaelic football is to survive, we need to *bring the football back into Gaelic football*. Consequently, I would like to see about half a dozen changes in the playing rules for our games but, in the interests of realism, I would like to propose the following five changes to the rules of Gaelic football:

(i) After a maximum of two successive hand or fist passes, the ball must next be played by kicking it. The argument that this would place too much pressure on referees is ridiculous: in Rugby League, the referee has to count up to six completed tackles before awarding a hand-over and in the Compromise Rules games the number of 'handballs' is restricted to four (using GAA referees). Why should all GAA referees not be able to count to two hand-passes even if far too many of them cannot count two hops – most miss one before going into the tackle and another coming out of that tackle.

(ii) A team must have at least five players in each half of the pitch at any time, when the ball is in play. Otherwise, it concedes a free from its opponents' forty-five metre line, straight in front of the posts; the linesmen should have responsibility for monitoring this.

(iii) A maximum of two opposing players should be allowed to tackle the player in possession, at any time.

(iv) Referees should give a straight red card to any player, who indulges in 'mouthing' at, or 'sledging' of, an opponent.

(v) In order to eliminate the cynicism which is creeping into our games, any player who commits a tackle which involves hauling down a player in possession should get a straight red card. One example of such a tackle received huge publicity and comment in 2013, but the fact that another team subsequently committed a number of similar fouls in the closing stages of one of our major games received virtually no comment. Why?

Essentially, I believe that Gaelic football should place a higher premium on skill and less on negativity.

The current rules and how they are interpreted by referees have led to the virtual elimination of high fielding, the reduction of the game as a spectacle and the creation of a totally defensive mentality. They have also led to a huge increase in fouling, especially in body-checking, made refereeing much more difficult and frustrated both players and spectators. All of that is unnecessary – none of it is essential to the game.

I have some sympathy with several of the other changes which have been suggested by various payers and ex-players from time to time, though I would like to see most of them tried out before they would be introduced as rules. I do not believe that our rules are perfect at present and I believe that changes should be introduced on a progressive and selective basis – not wholesale changes nor the introduction of more than one or two at a time. Nevertheless, some of those which have been suggested to me from time to time and which might be worth trying include:

- A reduction in team numbers to thirteen a side, with a related reduction in inter-county panels to twenty-two.

- A system of rolling substitutions, with a maximum of five or six interchanges from a designated starting panel of about twenty-two.

- A straight red card for a player who dives when he is obviously not injured, even if he has been hit (I would absolutely and unequivocally support that).

- Limiting the number of players who are allowed to contest the kick-outs as a way of retaining the art of high fielding.

- Introduction of the 'mark', as in Aussie Rules.

However, I agree entirely with Brian Cody when he demands we should leave hurling alone or, at most, introduce minimal change.

Furthermore, other than in very serious cases, I am entirely opposed to taking disciplinary action on any issues or events not witnessed by the referee or not reported to or by him, other than in very bad cases. Once the game ends, our existing disciplinary procedures should kick in, including the potential to exonerate a player, where there is doubt about the correctness of the referee's decision. On that issue, I believe the guidelines to Hearings Committees are far too stringent and I chaired a County Hearings Committee for four years; they should allow more scope to exercise greater leniency towards players who may have received harsh treatment from a referee because they make mistakes too.

But most of all, I believe that once the referee has submitted his report, it is none of his business how any committee deals with it. Once the police or Garda put their case to the prosecution services, they have no role in what happens thereafter. It should be the same with referees: referees should referee, disciplinary committees should deal with discipline, and never the twain should meet.

I watch many field sports, both live and on television. After hurling and football, I love watching track athletics, handball and Aussie Rules. But most of all, I love watching Rugby League: its controlled physicality (controlled mainly by the severity of the sentences on players who indulge in seriously dirty play), its non-stop movement, its players' capacity to take hard knocks without complaining, its sportsmanship and its lack of pretence, all attract me. I would never have been strong enough to play it but I think it is a wonderful sport and a 'working class' sport at that. I particularly appreciate the reality that its supporters do not have anything like the same level of aggression as applies in British soccer – in fact, they are wonderful supporters.

Ultimately, I have a very major concern that, in the current straitened national and international economic circumstances, failure to address our deficiencies will cost us dearly. In my opinion, 'doing nothing' is not an option – in both our administrative structures and our playing rules.

23

In the End

For me, the GAA is ultimately about two aspects – the games and the local community.

While county affiliations are important, they do not provide the same sort of robust foundations as the club and its community can create, nor do they generate the same commitment or passion. When we add culture and language to that mix, it produces a cocktail of enormous potency. It is that cocktail which has made the GAA so successful over the last century and a quarter.

The question is, will it continue to do the same for the next century? It should. It could. It might.

Then again, it might not.

One thing is certain, whatever we may have achieved in the past the future will be different. It will be a foreign place with new demands and new challenges. And those demands and challenges will be answered by a new generation and by generations as yet unborn.

Given where we came from, we can and should never forget our past, including our heritage, our quintessential Irishness, our social role and our community base. We should commemorate our successes and our contribution but we should also remember and learn from our mistakes and our omissions.

Obviously in expressing some of these views, I run the risk of being accused of being biased and even blinkered, and that is something which I am willing to accept. But, in my view, no other organisation better reflects the history, the mood and the aspirations of the Irish people than the GAA. It is rooted in its communities and has given them a sense of identity and of place which cannot be replicated in any other way, or by any other organisation.

In the future, that will have to be a more inclusive identity, especially in the North, but right across the rest of the island, too. But even then, it should still be an Irish identity – 'new' Irish, 'old' Irish, or ideally both, but Irish anyway. Thankfully, we now have the base and the resources to do that successfully, and I am confident that we will succeed.

But we will succeed only if we are united; ní neart go chur le chéile. That has been part of what we were and what we stood for since we were founded. I hope I am wrong but, right now, I detect greater division within our ranks than existed when I was more involved, or long before I ever became involved. I realise that there is always the danger of the infamous rose-tinted spectacles affecting one's view of the past. But, unless I am greatly mistaken, there is now a feeling of isolation in Ulster, especially in the six counties, which did not exist two decades ago, or even less than that.

It is not exclusively a GAA thing – it is probably even more of a national thing. But it exists within the GAA, too. The constant sniping at Ulster football, some of which is justified, has not been balanced by similar criticism of others. Armagh in 2002 and Tyrone in 2003 won All-Ireland finals for which they received only grudging recognition – 'puke football', 'typical Ulster football', 'defensive football', 'negative football'.

Firstly, Armagh and Tyrone played very different styles of football so they should not be branded together. Secondly, in 2008 Tyrone won another All-Ireland playing a very different style of football – a much better type of football – but they got no credit for the change. And thirdly, some of the worst football played in 2011 was played at the beginning of the last quarter of the All-Ireland final, but that is never mentioned by the many of the pundits who criticise 'Ulster' football, just as the closing ten minutes of the 2013 final was not great either.

Over the 18 years from 1991 to 2008, more than half of the All-Ireland senior football titles have gone to Connacht or Ulster. Yet there are pundits who, in that entire period, never once tipped an Ulster or Connacht county to win the final, after the finalists were decided. The sole exception was 2003, when there was no alternative. That pattern of favouring Leinster and Munster counties could be coincidence, but as a statistician, I would have to say that it is statistically improbable.

Whether we like it or not, our members in the North feel more marginalised now than they ever did during 'The Troubles'. They see themselves as completely Irish, just as much as the people who live in any of the other three provinces. They support the Irish rugby team and the national teams in other sports; the majority of them also support the Republic's soccer team because they feel that it better reflects their identity than the team representing the North. The recent Presidential campaign (aspects of which were a disgrace) confirmed what northerners were already beginning to realise – that they are no longer wanted in the New Ireland. Unfortunately, within the GAA, too, that 'anti-Ulster' attitude has become more pervasive in the recent past or, at least, that perception now exists in the North.

Mary and I have lived in three of Ireland's four provinces (as well as in England), since we married. We have five children. Two were born in Leinster (Dublin), two were born in Connacht (Ballinasloe) and one was born in Fermanagh before being educated in three provinces (plus the United States), going to university in Belfast and spending all his working life in Dublin. My daughter, Miriam's career and her future were destroyed by her accident but three of the other four live and work in Dublin and support Dublin, except when the Dubs are playing against Fermanagh. They see themselves as being completely Irish, and so do we. Interestingly, none of them ever considered it worthwhile to register to vote in either jurisdiction as they have nothing but contempt for politicians. For us the border is a political concept which has no impact on our Irishness, nor on our commitment to our country – as we define our country.

That is why the growing sense of alienation upsets me. In reality, I cannot either understand it or accept it. It particularly annoys me that it appears to have extended into the GAA.

The perception in the North is that the situation has worsened over the past decade. If the Association is to fulfil its potential, someone has to take a stand and reverse that trend of isolationism and the anti-northern attitude which gives rise to it – whether they are merely perceived or not. Those views have grown dramatically in recent years – they may even be other negative legacies of the Celtic Tiger. Having been through the media-led, anti-northern bias of twenty years ago, I understand the feelings of those who are concerned about these divisions.

I am convinced that the Association needs to take a lead on this issue. I am also confident that it has the background, the strength, the conviction and the courage to provide the leadership needed in resolving such differences. It may well be that the demise of the Celtic Tiger will provoke the changes necessary to create the psychological and communal unity which is much more important than any political unity, though that too would be helpful.

Ireland now needs a few years of positive leadership to create the necessary change in attitudes. If the GAA should be in the vanguard of any movement for change in the national 'psyche', this is the one.

Like the overwhelming majority of other members, I joined the GAA because of its games. I just wanted to play Gaelic football – for Teemore and for Fermanagh. I survived for a reasonable time at one level and for only a short time at the other. But I enjoyed every second of it. Later, partly because of need, local social and economic disadvantage, and my club's loss of players through emigration, I embraced the communal and cultural dimensions of the Association, too.

But I have never been under any illusion: without the games, we are nothing and without a united front, we run the risk of becoming nothing.

*****

I would be a complete liar if I was to deny that I considered it an honour both to serve the Association and to lead it, for three years. But when I look at those who preceded me, I am embarrassed by the comparison: Paddy Buggy and Con Murphy; Pat Fanning and Jim Ryan; Alf Murray and Pádraig McNamee; and several others, including more recently, Séan McCague.

I was never in their league. I knew a bit – but only a bit - about business and finance and construction, but they knew so much more about Irish life and the role of the GAA.

For me, the road to Croke Park was riddled with potholes, whichever direction I was travelling. But I survived it. I can look back and ask myself some very fundamental questions about my time as President.

Do I regret it? Not for a minute – and I never have, even on the worst of days.

Am I glad I did it? Absolutely, without a doubt.

Did I enjoy it? Yes – most of the time, but not always. Any time I was not enjoying it, it was not the Association or its members which detracted from my enjoyment. It is a wonderful organisation and I am very proud to have been involved with it at a high level.

Have I become disenchanted with the Association since my term ended? Possibly somewhat on a few aspects, but I am still very committed to it. I believe the GAA to be a major force for good and for progress but, most of all, I see it as a force for communal cohesion in most of the island and a force for potential cohesion in the rest of it – though that will take time. I am far from disillusioned with the GAA or any of the things for which it stands and I know of no other organisation in Ireland with greater potential in those areas. It is, in my view, the only organisation in Ireland which has any chance of making up for the abject failures of our political systems – North and South.

If I had known in 1986, what I know now, would I have stood in two elections for the position? Not a chance in hell! I would have opted for something very different. There are worse things in life than anonymity.

For all practical purposes, I am no longer involved in GAA administration. While the Association is just as important to me as it ever was, I have no interest in being part of its administrative structures. I no longer attend Congress and haven't done so for well over a decade now. I do not get involved in County Board affairs, though I spent four years chairing the county's Hearings Committee. However, I still spend most Sundays watching a GAA game somewhere and I still derive huge pleasure from that.

Effectively, I have taken a decision to move on. I became immersed in other things, but that's another story. Those who know me, know that I have never left the GAA and, until I am carried out in a box, I never will.

But, once an outsider ... That is a reality with which I have had to live.

I could and I would.

And I did.

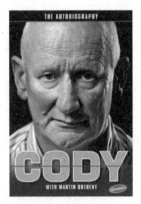

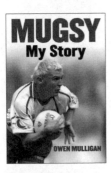
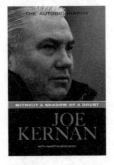
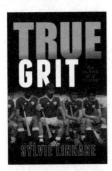
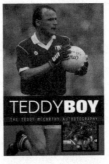

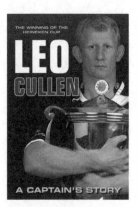

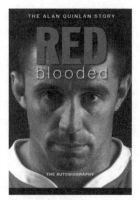

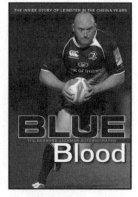

Leo Cullen: A Captain's Story
Leo Cullen
ISBN 978-0-9563598-7-2
€15.99

In May 2011, Leinster won the most remarkable Heineken Cup title in rugby history, coming from 22 points down at half time in the final at Cardiff's Millennium Stadium to defeat Northampton, and capture Europe's premier rugby trophy for the second time in three years. A year later, Leinster retained the Cup, making Leo Cullen the first captain to raise the Heineken Cup an amazing three times. An Irish International and inspirational leader, the captain of perhaps the greatest team European rugby has ever seen, recorded his incredible journey in 2011 in intimate detail in *A Captain's Story*.

Red Blooded: Alan Quinlan
Alan Quinlan
ISBN 978-0-9563598-3-4
€19.99

Red Blooded is the story of Munster rugby's most-capped player ever, Alan Quinlan, and his battle to reach the peak of the professional game of rugby. One of the bravest and most honest accounts ever written about the modern game, Red Blooded recounts Quinny and Munster's stories. It details how he has confronted professionalism, tough opponents, devastating injury and personal doubts to become one of modern rugby's toughest, and greatest, characters.

Blue Blood: Bernard Jackman
Bernard Jackman
ISBN 978-0-9563598-2-7
€19.99

Blue Blood is the story of one man's passionate, thirteen-year fight to reach the highest level of the professional sport of rugby. It's the inside story of Leinster's five-year journey, under their then manager, Michael Cheika, to become the No. 1 team in European rugby. In his revealing autobiography, Bernard Jackman, offers the inside story of that quest and lifts the lid on Leinster in the Cheika years. *Blue Blood* lays bare the ruthlessness required to reach the top of one of the greatest sports in the world.